VARNISHED BRASS

ALSO BY BARBARA GELB

On the Track of Murder
So Short a Time
O'Neill (With Arthur Gelb)

VARNISHED BRASS

THE DECADE AFTER SERPICO

BARBARA GELB

G. P. PUTNAM'S SONS
New York

A few of the incidents in this book were described in different form in
The New York Times Magazine, April 16, 1978, under the title
"The Purge of the Chiefs."

The author gratefully acknowledges permission from Harold Ober
Associates Incorporated to quote from "Conversation Piece" by
Muriel Spark, copyright © 1981 by Copyright Administration
Limited. First appeared in *The New Yorker*.

Designed by Richard Oriolo

Library of Congress Cataloging in Publication Data

Gelb, Barbara.
Varnished brass.

1. New York (N.Y.)—Police.   2. Police administration
—New York (N.Y.)   I. Title.
HV8148.N52G44   1983   363.2'09747'1   83-4568
ISBN 0-399-12871-9

Printed in the United States of America

For Artie with all my love

NEW YORK POLICE DEPARTMENT HIERARCHY

RANK	INSIGNIA	NUMBER IN NYPD
Police commissioner	civilian	1
First deputy commissioner	civilian	1
Chief of operations	four stars	1
Bureau chief (Superchief)	three stars	5
Assistant chief	two stars	10
Deputy chief	one star	20
Inspector	eagle	38
Deputy inspector	oak leaf	83

VARNISHED BRASS

★ ONE

★ To be a big-city cop in America was to be an alien and Assistant Chief Daniel J. Courtenay knew that as well as anyone. When I first met him in the mid-1970s, Courtenay was a high-ranking, college-educated career cop—right up there, close to the top—in a very big city, maybe the toughest in the world to police. Like his peers, he felt a certain sense of isolation from his fellow citizens, for the ordeal that formed the Police Experience was savage and brutalizing and it dug a moat between cops and the rest of the world. But along with the best of his colleagues, Courtenay rose above the squalor and despair of his profession.

In the picture I conjure of Courtenay as he was in the early months of our acquaintance, I see him on patrol in the city he loves, the symbol of a proud police department that just a few years earlier was locked in scandal. He is a youthful fifty. Appointed not many months since to the rank of assistant chief, Courtenay wears his cap, its licorice-black peak gleaming with gold braid, cocked ever so slightly to one side. He is Top Brass, his rank trumpeted by twin golden stars pinned to his broad navy blue shoulders. In America the police go armed, always, and Courtenay does not feel fully clothed unless his service revolver rides his hip, snug in its well-worn leather holster.

Unlike the British police, who mostly go weaponless, the

American police do not conceal their alienation. They need to feel armed, conscious that ours is a society founded on violence. His loins thus girded, Courtenay, a strapping man—tall, brawny, and gun-barrel straight—is a presence. Street-bred, he is ever aware of his beginnings and does not mind being called "a big son of a bitch" as long as the tone is respectful (he would really prefer reverential). Imperious, like Trollope's Prime Minister, he carries his empire in his eye.

The eye is icy blue and seldom thaws, even when warmed by his good smile. Dan Courtenay smiles but keeps his distance, like the sun in winter. In the street, commanding his troops during a political demonstration, the kind of massive protest for which his city is famous, he strides up to a subordinate commander, claps him on the back, winks, shows his teeth in an ironic grin, and issues his standard greeting: "You're doing a helluva job, I've been watching you!"

The phrase condenses his philosophy of policing and also satirizes it. Courtenay is serious about his work though never solemn. He holds few illusions about The Job, but he never has outgrown the tug of its romance. To him policing *is* romance, although it would embarrass him to say so.

He knows that he and his fellow police are our last defenders, the only real-life heroes left in our trembling cities. He believes, too (perhaps prays), that he and his fellow commanders (most of them, anyway) are truly doing a helluva job. And if their theme song is the piteous howl of a prowl car, if they patrol to the rhythm of a city often in pain, if even the courts and the judges sometimes seem to be their enemies, still they are hopeful men. Optimism is the bulletproof vest of big-city police commanders—optimism and a strong (sometimes bleak) sense of humor about their city, its politicians, and themselves.

The men who reached high police command during the politically explosive 60s and the rampantly felonious 70s were, all of them, including Assistant Chief Dan Courtenay, walking a beat as rookie cops in the late 40s and early

50s. Many of them joined the police after serving in World War II, mostly in noncommissioned ranks. Having chosen policing, they were burdened with—indeed they embraced—the isolating symbols of their trade: the dark blue tunic that rendered them anonymous; the shield, arrogant in its symbolism; the mandatory gun, the club, and manacles; and the unspoken law of Brotherhood to protect the deficient and the twisted among them. They inhabited a region of the mind that, like shrouded Tibet, was largely impenetrable to outsiders. You stepped across the close-guarded borders of the Police World at your peril.

But if we feared them, they in turn were wary of us—the middle-class civilians, the professional watchdogs, the journalists and writers, the civil libertarians. We were the solid citizens who wanted (so we said) an aggressive but humane police, an honest and accountable police, in a world where chicanery often was rewarded, especially at the top, where even our duly elected President turned out to be a closet crook, not only forgiven but also lionized.

Police commanders, with reason, *preferred* not to be known. Traditionally, the police operated behind closed doors where mismanagement and misbehavior often went undetected, where instances of brutality, racism, or thieving could be quietly contained and covered up, just as in the real world. Dan Courtenay's police department recently had emerged, somewhat humbled, from a nationally publicized criminal investigation. And so I was not really surprised when Courtenay admitted (after I'd known him for several years) that he was unnerved to find me, an outsider and a writer, established as a fixture at headquarters in the office of his boss, the four-star chief of operations. He tried to hide his resentment, to cover it with the sardonic humor that was as much a shield as his official gold one, but for a long time his displeasure hung in the air between us.

Their humor may have been what initially attracted me to the police—that and their Victorian sense of virtue. I began studying the New York police in 1973, three years after a rebel cop named Frank Serpico exposed a pattern of entrenched corruption and cover-up in the department. The scandal led to the celebrated Knapp Commission investigation and brought in a reform commissioner, Patrick V. Murphy, who purged the department, set up machinery to keep it clean, and declared it "open" to inspection, thereby reversing a century-old policy of evasion and secrecy. I started my research among the detectives, traditionally the most secretive members of any police department, and gradually worked my way up to the high command.

Courtenay and other commanders I came to know, those who were left after Commissioner Murphy's purge, were convinced they could impose order in their turbulent city largely by setting an example of old-fashioned honor, responsibility, and duty. It was the kind of order that emerged, predictably and delightfully, in the works of the Victorian novelists under whose spell I grew up. Police culture resisted change with all the conviction of a Victorian spinster: the old ways were the best ways. Good and evil were clearly defined. There was always a struggle between the two, sometimes violent, and there was usually sacrifice. There was no question, though, that Sydney Carton would go to heaven. The police commanders I studied were firmly religious in the Victorian tradition and could face hardship and other tests of courage with Victorian stoicism. They saw themselves quite literally as the ultimate Good Guys.

Few citizens saw their police in that light, however. Most of us saw our police—how could we help it?—against the background of their historical and mythological wickedness. Not dreaded, of course, as they were in totalitarian countries—but definitely tainted. For we knew of their past and possibly present willingness to be manipulated, to abuse their trust, their power. We saw them as menacing, sadistic. But they saw themselves as the narrow line between us and the jungle, licensed to kill for us and permitted to die for us. They were fascinating because they stood for the good/bad split in all of us. They embodied, as one

New York police commissioner remarked as he was about to take office, "the very best and the very worst."

In the big cities like New York and Chicago, the same working-class neighborhoods spawned both cops and criminals; sometimes they were childhood friends. A good cop's guard rarely went down. The more honest the cop, the more aware he was apt to be of his own darker side, his potential for becoming the very criminal he had sworn to lock up.

News item: In New York, on July 15, 1976, the Manhattan District Attorney announced that five police officers had been indicted on charges of stealing more than $30,000 from suspected narcotics dealers and assaulting some of them. The five officers were among the most active in making arrests in a Lower Manhattan precinct.

The chiefs knew well enough how we viewed them. They said things like, People have this stereotype of us. Bitterly, they said, People think we're gorillas. But even the more articulate among the chiefs despaired of being able to convey to anyone not a cop what the Police Experience really could do to a man. And we were content, mostly, to leave them in isolation. (Well, would you want your daughter to marry one?)

We've watched as city after city—New York, Chicago, Philadelphia, Los Angeles, Houston, Detroit, Miami—cringed under police scandal. We've been appalled, terrified, sickened by revelations of brutality and corruption in the ranks, cynically overlooked or even condoned by the Top Command. Were we being punished? Did we, as a society, get the police we deserved?

The police thought we did. And they were smug in the knowledge that they were the only police we had. Who else, the chiefs demanded, would do our dirty work? Who else would deal, as Courtenay liked to ask, with "the sewage of the city"?

Courtenay believed in his calling; for those who stayed
with it, policing was more a calling than a profession.
Courtenay once said that if he were commissioner he would
try, above all, to "keep our image proud." When I met him
toward the end of 1975, he was one of the Generals on the
biggest police force in the United States. It had shrunk to
27,000 but was still more than double the size of its closest
competitor, Chicago, and more than triple the size of the
Los Angeles force, which was America's third largest. Big
as it was, the New York Police Department thought of
itself as the country's most enlightened. Dan Courtenay's
police were so humane, in fact, that they professed to flinch
at calling themselves a *force*. They preferred *service*. New
York, by the mid 70s, had become the fountainhead of
American policing. Between 1972 and 1982—the ten years
that I studied the department—it evolved from one of the
most corrupt and brutal into one of the cleanest and most
judicious.

Courtenay was quoted by name in the press, he was
asked by television reporters for his comments on policing
in a time of savagery. He could look you in the eye right on
prime-time local news and make you feel ashamed. "Did it
ever occur to you," he was likely to say, "that if *we* weren't
the police, *you* would have to be?"

At the end of 1977, which was also the end of Courtenay's thirtieth year on The Job, a new mayor was elected
in New York. That meant a new police commissioner was
about to be chosen. And Courtenay's name was on a list of
twenty from which the mayor-elect's search panel would
make a recommendation to the Mayor-elect, Edward I.
Koch. Koch was a curious cross between a Wild West
maverick and a precocious Bar Mitzvah boy, and as rooted
in New York's sidewalks as its pigeons. No one in the
police department had a clue what he really wanted in a
commissioner. All they knew was that he didn't like the
incumbent and wanted him out.

When Koch was elected, he immediately pledged to

undo all the terrible things that preceding mayors had done. His predecessor was Abraham D. Beame, programmed early in life in the virtues of clubhouse politics, who had inherited a recently cleansed police department; and before Beame, John V. Lindsay, who seemed at sea in the confrontational politics of New York. It was in 1970, early in Lindsay's second term, that the police department erupted in scandal and subsequently underwent its radical shake-up. In the years following, the department achieved an image of relative stability and honesty. But Koch now wanted something more, a something he never clearly defined.

Immediately after the election, Koch announced that one of the first things he would do was fire Police Commissioner Michael J. Codd. Koch could not, in fact, legally do any such thing. The commissioner was always appointed to a five-year term, as against the mayor's elected four-year term. This was supposed to take the politics out of policing in New York. But it was the rare commissioner who had the bad grace to hang on knowing that his boss, the mayor, wanted him out. Every mayor, in practice, appointed his own commissioner and put the politics right back in.

Even as a nominee, Koch had talked the habitual tough clichés about controlling crime—as, indeed, had both Beame and Lindsay. Koch promised to appoint a commissioner who, among other things, would put more cops in the street. *All* mayoral candidates promised to put more cops in the street. Crime continued to rise, though, and the police force continued to shrink as fiscal disaster engulfed New York (and many of the nation's other cities soon after). The department went from 31,600 in 1974, the year Mayor Beame took office, to 25,500 in 1977, the year Koch was elected.

The incumbent police commissioner, who had been called out of retirement by Mayor Beame, did not wait to be fired by Koch, in spite of his legal right to stay on. Michael Codd was a career cop, once the department's chief inspector. A month after Koch's election, Codd announced he would resign and took himself quietly off to his home in Queens—New York's Cop Country—where he worked in his backyard garden, applied for an extra pension to compensate for what he said was a job-related strain on his heart (accompanied by a minor public outcry), and cultivated a splendid beard (an indulgence he never would have permitted himself as commissioner).

Codd, in Mayor-elect Koch's crotchety opinion, had lacked a spirit of innovation and experimentation. But largely it was a matter of style. Koch's free-wheeling, shoot-from-the-hip approach to city management, his uninhibited conversational and platform manner, clashed with Codd's remote, stiff-legged, rigidly traditional approach to policing. The police department was the mayor's toy and, more often than not, the commissioner became the mayor's puppet. The new mayor's appointment of a citizen's search panel to help find him a commissioner was taken seriously by the police department, and with restrained skepticism by cynical New Yorkers who followed such matters. The search panel members were lawyers, educators, and community leaders, most of them with backgrounds in some branch of the criminal justice system.

All the Top Brass of the police department were, in theory, candidates for the job of commissioner. But if a member of the Brass were named, he would have to put in his retirement papers, for the PC could not remain a uniformed member of the department. The mayor-elect, who would formally take office on January 1, 1978, wanted the panel's recommendation by December 7, 1977.

Even to be among those *considered* for the job meant you had made your special mark in the huge and furiously competitive NYPD. On the search panel's list, in addition to Courtenay and nine other high-ranking New York commanders, were several former NYPD chiefs, some of whom now headed smaller police departments in cities such as Hartford and Baltimore. Courtenay knew the competition was fierce and he told himself that if someone else were chosen as PC this time around, he would likely have another shot at the job within the next few years. The mandated retirement age for the New York police was sixty-three and Courtenay was now fifty-one—"a young fifty-one," he liked to say. He had time. Meanwhile, he certainly could expect to achieve three-star rank, possibly even the four-star rank of chief of operations, although that was almost as elusive a goal as commissioner.

For three months, Courtenay had been the Manhattan South area commander—the most visible of New York's seven area commanders (two for Manhattan, two for Brooklyn, and one each for the Bronx, Queens, and Staten Island). Assistant chiefs like Courtenay were the department's strategists, the field generals, heading armies larger than those of some small countries.

Courtenay commanded ten precincts manned by 2,700 cops and 300 civilian clerks—a force larger than the entire police department of Boston or, for that matter, Cleveland, Dallas, Milwaukee, or St. Louis. On his personal staff were a deputy chief (his executive aide), three inspectors, six deputy inspectors, and three captains; and the commanders of each of the ten precincts—captains and deputy inspectors—reported to him as well.

The job was a fitting celebration of Courtenay's thirtieth year with the NYPD. His turf was the city's undisputed center of action: tawdry Times Square and the glittering theater district; the United Nations with its frequent demonstrations; the East Side's foreign consulates with their sudden bomb threats; Little Italy with its revenge executions; Chinatown with its gang killings; Greenwich Village, Soho, Chelsea—all with their fluctuating middle class and their struggling poor, their bohemian and homosexual colonies; Bellevue, the city's busiest hospital; the Port Authority Bus Terminal with its runaways, prostitutes, and derelicts; Madison Square Garden with its giant political rallies and its rock concerts and rowdy sporting events; Grand Central Station, the Garment Center, Wall Street, Police Headquarters itself—not to mention the mayor's own workplace, City Hall. The Manhattan South area began at 59th Street, just below the vast, unsafe beauty of Central Park, and extended to the Battery, Manhattan's southernmost tip. It was the business, entertainment, fashion, financial, and political center of the city and—to some degree—the world.

Courtenay relished the command, but he'd had his disappointments. He was still two uniformed ranks away from the top. Less than a year and a half earlier he had been entrusted with the demanding job of organizing and running the police department's security operation for the 1976 Democratic National Convention, and he had done the job impeccably. But instead of being rewarded, as he had hoped and expected, with another challenging command— or, better still, with a promotion to three-star rank—he was given a make-work assignment at headquarters that lasted for a full tedious year. During that time the commissioner made shifts in the top ranks but Courtenay, deeply to his dismay, was overlooked.

What he had wanted and still did want, what almost every career cop who made it past the civil service rank of captain wanted, was to be named chief of detectives, the most glamorous job in the department. The chief of detectives was one of the department's three-star bureau chiefs, known at headquarters as Superchiefs, and sometimes as Dinosaurs, because in the view of most field commanders (until they themselves became superchiefs) they simply created red tape and were essentially obsolete. Above the five superchiefs in lonely Top Command, was the four-star chief of operations, answerable only to the commissioner and his handful of civilian deputies.

Courtenay believed that the incumbent chief of detectives was likely to be a casualty of the new administration, along with the already-departed PC, and he thought his chance of succeeding to that job was as good as or better than any of the eleven other assistant chiefs. While a qualified commissioner could be recruited from outside the department, all uniformed commanders had to be named from within the ranks. Everyone who became a New York

police commander had to begin as a patrolman after completing Police Academy training. The Academy was not a
West Point that turned out ready-made junior commanders. What the Academy produced, after conducting a six-
month course, were rookie patrolmen, most of them with
little more than a high school education. To become a police commander you had to grow On The Job.

The chief of operations and, usually, the headquarters
Superchiefs were closely identified with the PC; a new PC
was expected to sweep away the whole top echelon and
promote his own choices, who would be loyal to him. The
civilian PC could be recruited from another city. In 1970
the commissioner was Howard R. Leary, former Philadelphia PC and a stranger to the New York police. He was
followed by Patrick Murphy, the commissioner of Detroit's
police, who had earlier been a New York police captain.
The PC could also be an attorney with an interest in criminal justice—Vincent L. Broderick, who preceded Howard
Leary, was a chief assistant U.S. attorney and had never
walked a police beat.

The present chief of operations, James F. Hannon, was
appointed by Commissioner Michael Codd and was regarded (how could he not be?) as Codd's man, and so were
the present chief of detectives and the four other Superchiefs: the chief of patrol (at the moment, Courtenay's immediate superior), the chief of inspectional services, the
chief of personnel, and the chief of organized crime control.

But Courtenay prided himself on not playing politics,
and as a two-star chief he didn't have to. "I've never been
the police commissioner's man, or the first deputy commissioner's man, or the chief inspector's man," he liked to say.
"I work for the department. I don't believe in buttering,
because if you have to butter to get it, you have to butter to
keep it." (The chief inspector's title—from the British—
had only recently been changed to chief of operations, and
many old-timers in the department still used the old title.
The department was always taking a new look at its image
and revising its nomenclature, and Hannon was in effect

chief inspector or the police chief of New York, though he might just as well have been called Police Boss or Top Honcho. But, in fact, the designation *chief* corresponded to the military *general*, and the rank was graded, as were army generals, by stars.)

While Courtenay hungered for the detective chief's rank, he would not have said no to chief of patrol or organized crime control. If the mayor's search panel regarded him as a candidate for commissioner, Courtenay thought that was a good indication that his masterly job of patrolling the Democratic National Convention a year and a half earlier was not forgotten after all.

Not an immodest man, but aware of his strengths, Courtenay believed he'd been uniquely qualified for the job. Who but he could have handled—with such superb calm, such tact, such *generalship*—the truly dazzling police work that secured the safety and comfort of the convention, not to mention the world's press and every citizen's group with a grievance? He'd had to deal with the jealous presence of the Secret Service and the convention's own security operatives; with out-of-town, gun-toting police types; with the threatened participation of the National Guard; with the NYPD's own comically sinister intelligence division (Mel Brooks might have invented its operatives) and a contingency arrest team. The arrest team, created by Courtenay himself in one of his aberrant moments as Oberführer ("We'll keep them lean and mean!"), looked like shock troops when they drilled, were kept hidden in a cellar of Madison Square Garden, and surfaced only once in a quickly aborted sortie.

Now that it was over, Courtenay could reminisce in tranquil satisfaction. Dozens of delegates had written to the mayor praising the police work during the convention, as had attending governors, senators, and mayors. The presidential nominee himself called New York "the greatest of all cities" because he found it so well policed.

Courtenay worked on the convention's security plans for eight months, operating out of a cramped, glass-enclosed space improvised for him at headquarters, at one end of the large reception area outside the thirteenth-floor office of Chief of Operations James Hannon. It was under Hannon's supervision that the plans were made, second-guessed by Commissioner Codd.

Courtenay had been obliged to invent the rules as he went along, for there had not been a presidential convention in New York for fifty-two years, and policing had changed greatly since then. The most radical change of all was in the police attitude toward civil rights, and New York was out to prove that this presidential convention, unlike those in Chicago and Miami, could be policed without violent confrontation.

In the post-Serpico NYPD, the Brass was ever alert to incipient brutality, as well as corruption, and they aimed to show the world how New York's police could keep crowds under control with benevolent firmness, with patient strength. New York's police would employ strategy, electronic technique, and psychological indoctrination of its troops. The police would be prescient, sensitive, tolerant, and benign. They would carry their guns and clubs and be *prepared* for the worst, but not provoke it. There would be no unthinking brutality, no abuse of power.

Courtenay, with his deep sense of pride in his city and its police, his imposing personality, his pragmatism and tact, was the perfect choice to implement this ideal security force. It became his ruling passion to show off New York as a civilized city, and its police as urbane peace-keepers. His goal was for *nothing* to happen. He hoped to demonstrate that his city could host a tumultuous political convention for four days without even one cop having to use his gun or his club.

And as it transpired, those four days in July of 1976 afforded Courtenay the greatest professional joy of his life. He still glowed when he thought about it.

On Saturday, July 10, 1976, Dan Courtenay was changing into his uniform. It was two days before the Democratic

National Convention, and he was in his temporary field headquarters at Madison Square Garden. He was getting into uniform because a television crew wanted to interview him, and Commissioner Codd, a man of faultless military bearing himself, preferred that his field commanders *look* like field commanders when on public view. There was enormous self-assurance in all of Courtenay's movements, even though he was actually having to steel himself. He'd been interviewed often during recent months about the security arrangements for the convention, but interviews always made him nervous. He did not like to admit that.

In the room with Courtenay was Michael Shilensky, a young detective, wearing civilian clothes and a gun. Shilensky had a law degree and was on loan to Courtenay from the office of the deputy police commissioner for legal matters, which dealt, for the most part, with keeping the city's cops from tripping over anybody's civil rights and getting sued. Shilensky sat at a desk, speaking on the phone with lawyers representing a wide range of civil action groups— from anti-abortion to gay rights—who had achieved or were seeking permission to demonstrate in strategic times and places likely to be covered by the armies of the press, and particularly by the insatiable legions of television. The arrangements were complex and had been intensely negotiated during the past months. Shilensky was arguing about last-minute disputed territories that had or had not been granted by the police.

When Shilensky hung up, Courtenay said, "Tell the cop outside that I'll meet the TV people out front. I don't want the cameras in here, on my charts or my television monitors."

Courtenay was a benevolent spider, presiding over a web of electronic equipment. His Madison Square Garden field headquarters was a windowless cluster of small rooms, borrowed from the Garden's boxing office for the duration of what he and his staff referred to as "the DNC." The rooms were equipped with closed-circuit television to monitor the streets immediately surrounding the Garden; hot-line telephones to various strategic command and communications posts in Manhattan; and a squat computer terminal nicknamed Fat Nelly, that unrolled printout after printout of Copspeak. Commander-in-Chief Courtenay was ready to go to war, if necessary.

A lot of time and money had been spent to make the DNC a happy and proud event for New Yorkers and visitors alike. The police knew that the best way to avoid a battle was to be visibly and unmistakably prepared for one. To that end, $2.6 million was budgeted for security arrangements—this despite the fact that the city, since the summer of 1975, had been near bankruptcy. (Some of the money came from Washington.)

The room Courtenay chose as his own was equipped with a lumpy red rug. Rugs of any kind were scarce, even among the Top Brass down at police headquarters; the chief of operations had a deep blue carpet in his office at headquarters, but Courtenay's makeshift pre-DNC glass booth adjoining the chief of operations' reception area had a drab linoleum floor. Here at Madison Square Garden, even though the arrangement was only temporary, Courtenay finally had achieved the status of a carpet.

On the rug were three desks, a sofa covered in black vinyl, a metal clothes locker, a coat rack, and a color television. Closed-circuit monitors lined the rear wall behind Courtenay's desk, and above them was mounted a large bulletin board with an artistically rendered map of various strategic areas surrounding the Garden. A chart that hung over a row of telephones on Courtenay's desk listed the numbers for intelligence division, traffic area, Statler Hilton security, and other command posts—and for the National Guard, just in case. New York cops tended to view most other law-enforcement units, including the FBI, as provincial and unsophisticated; and they particularly mistrusted the National Guard, which they regarded as trigger-happy.

At the desk next to Courtenay's sat Inspector Herman C. Reed, borrowed for the DNC from the police narcotics division. Reed was a quiet, serious, middle-aged career cop, with whom Courtenay had worked comfortably before. Reed had no street duties for the time being and wore a short-sleeved shirt and slacks (and, of course, a gun). Reed was operations commander, assigned to help Courtenay with the day-to-day planning and running of DNC security.

"Is the white phone the hot line to Cliff Cassidy, upstairs?" Courtenay asked Reed. Clifford Cassidy was the DNC's own man in charge of security, reporting to Democratic National Chairman Robert Strauss. And Strauss was nominally the final arbiter in all major decisions concerning security. Courtenay, however, knew he would probably not consult either Cassidy or Strauss should a sudden emergency arise; there would not be time. But to the degree that it was possible, Courtenay maintained a diplomatic show of deference to the politicians who were pulling the strings from their more luxurious offices in the Garden's upper reaches.

Inspector Reed said yes, the white phone was a direct line to Cassidy, and as though on cue, the white phone rang. Confidently, and in the singsong voice he sometimes affected when he knew who was on the other end of the line, Courtenay lifted the receiver and said, "Hell-*oh, Cliff*-ord!" There was a chagrined pause. "It's *not* Clifford? Oh, it's Secret Service?" He recovered his aplomb. "Well, thanks for checking in." Grinning, he hung up and winked at Reed. "That's what this is all about! We have time to settle down and check the system!" The telephones serving the DNC had been installed in late June while the circus was still playing Madison Square Garden. Large enough to serve a good-sized town, the system encompassed 13,700 miles of wire, 7,000 lines and circuits, and 7 central offices.

Earlier in the morning—just as Courtenay was moving the last of his men and equipment into place in the Garden—Commissioner Codd had telephoned him.

"Dan," the PC said, "if this operation is a success, Jim Hannon and I will end up smelling like a rose. If it's a failure, *you're* dead." Courtenay knew the PC meant to be jocular, but still he was a little unnerved. Beneath his bravado was a layer of healthy insecurity.

Chief Courtenay had a tendency to overplan—at least that was the opinion of some of the commanders who'd worked under him. But this was such a big operation, not like running the St. Patrick's Day parade or patrolling a rock concert at Madison Square Garden, which he could do almost by rote. Understandably, Courtenay wanted to leave as little as possible to chance.

He knew, as did all police commanders, that no one could possibly foresee *every* contingency, or prevent—even with $2.6 million of the tightest security available—a determined terrorist attack or assassination (if the attackers were willing to die in their attempt). Still, some of his planning revolved around pretty wild possibilities: the kidnapping and hostage-taking of candidates; a sharpshooter crouched in the eaves of the Garden, as in *The Manchurian Candidate;* the introduction of poison pellets into the air-conditioning system; bombs in the tunnel under the convention floor that linked the Garden with the Statler Hilton Hotel, which was a DNC caucus center directly across from Madison Square Garden on Seventh Avenue.

Courtenay followed the news as closely as any politician, and he was aware that Jimmy Carter's nomination was regarded as a sure thing. He realized also that the decade of militant activism was in eclipse, and that much of the fight had gone out of the protest groups of the late 60s and early 70s. There was no Vietnam, and the issues of feminism, homosexual rights, and higher wages did not often ignite huge groups of activists into risking physical confrontation with the law and possible jailing.

Still, there had been requests by numerous groups that wished to rally in the streets outside Madison Square Garden during the four days of the convention, as well as on the Saturday and Sunday just preceding. These groups ranged from the sizable, well-organized Right to Lifers, to an amorphous collection of individuals claiming allegiance of a sort to the Yippies, who wanted to live in tents in Battery Park and be given free blood tests. Most of these groups were straightforward with the police about when and where they wanted to show up, and were given formal permission and promised protection for peaceful demonstrations or marches.

"We must give the demonstrators a chance to be seen and heard," Courtenay said. "The worst thing is to frustrate them." But there were other groups such as the municipal hospital workers who wanted higher pay and were threatening to strike; they were regarded as somewhat militant and (the police knew from experience) might try to demonstrate at the last minute, with no warning. There was always the danger of spontaneous confrontation, and that was the one thing Courtenay wanted fervently to avoid. "You gain nothing," he said. Courtenay (only a captain then) had followed with dismay the confrontations in Chicago between police and demonstrators. Wanting the benefit of their hindsight, he recently had flown to Chicago to consult with police officials there. "In Chicago, if anyone was wrong, *everyone* was wrong," Courtenay said, explaining that the youthful protestors had deliberately provoked the police and the police had wrongly allowed themselves to be goaded into a brutal response.

But crowd control was something the New York police had developed into an art, as Courtenay was always proud to point out. No city had bigger crowds to control; the NYPD had had lots of practice and had learned from some of its own shameful mistakes, such as the Columbia University riots of the 60s. The police, then, like other segments of the Establishment, had simply been unprepared for the phenomenon of privileged students actually wishing to provoke violent confrontation with their armed police. Since those days, the police had incorporated "sensitivity training" into their curriculum. They showed their troops training films, in which their brother officers (role-playing) were taunted and verbally abused in a simulated street demonstration. The idea was to inure them to such flash-words as *Pig* (the mildest of the epithets hurled at the role-playing cops by the role-playing demonstrators).

They were trained to shrug off verbal abuse, but they did not go so far as to give up their clubs (which they preferred to call batons). It was all but inconceivable that the sophisticated New York police would fire their guns into an unruly crowd. They were drilled to rely on their wits, on the authority of the uniform and, as a last resort, on physical restraint short of killing (what the public called brutality and the police called necessary and reasonable force).

The one thousand police officers assigned to special duty during the four days of the convention were given special training, and on June 18, three weeks before the Democrats were to convene, I spent a day at the Police Academy, where the training took place.

In the auditorium at 8:30 A.M. with almost every seat taken, Mike Shilensky stood on the stage and, to the accompaniment of groans, grumbles, and heckling, remarked that everything he was about to say was "subject to change." ("Naturally," groaned the cops.) Shilensky described the parameters of the demonstration areas, still being contested in court by lawyers for some of the demonstrating groups. He said there would be no room in the area for cops to park their own cars ("Call the P.B.A.!" cried a cop heckler). There would be no lockers provided for cops' equipment (groans).

"The uniform will be hats and bats," Shilensky said (meaning battle helmets and nightsticks), "but the PC says you can bring along your soft hat, too."

"God bless him!" came a sarcastic voice from the rear. (As it turned out, it was not necessary for the cops to wear their helmets.)

"When the gays demonstrate, do we get an early blow?" asked a cop, barely suppressing a snicker.

"If that's your preference," Shilensky replied calmly (raucous laughter).

Inspector Herman Reed joined Shilensky onstage and

apologized for Chief Courtenay's absence, explaining he had been called to a conference in the mayor's office.

"We have a tough mission," Reed said. "I wish I could share your levity. I hope I can laugh along when it's over, but we've been working and planning for months." He emphasized the police's duty to insure the safety of the "mass of humanity" expected during the four days in the area of Madison Square Garden. "Several thousand of the media will be looking at us," he warned, "and we must present a good image. You gentlemen will be the focal point." The hall was growing stuffy from body heat and cigarette smoke.

A cop wanted to know if any provision would be made for meals. "If you have a problem, see me and I'll take you to lunch," Reed said; then he added that the Patrolmen's Benevolent Association (PBA) would have a canteen in the area.

Shilensky explained the arrest procedure to be followed.

Cop: "Can we use the Eichmann defense—that we're just following orders—when we make an arrest?"

Shilensky: "You must witness the offense."

Cop: "Will anything be set up for injured police officers?"

Shilensky: "There will be a medical station with a nurse inside the Garden."

Shilensky and Reed were succeeded onstage by an intelligence officer who was an expert on demonstrations. After listing the groups that were known to the police and were cooperating with them (more or less), he mentioned such groups as the FALN (a small nationalist group of Puerto Rican terrorists) "who don't tell us their plans; they are the ones to worry about." Then there were the Yippies.

"They're the ones you'll come head to head with," he said. "They're great organizers and potheads. They'll be the street fighters, they'll go to the hotels. The Yippies once did a puke-in. Fifty of them went to a hotel and threw up in the lobby."

After a lunch break, the cops gathered in the third-floor

muster room for a refresher course in the uses of the night-stick. The instructor, James Smith, paired off his students. First they practiced a two-handed technique for hitting an attacker in the face; next they learned a one-handed method, with the left arm protecting the face; finally, they practiced defending the nightstick against an attacker who grabs it. The cops alternated as attackers and defenders, enjoying the physical exercise, laughing and sweating.

Smith explained to me, "You have to try to give them a mature balance of outlook." He tried to deal with the conflict between teaching what amounted to a method of violent attack and the stress on peaceful control.

Smith herded his group onto the roof, where there was more room. He had several cops lie down to show how to pick up a prone demonstrator. "It's too hard to lift a heavy man. The idea is to create a little pain, so he'll want to stand up by himself. What you do [he demonstrated] is to turn his wrist palm up, and with your other hand press under his elbow." The cop on whom he was practicing grunted and scrambled to his feet.

Smith illustrated the technique for getting a demonstrator who was sitting-in out of a chair: hold him around the neck with your right arm, press his head to his chest, press your left thumb under his ear lobe (the mastoid bone). "Once he feels pain, he'll stand up," Smith said, proving his point.

By now, dripping with sweat, the cops were herded back indoors for a session of what the police called "transcendental analysis." The instructor showed a film clip on television that purported to depict a white male provocateur ("Watch out for the small radical groups") haranguing a black cop from behind a police barricade. The black cop was too smart for him. Looking into the camera, he declared, "He's not going to break my chops. I'm OK now, I know where he's coming from." The watching cops snickered; they thought the film simplistic, if not asinine.

Next, they watched a film that showed a man taunting a white cop about his wife (what do you think *she's* doing while you're out here doing your job?). The language was nasty, but the cop (he knew where it was coming from) remained unmoved. The watching cops thought that film asinine, too.

The instructor suggested that any cop who might find himself getting hot under the collar in the face of provocation from a demonstrator should ask his sergeant's permission to walk down the block for a few minutes.

"Then you're giving in," protested a cop.

"No, you're keeping your cool. And if the guy follows you, you can arrest him for harassment. We must react not when *they* want us to, but at *our* discretion."

("We're not out for collars," Chief Courtenay had instructed his top bosses. "We have to select our commanders very, very carefully. If we see two cops whispering together—if we hear them saying, 'If that cat comes over the barrier, he's mine'—we have to *get him off the line.* We have to select the kind of captains who fit the mold we're looking for. We want no hard-noses out in the street. When you have an intermediate commander who doesn't like Yippies or gays or whatever—that attitude carries down the line. And when guys go to a meal, make sure it's a sergeant and five [Copspeak for a supervisor and five police officers]. We are not an attacking force. We are not an avenging force. This is the message we are giving our men in training sessions at the Police Academy.")

Finally, the cops were shown a film about the history and anatomy of riots. It began with Marc Antony's speech and went on to the storming of the Bastille. It was about the art of exploiting discontent; a police term for agitator was *Leninoid.* The film was more sophisticated than the other two, and it held the cops' attention.

The size of the convention, the concentration of visiting celebrities from all over the country, the presence of the news media from all over the world—and the opportunity for every fringe group and cultist advocate to be seen and heard—contributed to the tension of Dan Courtenay's assignment.

The responsibilities that went with being a high-ranking police commander in New York could be scary, but Courtenay had never been unwilling to accept responsibility. From the time they began patrolling a beat as rookies, all cops had to assume responsibility for firing their guns, and that was a matter of life and death, possibly their own.

Courtenay was the sum of his thirty years of Police Experience; like Tennyson's Ulysses, he was a part of all that he had met. He had started at twenty-one as a street cop just after World War II, fresh from a two-year tour on a naval destroyer in the Atlantic. He studied nights, on his days off, and once in a while, guiltily, on the job, in order to pass the Civil Service exams for sergeant, lieutenant, and captain. That took him eighteen years. And then, nearly forty, he went to college at night to earn the degree that as a youth he hadn't known he wanted. Even now, he wasn't sure what had impelled his quest for a higher education. "I honestly don't know why I decided to get my degree," he explained. "Maybe ego." Nonetheless, he was going on for his master's degree—in labor management. And he still believed that for police work, "street knowledge is in many ways more important than a college degree." With all his laboriously earned rank and his late-acquired education, he was still the tough street cop from Queens, with his inherited working-class values, his unflinching belief in Family, Service, God, and the Democratic way of life.

True, he had *unlearned* some of the traditional prejudices cherished by cops. He accepted the fact of high-ranking blacks on the police force. When he joined in 1947, a black police chief was unthinkable; just recently he had been outranked by a black three-star chief of patrol, and his opposite number, the Brooklyn North area commander, was a black assistant chief. Courtenay had to swallow the idea of women patrolling the streets and confronting the same haz-

ards he confronted. He'd been raised (like the heroes of
Victorian literature) to feel *protective* toward women, not to
use coarse language in front of them, to shelter them from
precisely the sort of besmirching experiences that lurked in
the streets, that only men (or prostitutes) should have to
deal with.

And finally, courageously, he had accepted the possibility of homosexuals on the force, probably the greatest
cultural wrench of all. He taught himself to use the officially sanctioned word *gay* and could almost say it without
choking.

"I'm not concerned about gay cops," he said. "Some cops
may be concerned, because it challenges their masculinity
to be shown that a homosexual can do the same job as they
can; we've already seen that women can do the job,
though—why not qualified homosexuals?" (It fell to the
eminent choreographer George Balanchine to poke through
the hypocrisy of the issue. Regretting the lack of tradition
for male ballet dancers in the United States, he commented
in 1980, "In America it wasn't allowed for boys until recently. American boys wanted to be football and baseball
players, policemen and firemen. Nobody knew how many
sissy policemen there were. . . .")

Courtenay also had learned how to stride past a police
barrier that bounced with pot-smoking Yippies and feel
hardly any urge at all to smack them around. Coolness and
a sense of proportion had to be worn with a New York
police chief's stars in the late 1970s. Shortly before the
DNC, when 1,500 marchers celebrated National Marijuana
Day by openly smoking pot in Central Park, the police
ignored them, acknowledging they were outnumbered.
Courtenay personally disapproved of marijuana as a harm-
ful drug (unlike alcohol in moderation, which he considered
sociable and relaxing).

Courtenay regarded himself as a man of the world. And
yet, within the broad, proud, navy blue breast, hung with
its discreet rows of commendatory ribbons, lay a slumber-
ing street cop, one eye open—a police animal, the best kind

of cop. It was possible to hunger for power without being greedy, and possible to hold the kind of limited power a police commander could attain in libertarian, urban America, without being corrupted. It was possible, and Courtenay managed nicely. He enjoyed his life. And he tried not to think too much about the darker side of the Police Experience. It took a lot of surviving out in the street—and off duty, too. Not everyone made it.

> News item: In White Plains, a suburb of New York, on May 9, 1979, a 39-year-old off-duty police officer named Jose Torres tried to shoot his estranged wife while the couple were awaiting a court hearing. He missed his wife and critically wounded a woman bystander, and then was himself shot and killed by an armed officer of the court. Torres, ten years in the NYPD, had recently been returned to active duty and was assigned to the Bronx youth gang squad. Two months earlier, his service revolver was taken from him and he was placed on restricted duty, after he had twice threatened his wife, Carmen, with a gun, and once assaulted her in her home in Peekskill, N.Y. The police medical department had determined less than a week earlier that Torres was fit to return to active duty and gave him back his gun.

Torres was only one among many cops who found it hard to leave behind the stresses of the street; career frustrations and anxieties spilled over into their personal lives. At the end of their daily or nightly tours, these cops slipped back to their closed world (most often a neat house in Queens, but sometimes an apartment in Manhattan), where frequently their households held wives who were having nervous breakdowns, delinquent children, checkbooks that didn't balance. The grinding isolation and daily tensions of The Job often impelled these cops to drink too much, drive too fast, gain too much weight, have illicit love affairs, blow up, blow away a kid with a toy gun who happened to be the wrong color in the wrong street at the wrong time, blow their own brains out. Was it the stress of The Job that resulted in marital discord, panic-shooting, suicide? Or did the police department, like prisons and psychiatric hospitals, attract men whose psychic systems were programmed for anger and hostility?

Divorce was high among the police and so were the other symptoms of alienation: alcoholism, rage, cunning, suicide. A survey by a faculty member of the New York Police Academy revealed that during a five-year period ending in December 1975, twenty-eight cops took their own lives, most of them shooting themselves with their service revolvers. Was it the good guy in them trying to annihilate the bad guy? Or the other way around?

Cops could both sympathize with and despise the criminals they confronted. Cops were closer to duality than most of us, because of that dark affinity. That was why the collision between cop and thug could sometimes be savage. The cop was trying to beat his own evil impulses into submission. Probably the most thieving and corrupt cops were also the most brutal. The very word *cop* was dualistic. The original Anglo-Saxon meant the head or crest; but the slang meant to steal or rob.

American cops were understandably ambivalent about their guns. It wasn't that they were unaware of the cultural symbolism of the gun as sex organ. But they weren't sure if they should feel good or bad about having that symbolic secondary organ. And the culture—insofar as it was represented by some of our leading male novelists—was not much help with the problem. These novelists couldn't even think straight about their *primary* organ. Some of them dodged the issue by describing this organ coyly, as their "member," while others swaggered and used blunter words. But to a man they dwelt obsessively on their member's condition and behavior.

Joseph Heller, in *Something Happened*, described for 569 pages a quintessential little boy, howling from within his mature man's frame that he couldn't tolerate growing up. A huge part of the protagonist's problem was, predictably, his infantile castration fear. "I get the feeling when I'm alone in strange American cities that I have no inner resources and no cock," wrote Heller in his hero's guise.

And John Cheever, describing the baffled, middle-aged hero of his final novel, *Oh What a Paradise It Seems*, wrote with a kind of reverential irony (and, in this instance, eschewing the vernacular): "Putting his genitals into his trousers, Sears seemed to think he was handling history."

I won't begin to list the frenzied complaints ascribed to Portnoy by Philip Roth. These novelists reflected their own kind: non-gun-bearing, upward-striving, gifted, eloquent, grown-up-seeming equivocators, all of them struggling to keep their one and only member fully functional, all of them striving to live up to their self-invented coat of arms: a Glorious Penis Rampant.

How much more bewildering, then, having to cope with a second, symbolic organ. The cop's burdensome coat of arms, perforce, was a squamate lizard. Male squamate lizards—first cousins to the snake—had two penises, each linked to a corresponding testis; a recent study by Harvard revealed that the lucky lizard felt free to use either penis at random when mating.

If I seem to exaggerate the sexual significance of his gun as viewed by the American male police officer, let me refer you to yet another prominent male novelist who was for fourteen years an American police officer. Former Lieutenant Joseph Wambaugh of the Los Angeles police department was a writer admired by the New York police (although there was much they did not admire about the LAPD itself). They thought that Wambaugh sometimes embroidered for effect, but they also thought he mostly told it like it was.

Early in his novel *The Glitter Dome*, Wambaugh began a scene in which his hero contemplated suicide: "It was six inches long. He stroked it lightly, but he could not conjure an appropriate response: eroticism, revulsion, fascination, *terror.* . . . He stroked the thing again. It had hung on his body for too long. More of a cock than the other one."

Wambaugh's was an authentic cop voice, the only such voice in contemporary American fiction. He chose policing but discovered he was a born writer. When he described a policeman's gun as "his unfailing surrogate cock," he knew what he was talking about. He knew that their gun-given sense of double-virility did much to explain the character of our police. The language of male sexuality and the language of the gun were often interchangeable. The cop's phrase for a fellow cop who shot himself through the roof of the mouth—the surest way, though unpleasant for whoever found the body—was, "He ate his gun." The phrase was vivid and ugly and apposite.

Cops of all ranks have told me how they felt (at least superficially) about their guns; I didn't expect revelation. One said he never thought about it, he carried his gun as casually as a pocket comb. Another said he would, in a way, prefer *not* to carry a gun (like most of his British cousins), adding that cops probably got into more trouble having guns than not. I knew a detective who quite often carried his gun in a brown paper bag, and an inspector who carried his (on social occasions) in a neat leather attaché case. An about-to-retire chief told me, "I'll be very relieved when I don't have to carry a gun anymore." But a retired captain, rather alarmingly, told me, "I wouldn't dream of *not* carrying a gun; the city is a scary place—I *know!*"

Most cops who made it to the top in New York had never fired at anything but a target on the rifle range. "I can hit the target when I aim at it," Dan Courtenay once said, "but I've never had to shoot anybody—and that doesn't make me feel any less whole." Courtenay did have the quirky habit, when not in uniform, of strapping his off-duty revolver to his ankle; it had earned him the nickname Popeye after the character in *The French Connection.*

Big Dan Courtenay was a balanced man, well married, devoted to his family, fulfilled in his job, and on this Saturday, July 10—two days before the opening of the DNC—he was having fun.

"Mrs. Jimmy Carter is coming in with three Georgia cops, one of them a former New York City cop." Deputy Chief James B. Meehan offered this bit of information. As a deputy chief, Meehan was entitled to wear a single star on his shoulder boards, and an oak leaf garland on the peak of his cap. But Meehan's present assignment didn't call for a uniform, and he was wearing a conservative business suit. Meehan, who headed the department's intelligence division, was wry, wary, a bit supercilious, and even more sarcastic than Courtenay. He brought a slight chill into the atmosphere of bouncy bonhomie with which Courtenay generally managed to surround himself. He added, glumly, "The PC wants *us* to cover her, too."

"If that's what the PC wants," Courtenay replied evenly.

Chief Meehan's staff had worked out a code for radio transmissions in the street. A confidential memo to Courtenay read: "The use of this system will not obviate the interception of transmission, but it will prevent an interceptor from discovering the meaning of the messages." The overall code name for the DNC security operation was Overlord, and Courtenay's code name was Madison Leader. Meehan's was Overlord Chief.

Madison Leader sat at his desk consulting with Detective-lawyer Shilensky, carefully pasting bits of tape on his charts to indicate where protesters would be allowed to demonstrate. On Sunday, the day before the convention, 100,000 Right to Lifers would march around Madison Square Garden at noon, and at 3 P.M. between 5,000 and 10,000 members of the New York State Coalition of Gay Organizations would follow suit. The pro-lifers wished to demonstrate for a constitutional amendment to overturn "the Supreme Court's infamous abortion decisions" of 1973, and the gays wished to demonstrate for repeal of "all consensual sodomy laws."

The police were sensitive to the civil rights of the populace, an attitude they held less from humanity than from fear of legal retaliation. The department's behavior was being monitored by the American Civil Liberties Union and other watchdog groups, and that was why Courtenay was being legally advised almost minute by minute by Shilensky. Anticipating what could happen in the courtroom was an ongoing and serious part of all cops' thinking. Courtenay would keep Shilensky at his side, even in the street. *Especially* in the street.

Inspector Milton Schwartz and Captain Robert Hartling breezily greeted Courtenay. Inspector Schwartz was on loan to Courtenay from the Manhattan South area command, and for the duration of the convention he would be Courtenay's commander of uniformed street troops, as Inspector Reed was in charge of staff. Schwartz was wearing the commander's hot-weather uniform of long-sleeved, blue dress shirt and black tie, with no jacket. The eagle of his rank was pinned to the points of his shirt collar. He was smoking a cigar—a *good* cigar.

Captain Hartling, a chubby, gruff-sounding, no-nonsense, old-time cop and an expert logistician, had been working for weeks on the rosters and duty charts designed to create the maximum coverage at the least expense with 1,000 cops. Because of New York's fiscal crisis the police were under instructions to be thrifty. On July 1, 1975, Mayor Beame had ordered Commissioner Codd to fire 5,000 cops (3,000 sanitation department workers and 1,500 fire fighters were also dismissed). Two days later the governor gave the mayor enough money to restore to their jobs all the laid-off sanitation men and some of the firemen, as well as 2,000 cops. Still, the department was depleted. Its commanders had to be resourceful, and they were. "We do things with mirrors," Courtenay told me, explaining how you could make a dozen mounted police seem like three dozen if you had them show up quickly in a new location before their absence was noticed in the old one, and then returned them rapidly to the first location, and so on. The best trick, though, was the Driverless Van. Some mechanically skilled cops had rigged up a small van with a periscope and a special driving mechanism, so that the vehicle could be operated by a cop who crouched in the rear and was invisible to anyone in the street. Rolling resolutely along, the Driverless Van was designed to strike terror into the hearts of unruly demonstrators and cause them to fall back submissively.

With a reduced force and budget, the police department could no longer assign men as lavishly as had been its habit in years past. Promises of a smooth operation had been made to the convention's leaders in the summer of 1975 while the city was laying off cops with one hand and keeping its fingers crossed with the other. When Chief of Operations Hannon told me late in August that approval was momentarily expected from the DNC, I asked him if he wasn't worried about policing such a major event with his depleted force.

"If it supports the city, then I'm for it," he said. "We can handle the problems and we'll find the money somewhere."

Two hundred sergeants, for instance, were going to cost the city—with overtime and fringe benefits—$378,132.30. Some of the money would come from Washington, but only if the convention's 1,000 cops represented an ethnic balance, reflecting the city's population of blacks and Puerto Ricans. Courtenay had wrestled with that requirement at headquarters many months earlier, during conferences attended by both Inspector Schwartz and Captain Hartling.

"If we can't get ethnic balance," Courtenay warned them, "we get no federal bread."

"You have me, for a start," Inspector Schwartz said helpfully. "Jews are a minority group."

"So are assistant chiefs," Courtenay said.

Captain Hartling had merely smiled and set to work. He smoked steadily with the obstinacy of middle age, and bummed cigarettes from Shilensky, who also smoked steadily, with the heedlessness of youth. Hartling's assignment, like Reed's, was mainly indoors, and he was dressed in sport shirt and baggy slacks.

Schwartz and Hartling informed Courtenay that they had just completed a check of street barriers, those gray wooden sawhorses (soon to be repainted robin's-egg blue) that bore the stenciled warning POLICE LINE DO NOT CROSS, and that were a psychological (certainly not a physical) deterrent to the sudden swell of a human tide. Schwartz said that in the area where the main demonstrations were to take place—Eighth Avenue, between the Garden's rear entrance and the two-block-square U.S. Post Office across the avenue—there were nowhere near the number of barriers that were ordered and promised.

Courtenay turned to Inspector Reed.

"Herm, see if you can get Lieutenant Frawley at home." Courtenay's tone was sardonic. "Try current situations, they should have a number for him." Frawley was the man Courtenay had put in charge of delivering the 1,000 barriers deemed necessary for the DNC operation.

"Of course, they may have been set up in the wrong places—but the total count, all we could find, is way under the thousand we were promised," Schwartz said.

The fourteen-foot-long barriers, costing $40 apiece, were transported by special trucks that held sixty each, and whose rear ends were equipped with a hydraulic lift. The mechanism frequently did not work, the barriers often were not in their storage places when the trucks came for them, and cops hated loading and unloading them. Setting up barriers was a dirty job that soiled uniforms; cops paid their own cleaning and repair bills. Another problem was theft—the department lost about 1,000 barriers a year to vandals and derelicts, who built outdoor fires with them. Often, when large numbers of barriers were required, they did not materialize until the last minute. On the other hand, when only a small number were needed, such as the dozen or so to cordon off the streets bounding a crime scene, they seemed to appear within minutes from nowhere (or from out of whatever magic hat the cops pulled their black slickers at the first drop of rain, or the money to buy an informant in a homicide case).

"You better get another count, Mickey," Courtenay said.

"And tomorrow see if you can get some men in plain clothes to move them around."

Schwartz turned to Hartling. "Let me have your map. I'll send someone out to count again."

Inspector Schwartz was ten months younger than Courtenay and two ranks lower. He had been an inspector for three years and thought he was overdue for promotion to one-star deputy chief. He sometimes wondered if he would have risen faster had he been part of the Irish Catholic majority that had always dominated the New York police. While he had the presence and authority of the born police commander and could trade barracks wisecracks unself-consciously with Courtenay, there was a melancholy just under the surface. It showed when he was unguarded, in his eyes, which looked haunted, and in the haggard lines of his face. He was under particular stress because of a troubled personal life, and he tended to overcompensate in his work.

Mickey Schwartz was a trim five feet eleven inches and had a head of thick, dark hair (Courtenay's was receding). Also, he watched his waistline more carefully; he had half of Courtenay's bulk. Were Schwartz not a first-rate commander, Courtenay would not have requested him for his DNC team. Courtenay was a practiced judge of character, and Chief Hannon had given him his pick of inspectors.

Courtenay was on the phone by now with Lieutenant Frawley, ordering him to "*find* and *deliver forthwith*" the rest of the promised barriers. Hanging up, he told his team, "If we can't get what we need, I'll call Chief Hannon, and we'll go out and pick up barriers ourselves."

A uniformed cop put his head in the door.

"Chief, the people from CBS are here."

Courtenay winced, then covered the gesture. He opened his steel locker and took out a pre-knotted black tie. Like Schwartz, he wore the summer uniform of blue shirt, navy blue trousers, no jacket. He clipped the tie under his collar. In the nearly three decades since he'd first begun walking a beat, he had learned many small ways to keep the enemy off balance and himself uninjured. A clip-on tie was one of those small ways.

"More police should wear this kind of tie," he said. "You don't go *with* it if someone grabs you by it."

He settled his cap, tilting it slightly, aware that it flattered him. He and his fellow chiefs—those entitled to wear the parenthesis of golden oak leaves on the peaks of their caps—called the ornamentation "scrambled eggs," a form of self-deprecation that was really bragging.

Reflexively, Courtenay patted his hip for its service revolver and slipped a stick of gum into his mouth. A reformed cigarette smoker, the General chewed gum at moments of stress.

And now, orgulous and bellicose, Big Dan Courtenay strode down the narrow passageway of his cavelike network of offices toward the street, to the painful but necessary chore of the television interview. (Chief Hannon, Commissioner Codd, the first dep—even the mayor—would likely watch the interview on the evening news; if Courtenay misspoke, they might jump on him.)

On his way Courtenay passed Captain Hartling, who told him, "You were right, Boss, about the barriers. Chief Sachson went out after Operation Sail last week and glommed everything in the street." (Jules Sachson was the commander of Brooklyn South, where large crowds had gathered on July 4 to watch the procession of tall ships celebrating the nation's Bicentennial.)

Courtenay grinned distractedly and kept moving. He stepped into the street, his large uniformed presence exuding benign reassurance. The television crew closed in and he was asked if the numbers of cops assigned to DNC security would leave the rest of the city without adequate protection in view of the recent manpower cuts. (Of course not. The extra manpower was being mustered through overtime assignments.) He was asked who would decide whether Madison Square Garden would be evacuated in the event of a bomb threat. (The Democratic National

Chairman, Robert Strauss.) That question and answer pained him. Just a few months earlier—well into the planning for the DNC—Courtenay had told Chief Hannon at headquarters: "Dealing with political types is very different from dealing with police types. They introduce unexpected elements. They are willing to accept a lower level of security, they want no metal-detector wands, no bomb-sniffing dogs on display."

Courtenay considered disguising a bomb-sniffing dog as a seeing-eye dog by giving the handler a white cane and glasses. He was particularly concerned about the right procedure in case of a bomb threat. And while he maintained publicly that he and his staff were "adjusted to the fact that it won't be our decision," he privately told Hannon that if he were convinced that a genuine bomb threat existed, he would personally order the Garden evacuated, "no matter what Strauss says."

Of course, he said no such thing to the television cameras that stalked him and occasionally caught him during the next few days. For them he flashed a reassuring tiger's grin, quickly said something upbeat—"We're in good shape, we anticipate no problems"—and signed off, leaving the viewer, like Alice, with nothing but the grin.

TWO

★ Chief of Operations James Hannon, the department's top uniformed commander, was one of the ten police officials whose name, along with Courtenay's, was on the search panel's list of candidates for commissioner. (There was one three-star headquarters bureau chief on the list, and the other seven were of two- or one-star rank.)

Jim Hannon was New York's forty-second police chief since 1803, when the first was named. Although that worked out to an average four-year term, most police chiefs did not last even that long. Like commissioner, they were subject to the political whims of city government.

In his office the morning of December 1, 1977, Hannon was trying to assess his chances realistically, to balance misgivings against hope. He had received a phone call inviting him to present his credentials to the search panel, and he had an appointment with its members at noon.

Hannon was not ready to quit the department. But if the new mayor didn't want him as commissioner, he might *have* to leave. Of course, he *might* be asked by whoever *did* become the new PC to stay on as chief of operations. That depended a lot on who the new commissioner was and even on whom the commissioner chose as his first deputy. Since the civilian PC and his civilian first dep, together with the uniformed chief of operations, were the triumvirate that ran the department, their styles had to mesh. Hannon, snugly situated until now, had come up through the ranks with the outgoing PC, who had valued him as a solid, traditionalist cop. And Hannon had a particularly warm personal relationship with the commissioner's first dep, James M. Taylor, also a veteran commander and a man cut from the same cloth as Hannon. Taylor was scheduled to leave with Codd.

For the past two and a half years Hannon had worked smoothly with Codd and Taylor. If the new commissioner were to be someone in Codd's mold or Taylor's, Hannon might well be asked to remain as chief of operations. Such a commissioner might even ask Hannon to be his first dep. Hannon did not want to think much beyond that. But the scenario was unlikely, in view of the new mayor's tilt.

I had often heard Hannon say things like, "The closer you get to the top, the more vulnerable you are," and "We know that in our jobs there is a built-in terminality." He had seen the High Command topple before, and he knew it would happen again whenever there was a change at City Hall. But, up to now, it had always happened to the other guy.

Hannon sat at his desk at headquarters, patiently turning the pages of *The New York Times*, which he read daily along with the *Daily News* and the *Post*. An inch under six feet, he was broad-shouldered and heavyset, with a straight spine and thinning, sand-colored hair. There was a worn dignity in his bearing, and his face bore the shuttered look that most police commanders assumed by the time they reached the rank of captain. After thirty-one years on the force, Hannon wore his police commander's mask—appraising, impervious, wary, unflappable, stoical, anticipating crucifixion—almost more easily than he wore his own face.

In the paper that morning he found a story that did not cheer him: According to sources close to Mayor-elect Koch, the job of police commissioner was about to be offered to a former Manhattan assistant district attorney, John F. Keenan. Named eighteen months earlier as special state

prosecutor by Governor Hugh Carey, Keenan had headed
the DA's Homicide Bureau and later served as chief assistant district attorney. Keenan was quoted in the story: "I
have not been offered the position of police commissioner."
Hannon did not know what to believe, but the article increased his unease.

"You'd think," Hannon said as he prepared to keep his
appointment with the search panel, "that anyone who's gotten to my rank in the biggest police department in the
country would automatically qualify as commissioner." His
voice was mild, but his smile was wan. He was so absolutely straight himself that he had an innocent faith in the
candor of others in high position. If he were not a strong
contender for commissioner, why would the panel interview him? It did not occur to him that the interview might
be a simple courtesy, a deference to his rank (and perhaps to
his imminent banishment).

For two and a half years I had been attending headquarters meetings with Hannon, accompanying him on his occasional trips into the field and, whenever he had an
uninterrupted moment, asking him questions about his life,
his job, and his attitude toward policing. I wanted to know
if there was such a thing as a cop mentality, to find out
whose side the Police Brass was really on, whether we had
any reason to trust them, if we really did have the police we
deserved.

I was mindful of Bernard Malamud's challenge: "When
you write a biography, you want to write about people who
will strain to make you understand them." Malamud was
speaking of D. H. Lawrence, admittedly a difficult fellow
to grasp, but—even Malamud would concede—more ac-
cessible than a police chief. Unattuned to many of our
cultural reference points, police chiefs did not have the
habit of easy revelation. They sometimes allowed their
wives to know them, but few others. Former New York
Commissioner Patrick Murphy once referred to the closed
world of cops as "the grossly insular, fragmented police
world."

Hannon and I first met in 1973 when I was writing a book about a newly formed squad of Manhattan homicide detectives. He was then the commander in charge of all Manhattan detectives and the first member of the police Brass whom I came to know. The new squad was small and experimental, a commando unit that operated under Hannon's direct supervision. There were 661 homicides in Manhattan in 1972, of which fewer than half were solved. Hannon decided which homicides the squad members would investigate, and they formed an unusually close relationship with their high-ranking boss. While Hannon, at first, seemed remote, I gradually learned to see him through the eyes of the detectives. I began to share their respect for him, and I found him, at last, approachable. The police were an acquired taste, like rhubarb.

Gaining access to the detectives in the first place had been possible only because then-Police Commissioner Patrick Murphy, who had conferred upon Hannon his second star in 1972, was willing to demonstrate that the New York police department no longer had anything to hide. He accepted and encouraged my investigation of the theretofore tightly closed (not to mention historically brutal and corrupt) Detective Bureau, at a time when most other big-city police departments and many smaller ones as well were still clamped shut. Indeed, as late as the summer of 1982, the 14,000-member International Association of Chiefs of Police threatened to expel Murphy for publicly criticizing the shortcomings of various police departments and for characterizing much of the Police World as "racist" and socially regressive.

News items from all over:

In 1979, things were so bad in Philadelphia that the U.S. Civil Rights Commission felt obliged to look into charges of condoned police violence and brutality. The commissioner also investigated the Houston police. "If a police officer decided he wanted to execute me, he probably could," said the Reverend Jack McGinnis, a Roman Catholic priest in Houston.

In Washington, D.C., that same year, the chief of detectives, William Trussell, was publicly accused of racism. According to some of his white detectives, Trussell had remarked—in a discussion about traumatic shock: "Not all people go into shock. Animals don't go into shock and neither do blacks."

In Miami, in 1980, there was widespread rioting in the wake of the killing of a black businessman by four white police officers.

In Milwaukee, racial tension was high by the end of 1981 as a result of the police killing of a black rape suspect who turned out to have been innocent. "It is a problem that has been festering for years," said Patrick Flood, the executive director of the Greater Milwaukee conference on Religion and Urban Affairs. "The problem has polarized city communities racially, with minorities viewing the police as a surveillance force in their communities."

In Los Angeles, the nation's highest paid police chief, Daryl F. Gates—his salary in 1982 was $94,500 for running a force of only 7,000—publicly defended himself for a statement made in an interview. "We may be finding," he said, "that in some blacks when the chokehold is applied, the veins or arteries do not open up as fast as they do in normal people." Earlier, he had stated that a major reason that more "Hispanic" police officers had not risen higher in the department was that they were "lazy."

Even with Commissioner Murphy's blessing, and later with Commissioner Codd's, it took months before the detectives stopped avoiding me. For at the time the New York police were just recovering from their trauma of corruption.

Murphy left New York in the spring of 1973 while I was still studying the detectives and was replaced (after a brief, interim tenure) by Michael Codd. Codd, while himself no innovator, endorsed most of the Murphy reforms and appointed Hannon his chief of operations. It never occurred to me that Hannon would become within three years of my meeting him the department's four-star chief and be in a position to grant me free-roaming access to the police hierarchy.

Of course, he had to be of a mind to do so. Early in our acquaintance I asked him to attend a small dinner party given for me by a friend to celebrate the publication of my book about the detectives. The guests were mainly writers and journalists, and Hannon was reluctant. In almost any social gathering, he said, he was likely to "end up having to defend the police." He did not find that restful after a day's work.

Cops tended to linger in their traditional cultural grooves, even when they rose to high officialdom. Police chiefs in New York fell into the demographic criteria established for the upwardly mobile middle class. A two-star chief earned $42,000 in 1976 (and nearly $59,000 by 1982). The chiefs were not socially easy in that bracket. They traveled abroad, they attended an occasional Broadway show with their wives, they read some, but spiritually they seldom moved out of Queens. Few of them grew up among books. They could acquire an academic education in middle age, but it was almost impossible to catch up on cultural references, to train esthetically the middle-aged ear or eye. Little things caught them. One day I was office-hopping at headquarters. From Chief Hannon's suite it was a short stroll to the office complexes of the chief of Patrol and the chief of Detectives, as well as that of the chief of Organized Crime Control. I overheard a high-ranking official dictating a letter to a clerical aide.

Official: " . . . for security reasons, I do not propose to go into detail, but there are myramid problems involved with . . ."

Aide: "How do you spell that, Boss? The word just before *problems*?"

Official: "My-ra-mid. The way it sounds."

Aide: "Right, Boss."

Every one of the chiefs fell into small errors of this kind, and the better-read among them were conscious of their own rough edges. Mostly, they spoke in the accents of working-class New York, and they had difficulty with a word like *precinct*, which usually came out "pre-sinnt" or "pre-sink." In a wide-ranging, general conversation, they would often feel insecure, and they were reluctant to ask questions that might seem naive or gauche. Yet on the subject of policing they could be amusing, eloquent, even rhapsodic. Most of their close friends, they told me, were "outside the department," lived in the cop-commander's neighborhood, and were, themselves, blue-collar–oriented. The rest of their socializing was done at police functions, of which there were myriad.

Despite Patrick Murphy's efforts to encourage openness, most of the chiefs preferred to stay behind their stony facade and say nothing. They made you pay your dues, if you wanted to know them. I soon found that many police officials were peeved by my presence at headquarters. They particularly mistrusted journalists (a category to which I only loosely belonged) who, they believed—sometimes with justification—hungered exclusively for news of police abuse and disarray and had no sympathy for police perseverance and dedication and service. Actually, journalists were one group of civilians with whom the police did, constantly, rub elbows; police and journalists fought a war almost as intimate and persistent as the war between police and criminals. Most cop-commanders suspected that the press perceived them as brutal, greedy, and arrogant. The press, these commanders thought, was skeptical of their honor and enjoyed nothing better than exposing them. With a zealous belief in their mission, police commanders felt that the press should support their efforts and serve their interests. They understood their own professional function, which, as the good cops among them practiced it, was honorable service to the vulnerable public. But they misunderstood the professional function of journalism and failed to grasp that the good journalist strove to practice unbiased and honorable service to the reading public. And while some of Hannon's subordinate chiefs remained permanently disgruntled and hostile, regarding my intrusion into their world as both impudent and threatening, some did, ultimately, surrender.

Doubtless my being a woman in what was still largely a male world gave me an edge. It was easier for a cop-commander to tell a woman about his personal attitudes and feelings; it was part of the cop credo to appear invulnerable to other men. I encouraged that. While I always respectfully addressed the chiefs by their titles, I allowed them to patronize me by using my first name. It came naturally to them to patronize a woman, and also to be playful, to show off.

After all, they were the ones who took the risks and kept the ghosts and goblins at bay for the sake of wives and daughters. They went into the dark and dangerous places, risking their necks (clutching their guns, covering their members). Their wives and daughters (and if they were still around, their mothers, too) waited and admired and, like Desdemona, thrilled to the tales of dangers passed.

Even the writer Muriel Spark, who seemed to me to be fearless and altogether self-sufficient in the independent life she lived, was not untouched by this masculine mystique. She obliquely conveyed in a poem something of this sense:

Of course, the idea of being seized is
A prehistoric female urge, probably, rising
Up from the Cave, which must have been exciting.
And perhaps, one would hope for a charming interrogator

Yes, I do agree, I wouldn't like it really.
It's only just an idea. . . .

All of the chiefs had a vested interest in their police careers, in their fattening retirement pensions, in their images. All of them were still haunted by the pre-1970 days of unpunished corruption and ignored brutality, the bad years, the pre-Serpico years. Those who submitted to my scrutiny felt profoundly secure in their professionalism and integrity and some of them had the sense of irony to feel challenged by the idea of an outsider observing them. After a while they began (as Hannon had predicted they would) to be at ease with me. By the time Mayor-elect Koch announced that he planned changes for the department, I was caught up in their destinies.

Dressed in civilian clothes and outwardly calm, Hannon left headquarters to keep his appointment with the search panel. Shortly after noon on that cold December Thursday in 1977, his black limousine, immediately recognizable as official by its stalks of silver antenna front and rear, slid up the ramp of the subterranean headquarters garage. Police headquarters was housed in a stark, sprawling, red brick building, its front entrance guarded by a monstrous, cast-iron sculpture. It was bounded on the north by Pearl Street, one of the city's oldest thoroughfares, and on the south by a short new street named Avenue of the Finest. Built under Mayor Lindsay at a cost of $58 million to replace the architecturally striking but obsolete Headquarters on Centre Street, it opened in the autumn of 1973, and a year later its terraces had already begun to crumble. The new headquarters was symbolic of the bureaucracy brooding within its walls: a mixture of decay and verve, of bungling and grace.

Gliding by the five slender mock-Greek columns incongruously planted at the rear of the building, Hannon's car swung past the stanchions of the Brooklyn Bridge and pushed uptown on the East River Drive. Hannon sat in the front passenger seat. His occasional frown was a fog closing in, hiding anger. Under stress he was betrayed by a habit of puckering and unpuckering his mouth, and he was doing that now. Resolute and impassive, Hannon was an exemplary product of urban street life, of Irish-immigrant, working-class roots, of a rigid religious upbringing, of his harsh police training.

First there had been the patrolman's rotating tours—a week of night duty, then a week of day duty—a disorienting routine at best, cruelly disruptive of family life. "The one time I thought of quitting the department," he once said, "was when I was a foot patrolman. It was lonely and sometimes frightening. My feet hurt at the end of the tour, but what I'll never forget is my backache. The strain from the hours of standing was terrible." Cops learned to wear elasticized stockings, and they used other techniques as well: wriggling their toes, taking little steps in place when standing at barriers, using the curb to stretch their toes and heels.

Thirty-one years on the force meant thirty-one years of struggle—slow progress upward through the Civil Service system, being yanked capriciously from one assignment to another, often by men less intelligent, less dedicated, less honest than he was. Hannon would always remember the pain of those days. "There would be times when I'd get my mail at 6 P.M. one day and find I'd been transferred as of 4 P.M. that same day," he recalled. "I was already two hours late reporting to my new command." In 1966 when he was a deputy inspector supervising public morals enforcement with the Seventeenth Division in Queens, where he lived, he was told, "There's a message for you in the telephone logbook." The message said he was transferred "forthwith" to the Sixth Division in Harlem as executive officer. (Even their language had a Victorian flavor. Sometimes they were ordered to report "forthwith" and sometimes "post haste"; they were wedded to the archaic word *perpetrator*, and their written reports and court testimony were filled with stilted phrases such as "He did aver" and "In the performance of my tour I did see.")

"It's more trouble for a commander to face a subordinate and explain *why* he's being transferred," Hannon said. "We try to be more human now about personnel. We feel the supervisors of the various outfits are entitled to have a face-to-face confrontation with regard to transfers. I wasn't treated like that, and I'll never forget it."

But if you were raised in the rigors and ceremonies of working-class Catholicism, the rigors and ceremonies of policing held the lure of the familiar, and Hannon endured. His father, a trolley-car motorman, died at sixty-three during the Depression. Hannon was only thirteen, the second youngest in a family of seven boys and two girls. All of his older siblings went to work, but Hannon continued in school, earning money after hours as a messenger. To grow up fatherless and poor in Brooklyn in the thirties was to grow up with low expectations and a narrowness of choices. But Hannon, a good student, decided to be a banker after graduation from high school and took a four-year course at the American Institute of Banking. Then, at twenty-three, not waiting to be drafted into World War II, he entered the Navy. First, though—concerned there might not be a banking job when he came out—he took and passed the examination for the police department.

He also got married to a Queens girl named Isabel Van Keuren, whose favorite uncle happened to be a cop. Hannon spent most of World War II in Virginia, forming crews for LSTs—"That's the bag I was in, I never got out of Little Creek." When he left the Navy in 1946 as a yeoman first class, a banking career no longer appealed to him and, although Isabel was unhappy with the idea, for her favorite uncle had been killed on the job, he joined the police. Twenty-nine was the age limit for joining the NYPD, and Hannon, at twenty-eight, was older than the average rookie.

While he began studying to advance in rank almost at once, it never occurred to him that he might one day reach the very top in a Police Department where the competition was ferocious and advancement often political and arbitrary. Hannon, unlike many of his colleagues, did not go to college on the job, although he was a natural student. He was weary of studying by the time he passed the exam for captain, the final civil service rank, at the end of 1960. He was nearly forty-three then. But even without a college degree, he had one high priority for advancement (apart from tenacity, a capacity for Spartan endurance, and his high native intelligence): he was an Irish Catholic during a period when the department was dominated by Irish Catholics. Willing to put in long hours, super-straight, totally unsentimental about his approach to command, almost frighteningly fair-minded, Hannon molded himself into his own ideal of an urban police boss step by disciplined step. Policing, after a while, became an act of faith. You just braced for the lumps you knew you'd have to take, and carried on like a Good Soldier.

Many of the men who came on the job with Hannon put in their papers after the prescribed twenty years. You put in your time and you retired on a good pension. You were still young, in your forties, and you could augment your pension with a second career. That was one of the lures of a police job, why it was considered a secure job, a short-term job, a job that promised (if you survived) a carefree future.

But some cops, like Courtenay, like Hannon, stayed on well beyond the twenty years. Long before he made captain, Hannon, a private man of almost monastic faith, had discovered his calling. Often the same Irish Catholic families that produced one son a cop produced another a priest; that was a cliché of the Police World. Making the decision to submerge yourself in the anonymous blue uniform of the cop was not unlike clothing yourself in the anonymous black suit and white throat rim of the priest.

Hannon was a stoical man, almost an ascetic, a man who could take deep comfort in his religious belief. Whenever he could, he went on department-sponsored religious retreats. He felt a genuine sense of service and absolutely no sense of greed. He had always exemplified the cop-commander, obeying orders from his superiors without demur, making careful, balanced decisions free of personal bias, asking for no quarter and giving none. His colleagues respected him for these traits, but there were those (usually younger and lower in rank) who found him overcautious, inordinately self-protective, unnecessarily rigid, even somewhat inhuman.

He waited patiently, always the Team Player, waited to be made deputy inspector (oak leaf), full inspector (eagle), one-star chief. Those and the higher ranks were not protected by civil service tenure, nor by the various "line organizations"—the Sergeants', Lieutenants' and Captains' Benevolent Associations. Those were ranks filled by the police commissioner at his discretion. Any inspector, any three-star chief, even the chief of operations himself could be reduced in rank back to captain.

As a high-ranking officer, you no longer could put in for overtime (chiefs were permitted to earn outside money by teaching or acting as consultants). Inspectors and chiefs were well paid, they were the first to say so, and they were willing to be full-time police commanders. As chief of operations, Hannon earned a little over $44,000. (By 1982, the job paid $62,000.)

Generally, it was only *after* reaching retirement status, *after* putting in your twenty years, that you began climbing the appointive ranks. That was why the police department's young tigers were all well into middle age.

Hannon's pale blue eyes gauged the traffic, estimating his time of arrival. He made occasional comments to his driver, assessing impending upheaval and its effect on his immediate future. He calculated his chance of survival in a career that meant everything to him, and couldn't help wondering if he was about to be skewered for the sake of political expediency. A month short of his sixtieth birthday, Hannon was only three years away from mandatory retirement. He asked little more of life than to stay a policeman those final three years, and then retire with dignity, with his pride intact.

To keep the appointment, Hannon wore a light gray business suit, a blue tie of sober pattern, and a white shirt. (He could leave the shirt on when he changed into his uniform again back at headquarters: winter dress required a white shirt under the navy blue jacket.) There was nothing flamboyant about him and nothing affected. His jacket hung open for comfort, revealing a paunch, as well as the .38 at his waist.

On his lap—heavy, powerful thighs toughened during the early beat-pounding days—lay a briefcase from which he extracted a tidy sheaf of papers. It was always a struggle to keep up with the volume of his paperwork, and since he was a well-organized man, he used his traveling time thriftily. As he rode uptown he forced his mind to his papers, making a marginal note here, placing a signature there, initialing this or that order. "I can live with this," he said, signing his approval, or "I have a problem with that one, I'll have to bounce it off the PC," putting it aside for further study. If a report indicated a disciplinary problem, he would say, "We may have to make a recommendation"— meaning punishment. Once in a while an instance of outrageously slipshod work or the hint of a cover-up caused him to voice his sternest expression of disapproval: "This is atrocious!" As, for example:

Hannon told me about two uniformed cops who hit a gambling operation and made several arrests. Hannon said that "smelled."

"Our uniformed men are not supposed to make indoor gambling arrests, we have a unit for that—public morals." The men in that unit were investigators who worked out of uniform and were seasoned cops, trusted for their demonstrated skill and integrity. "The opportunity for corruption exists," Hannon said, noting several other aspects of the report that rang false. The report said the cops had responded to a call for help with "a D.O.A.," which turned out to be unfounded. The report also mentioned that one of the arresting cops was injured when a door slammed on his hand, but there was no mention of medical treatment. "The lieutenant who signed this report is a dolt," Hannon said. "It looks to me like the cops tried to shake someone down and failed, and then made the arrest." (Hannon asked the Manhattan North area commander to investigate. One of the department's problems, he said, was unsupervised or loosely supervised personnel.)

The items that Hannon discussed with me from time to time ranged from the weighty to the ridiculous:

A letter from a police officer, with an attached note from a psychiatric clinic on Long Island where the officer lived; his marriage was collapsing and he requested a transfer out of the high-crime area where he was assigned, to relieve his stress and save his marriage. (Hannon checked the request yes—pending the PC's approval.)

A memo in an endless series regarding a dispute with the fire department—this one a complaint that the fire department failed to ask for police help in an arson case that the police department regarded as its jurisdiction; a meeting was requested by the fire department. "Both the fire inspectors and our own detectives investigate the same suspected arsons," Hannon said, "and that's a waste of effort." He assigned the three-star chief of patrol to attend the meeting—"The heavier the hitter, the better."

A memo from the chief of patrol asking Hannon's help with a ticklish problem. Should the uniform blouse (jacket) worn by female police officers keep its side zippers (to facilitate getting at handcuffs, club, and other paraphernalia), or should the blouse be zipperless, like that of the male police officer? Hannon chuckled and decided to ask the PC to make the decision. (It was ordained that the female's blouse should lose its zippered slits.)

A lengthy report about the arrest of John C., a detective first grade, for drunk driving as he returned home alone from an out-of-town wedding; the report included the detective's defense that he never drank because liquor interfered with the medication he used for a chronic minor ailment. Another report about an officer arrested and suspended from the force for stealing a park bench; and a report of a cop who shot an escaped monkey—did he use his gun within police guidelines?

Another in a series of memos about parades up Fifth Avenue; Hannon had met with the Fifth Avenue Association, whose members objected to the parades with their noise and dirt. He had also met with various ethnic groups

that wanted to know why *they* could not march up Fifth
Avenue on *their* national days of celebration, if the Irish
could march on St. Patrick's Day. The police department
followed local law holding that any parade established as an
annual event prior to 1914 had a perpetual right to march.
This did not satisfy the protesters. "Frankly, I don't know
how to deal with this," Hannon confided. "Personally, I
think it would be a good idea to call off *all* parades, as a way
of saving costs. The PC could do it. He would have to warn
the mayor's office, of course." Meanwhile, Hannon turned
down the current request, anticipating further protest. "I
always alert the PC when I take this kind of action," he
said, "so *he'll* be ready for complaints. I would hope anyone
below me would alert me, too, in something of that nature.
But you don't always anticipate reaction."

A report that parked vans equipped with couches were
being sighted around the city, where prostitutes were
"making meets" with their customers. Hannon recommended, "Get them on parking violations."

A request for Hannon's suggestion in the case of a "good
cop" who, his commanding officer felt, should be rewarded. The case had been the subject of a short but lively
discussion at headquarters among Hannon, Chief of Personnel Cornelius J. Behan, and a captain on Hannon's staff.
The cop—who had refused a motorist's proffered bribe of
five dollars and arrested him instead—wanted to go into an
anti-crime unit.

Captain: "He has a minor thing on his record; he got
drunk one day and waved his gun around. But he has no
drinking problem."

Behan: "He was very young, about twenty-two, when
that happened. But his record says he hasn't enough community understanding."

Hannon: "Where does he work?"

Captain: "In Harlem."

Behan: "That's understandable; he's Irish."

Hannon: "Why don't we let his own CO decide?"

Captain: "He's a good cop, but he's not a classy individual. He's a real good, sharp street cop who gets the job done. He missed getting his gold shield once because, *he* says, 'of my big mouth.' And that's probably true."

Captain: "He wants to go to polygraph school."

Hannon: "How much would that cost us?"

Captain: "Six hundred sixty dollars."

Hannon: "Would we get our money's worth out of him?"

Behan: "He has enough time left, maybe we would."

Behan meant that the cop had been in the department ten years and had another ten to go before he was eligible to retire on a full pension. He was sent to polygraph school.

Another case before Hannon—a cop in his twentieth year of service who apparently was trying to build up his salary average with "night differential" to be able to retire on a higher pension. Hannon's comment: "I think we're being used. If we look into his command and find he's going on steady late tours, heads will roll."

A problem with the captain of a Queens precinct, where corruption was suspected among some junior commanders. Reviewing the chief of patrol's final report and recommendation, Hannon decided he wanted Captain X. "in a low-level job, not as a leader." Hannon viewed the captain as "overly protective of his people," explaining:

"He is not showing leadership. He says the IAD [Internal Affairs Division] is picking on him, instead of admitting there's a problem and getting after it. There's something wrong with him, he's too close to his men."

Finally, Hannon read over notes on the investigation by the department's Internal Affairs Division of an incident in which several drunken officers had beaten up some residents in their precinct. Brutality was built into the system, but since Patrick Murphy's cleanup the New York police hierarchy did its conscientious best to expose and punish such instances, as it did with corruption. There were far fewer cover-ups than in the old days. (The officers, after a departmental trial, were dismissed.)

On his drive uptown to meet with the search panel,

Hannon listened with half an ear to reports on the police frequency: an accident or a protest demonstration building up somewhere in the city; a gun run (a report of shots fired, or a man with a gun); he took note of a signal indicating that the commissioner or the first deputy was "reaching out" for a particular commander or a special piece of information. His own call number was 201.

"You can sit in the car and not really hear the radio," Hannon said, "but when your own number is called, it's like an alarm going off. You *always* hear that." None of the voices crackling over the radio called for 201, though.

Occasionally, during the twenty-minute ride, Hannon glanced at his digital wristwatch. He was compulsively prompt—one of the marks of chieftainship—and he grew irritable when others were tardy. Few under his command ever trifled with their boss's compulsion.

Driving the car was Pete Cassi, on the force almost as long as Hannon himself. Cassi was fifty-five, gray-haired, with strong North Italian features—patient and loyal, a police officer of the old school. He and Hannon had known each other ever since Hannon, at thirty, passed the Civil Service examination for sergeant.

Cassi never had risen in rank, and he regarded it as a privilege to be Chief Hannon's driver—or, rather, one of the chief's two drivers who provided him with twenty-four-hour-a-day, seven-day-a-week service. Cassi was protective and solicitous of his boss, and felt it was an insult to ask the chief of operations to appear for what amounted to a job interview. It was like asking Dave Winfield to prove he could play ball.

Cassi pulled the limousine, its radio squawking, primly to the curb in front of a tall Park Avenue building. Hannon sat for a moment collecting himself. He removed his spectacles—they were too tight and left pale red grooves along his temples—and then absently replaced them as he entered the building.

Hannon and the panel members, many of whom he had met before, greeted each other cordially. His smile was pleasant but impersonal, giving nothing away. The panel's co-chairman apologized for the newspaper story naming the special state prosecutor, John Keenan, as Koch's choice for commissioner. But Keenan was, in fact, one of the ten lawyers on the panel's list of candidates. One of the panel's members had called the mayor for an explanation and been assured that no one had yet been offered the job, and no one would be offered it until after the panel made its recommendation four days hence. It *was* insulting to ask the chief of operations to audition, and the panel members must have been sensitive to the slight.

The panel had requested Hannon's résumé, not realizing that Hannon was probably the only ranking commander in the department who had never prepared one. He simply had never thought beyond the New York police. Most police commanders kept carefully updated professional histories, listing all their command achievements, their departmental commendations and college degrees, in the event that an irresistible, out-of-town police chieftaincy should fall vacant, or a challenging job open in federal or state law enforcement. Hannon wrote up a résumé just for the panel and did not even bother to keep a copy for himself, so wedded was he to the NYPD.

And the résumé was a stark listing that included his weight (187 pounds) as well as the fact that he had one child—a married daughter with three children. The two-and-a-half–page résumé, dryly documenting his steady rise in the department, had been glanced at by the panel members, but there was nothing in its rows of dates and lists of accruing responsibility to tell anything about who Hannon really was. And yet, he embodied most of the traits the panel members had drawn up, qualities they believed were required for a Perfect Police Commissioner, who had to have:

High Intelligence
Sensitivity to Race

Sensitivity to the Criminal Justice System
Sensitivity to the Morale of the Street Cop

And who had to be:

a Strong Leader
a Good Manager
a Problem Solver
Acceptable to the Rank and File
Able to Work Well with the Mayor

The panel members measured Hannon only cursorily, for they did not believe he met their final criterion: The Perfect Police Commissioner must be, in addition to all his other virtues, Conceptual and Innovative. And to the degree that Mike Codd was perceived as lacking in those attributes, so, too, was Jim Hannon. He *was* Commissioner Codd's man. It was Codd who had raised him, within the past three years, from assistant chief to superchief to Top Cop.

The session was pleasant, but brief and noncommittal.

Hannon, poker-faced, stepped out of the building and met Dan Courtenay coming in. Hannon had always been Courtenay's senior in rank, although he'd begun in the department only a year ahead of Courtenay; the eight-year difference in their ages—Hannon's edge in maturity— might have accounted for Hannon's more rapid rise. In 1960 he was a captain and Courtenay was still a lieutenant.

Hannon and Courtenay greeted each other with a mixture of sheepishness and bravado. It was the first time in their careers that they had competed for the same job. Hannon genuinely admired Courtenay, or he would not have chosen him for the arduous job of coordinating security for the Democratic National Convention. He regarded Courtenay as a Good Soldier and a Team Player, a hardworking career cop like himself.

Hannon was almost wistful when he contemplated Courtenay's ability to enjoy himself in the job of the moment, to milk a job of everything he could get from it, and give all of himself, at the same time. Courtenay's enthusiasm and sense of fun were contagious, and Hannon would sometimes find himself responding in kind. Once, during the planning of the DNC security arrangements, Courtenay was in need of a temporary driver as he spent his days hurrying from appointment to appointment. His regular driver was on the sick list, and Hannon told Courtenay he had the perfect replacement—a cop just suspended from the force, pending trial for having moonlighted as the driver of a getaway car in a bank robbery.

In the office where the search panel had gathered, Courtenay's qualifications were now cordially assessed. Out of uniform, in a dark blue suit and flowered necktie, Courtenay was trying to look like a police commissioner—although he, too, had been somewhat unnerved by that morning's premature announcement about Special State Prosecutor John Keenan. He later recalled that the questions were of a general nature—how did he feel about the level of education for police? Did he think the detective bureau could function more effectively in solving the rising numbers of murders, rapes, and armed robberies?

Courtenay gave generalized answers: he thought the standards of education should be raised, if possible; he thought that detective specialists should be balanced by detective generalists; and he volunteered that as commissioner he would encourage closer supervision all the way down the line in the matter of personal appearance.

"Supervisors are too lax," he said. "They should insist on their people looking good. When a cop *looks* good, he's more apt to *act* good, you get better work out of him." Courtenay advocated more professionalism, more dedication. The panel members, he believed, were "one hundred percent on the level about finding the right candidate to recommend to the mayor," but they were not police experts or theoreticians. "They just wanted to get a sense of how I handled myself," Courtenay said.

I had the opportunity to sit in on an earlier and far more

probing session during which Courtenay was obliged to present himself in the best light he could. That was when—on February 4, 1976—he was summoned for the annual evaluation that would determine if he should be allowed to continue in his present rank, be promoted, or be reassigned to a job he'd find unpleasant enough to cause him to put in his papers. At that high level of command, the questions were apt to be tough, almost hostile. His interrogator was Chief Behan, the three-star commander of the Personnel Bureau, one of the five headquarters superchiefs.

As an inspector Cornelius Behan had been a key witness before the Knapp Commission less than five years earlier. He had corroborated Frank Serpico's testimony that allegations of widespread corruption had been conveyed to the then-first deputy police commissioner, John F. Walsh, who had delayed acting on them for eight months.

Although privately affronted, Courtenay had agreed to let me sit in. He admitted to me long after, "When I saw you in Hannon's office I said to myself, this isn't right." Ultimately he understood why Hannon was being so open, and he decided that if Hannon could trust me to be discreet and fair, he would go along. Nonetheless, for many months he encouraged a certain austere distance between us, and I must say I found him somewhat daunting. Daunting? I approached him as warily as I might have Attila the Hun. And I tried to propitiate him with small attentions, such as a birthday plant for his desk (which to my surprise, he carefully watered for nearly a year before it withered). Although Courtenay eventually became—for a cop-commander—quite candid, he was at times instinctively evasive. Like all who got to the top of the NYPD, Courtenay was a canny survivor: of street wars, political pressures, departmental mismanagement and scandal, intra-departmental jealousies and the daily, unrelieved stress of The Job. Defensiveness against civilians was inbred.

The evaluation was held in Hannon's headquarters office. A conference table that could seat eight or so was surrounded by blue-upholstered chairs. Hannon did not

take his usual position at the head of the table, motioning
Courtenay to take it instead.

"You sit in the hot seat," Hannon said, his mouth
straight, but his eyes smiling. The decision, Hannon knew,
was foregone; the PC would not have approved Courtenay
as coordinator of security for the DNC had he not planned
to reappoint him as a two-star chief. All the department's
inspectors and chiefs served at the pleasure of the commissioner. At the yearly reevaluation ritual, headquarters' five
three-star chiefs sat in judgment on the department's twelve
two-star chiefs; those twelve, in turn (Courtenay, of course,
among them) evaluated the one-star chiefs, and so on, down
the line. The PC then acted upon those evaluations at his
discretion.

And all the two-star chiefs, like Courtenay, were waiting
to step into the shoes of the three-star chiefs, like Behan
(but the Personnel Bureau chieftaincy was not what
Courtenay had his eye on). And all twenty of the deputy
chiefs, with their one-star rank, were snapping at
Courtenay's heels and at the heels of the other assistant
chiefs, hoping they would make room by going up the
ladder, or taking early retirement, or dropping dead, or
being sexually indiscreet, or caught doing something dis-
honest, or taking to drink, or in some other way conducting
themselves unbecomingly and incurring the commissioner's
displeasure.

Hannon moved to shut his office door, which usually
hung wide open, shielded by a staff of clerks in the anteroom. The chief of detectives, Louis C. Cottell, stood on
the threshold. He and the other superchiefs frequently
strode into Hannon's office for consultation. Cottell was not
wearing his urgent face, and Hannon told him, grinning,
"You can't come in, this is very secret." He shut the door
firmly. In his quiet way Hannon enjoyed needling his subordinates. As the Brass never tired of pointing out, they
went back a long way together, all having risen through the
ranks, all having survived the harsh scrutiny of the Knapp

Commission, a scrutiny that some of their colleagues did *not* survive.

"Okay, Daniel," Hannon said to Courtenay, making a small joke, "I don't think either Chief Behan or I know you very well, so talk as though we don't."

Courtenay was ill at ease; his manner, for him, was subdued. He described his activities in his previous assignment, as executive aide to the superchief who had succeeded Hannon as head of the Organized Crime Control Bureau.

"I'd like you to postpone evaluation of my performance in the DNC job until July 17, when the job will be complete," he said ruefully. But Behan brushed that aside.

"You now have a college degree and you're interacting with politicians," the chief of personnel said sternly. "How has that changed you?"

Courtenay said he had been surprised that the DNC bosses seemed more concerned with appearances than with real safety. The basic difference between pols and cops was that pols were first and foremost image-conscious. Things were supposed to *look* safe, the delegates must not be alarmed by militant-seeming preparations. As for diplomatic relations, Courtenay admitted, "It was hard for me to accept at first that all command decisions would be made by Bob Strauss, on our advice." He was still brooding about how he would handle a bomb threat and he told Behan, unconvincingly, "We are now adjusted to the fact it won't be our decision."

His real problem with the job, Courtenay explained, was "the great length of time" allotted to the planning. On this point Behan was sympathetic. "Yes, we're geared to crisis planning," he said. Courtenay was worried that his people would "peak" too early, lose their momentum. That was a traditional concern of the military mind.

"We've never had so much lead time before," Hannon agreed. "Actually, we could do a hell of a job if the convention were next week." He and Courtenay reminisced

briefly about earlier events that had required massive planning—the 1961 visit of Nikita Khrushchev to the United
Nations, the Pope's visit in 1965, George Wallace's appearance at Madison Square Garden in 1968. "We lost Eighth
and Ninth avenues," Hannon reminded Courtenay. "That
was a bad one."

"At least we won't have to worry about policing demonstrators in Central Park," Courtenay joked. "We'll just send
in some extra muggers."

As to his recently earned college degree, Courtenay told
Behan he had chosen to attend Pace College, rather than the
John Jay College of Criminal Justice, the traditional cop's
college.

"I wanted a non-police environment and I wanted to be
with young people, because I thought it would help me deal
with people at a different level than I ordinarily deal with in
police work."

To Behan's pointed query about Courtenay's managerial
style, Courtenay answered calmly:

"My managerial style *is* probably authoritarian. I'm not a
pussycat. For me, that style is appropriate. I don't mean I
have to call the shots all the time. But if I see something
wrong . . ." He did not finish the thought.

Behan asked, "What do you regard as an ideal subordinate commander?"

Courtenay had no difficulty with that.

"One who will challenge me," he replied in perfect sincerity. "I don't need my ego flattered."

Behan asked, "If you were P.C., what is the single thing
you would do?"

Hannon, who had been listening in amusement, inter-
jected, "Send Neil Behan away."

But Courtenay knew how to be very diplomatic; his answer was ready and correct, the answer of a Good Soldier
and a Team Player.

"No," he said, responding to Hannon's smile. "Chief
Behan keeps you careful." Then to Behan: "I would try to
keep our image proud, make everyone feel pride in his

work, instill an attitude that you want to be of service."
Somewhat hesitantly he added, "We have shafted our people sometimes, not kept our promises . . ." He let the
thought trail off, having perhaps gone too far, remembering
that Commissioner Codd, unlike himself, did *not* encourage
subordinates who challenged him.

After about forty-five minutes Courtenay was dismissed.
Behan had been disarmed.

"He has improved enormously in his interpersonal deal-
ings," Behan said.

Hannon, seeing Behan so well disposed, could not resist
a small jape. "Dan *does* have an authoritarian style," he
remarked.

Behan commented that Courtenay was keeping too much
of the planning in his head, had not committed enough
about his plans for the DNC to paper. "What if he drops
dead tomorrow?" Behan asked.

Hannon defended Courtenay's methods, and Courtenay
was, of course, reappointed as an assistant chief by Commissioner Codd.

Courtenay expressed few of his deeply held convictions
to the search panel members, most of whom were not
equipped to discuss specific changes or technical concepts
of policing. They invited Courtenay to join them for lunch,
where they continued to converse casually about the commissionership. When he left, Courtenay, like Hannon, had
no better idea than before what his chances were.

In the late afternoon of Saturday, July 10, 1976,
Courtenay, in his windowless office at Madison Square
Garden, was on the telephone to the Manhattan South area
commander. He was inquiring about the delegates' hotels,
particularly the leading candidate's hotel where a demonstration was building. Many delegates had already arrived
and television vans were spewing their equipment into the
streets in search of action, and groups of demonstrators,
sniffing national coverage, were beginning to snarl traffic

and require New York's brand of (usually) benevolent control.

"What kind of reading do you get on the Carter rally on Seventh Avenue and 52nd Street? In excess of 10,000? OK, thanks." He looked across the room to Inspector Herman Reed sitting at his desk consulting work charts and muttered, "*Intelligence* should have given us that."

Scowling, he called Intelligence, asked if they could come up with a figure for the crowds at the rally. He drummed on his desk as they clutched for figures they evidently didn't have. "Five thousand? That's your best estimate? Thanks." He threw Reed a look of resigned disgust that quickly gave way to a grin of delight as Mary Courtenay entered. She kissed her husband lightly and greeted Reed by his first name. Mary Courtenay had been a company wife for a long time. Open-faced, poised, warm, and animated in speech and gesture, she was a woman who put others quickly at ease.

It was seeing Courtenay with his wife that first altered my perception of him. The Courtenays had been married twenty-seven years and had three children, and whenever Courtenay had mentioned his family to me, he had used his habitual caustic tone. Telling me about their early years when Mary was pregnant with their second child, he said that often he could not telephone her. "I was in plain clothes, in gambling, and would be out on a raid, and she'd think I was dead. But I was a cop *before* she married me, so she had an idea of how it would be." And he would say things like, "When I get a promotion, the wife gets one, too. She knows as much as a two-star chief without having taken any of the exams. She treats me like a peasant. My dog barks at me when I come home. I didn't mind him barking when I was an inspector, but you'd think my wife would have told him I got promoted." That kind of gruff humor about his family had misled me.

Mary Courtenay did not behave like a woman who was held at arm's length by an intimidating husband. She looked like a woman who was cherished and deferred to and who had bloomed under her husband's devotion. Observing them together, I saw Courtenay's softer side, and that helped me overlook the sarcasm he often directed toward me and others.

Mary Courtenay was planning to spend the weekend at a Manhattan hotel to be near her husband; he would be on call twenty-four hours a day until the convention's end, and unable to return to his home in Queens. Courtenay had asked her to drop by on the way to her hotel to see his field headquarters.

She looked around, perching on the arm of the office sofa, fearing she was in the way.

"You must have passed the Carter rally on your way here," Courtenay said to his wife. "Can *you* estimate what the size of the crowd was?"

"Ten thousand," she replied without hesitation.

Courtenay beamed. "We're gonna make you chief of intelligence," he said.

Inspector Mickey Schwartz arrived to remind Courtenay of the 4:30 briefing he'd called. Captain Hartling, also aware of the meeting, appeared, surrounded by a halo of cigarette smoke. "There are 10,000 people at the Carter rally," he announced. "And we just lost 52nd Street."

"Carl Ravens doesn't lose streets," Courtenay said. Assistant Chief Ravens, commander of the Manhattan South area, was Mickey Schwartz's boss. "The mayor probably asked him to *let* the demonstrators overflow. He was concerned earlier today that there wouldn't be enough people out for Carter." Mayor Beame was a Democrat; thus the politics of crowd-manipulation.

"All right, gang," Courtenay said, "let's have our briefing."

His wife stood up. "I don't think I should hear any of this," she said.

Pretending to misunderstand, Courtenay assured her playfully, "We won't use any bad words."

She giggled and kissed him good-bye.

The most urgent order of business continued to be the

barrier shortage. Hartling said that 150 had been spotted on one of the Hudson River piers—probably set up for the arrival of an ocean liner—and Courtenay ordered, "Get them here by eight tomorrow morning."

Mickey Schwartz had the latest recount of barrier strength. Dramatically he announced: "We now have out in the street . . . a total . . . of *740.*"

"You've got to be kidding," said Courtenay. "Well, if we have to go out and steal them, we will. I am *owed 1,000* barriers. We'll send out trucks. I'll use the TPF if I have to." The Tactical Patrol Force was designed to control street riots during the 60s, when it consisted exclusively of cops in their twenties and six feet or taller—a grim squadron of deterrence. Courtenay, as an inspector, had been its commander.

Captain Hartling, the pragmatist, grinding away at his logistical problems, now posed a hypothetical question:

"OK, we have seventy VIPs at the Statler on Monday for a cocktail party. How do we get them across the street after the party and into the Garden?"

"We may have to use the tunnel connecting the Garden with the Statler, if demonstrations have built up in the street by that time," Courtenay said. "If there are only a few people sitting in the street, we can move around them. If there are 500, it won't be that easy." He pondered the problem. "What I'd like to do is shut off the street to demonstrators during that period." He looked at Mike Shilensky. "OK, lawyer, what do you say?"

Shilensky: "If you can establish it's a *safety* factor, that the demonstrators are endangering lives, OK, you can move them out. But if their being there and our having to move around them is just something that makes our *job* a little harder—and we disperse them—we'll get sued."

Courtenay thought for a moment. Then, hopefully: "Look, we have to park the delegate buses nose to ass, and when they discharge, the delegates will fill more than half the sidewalk *and that's not safe!*"

Shilensky: "Is that a *fact?*"

Schwartz, intervening: "It's a judgment, not a fact."

Shilensky, who always had to discipline himself not to confuse his legal persona with his cop persona: "If on Monday night we have a problem getting the delegates into the Garden reasonably, then we can say it's a safety problem, and then on *Tuesday* night we'll shut the street—and screw them!"

Courtenay: "OK, I guess Monday night we'll just have to sweat it."

Schwartz jokingly suggested a sneaky alternative tactic: "We could underman the streets Monday, so the streets get lost, and then we have a precedent for freezing the area Tuesday." "Frozen" areas—anathema to civil liberties watchdog groups—were city blocks from which demonstrators were banned.

As the session broke up, Schwartz asked, "Are we getting sandwiches sent in?" Forlornly he added, "I haven't eaten anything with a knife and fork for three days."

Back in Courtenay's office, Inspector Francis D. Burke, Chief Meehan's intelligence liaison with the DNC security operation, was studying Courtenay's wall map. Drawn in meticulous detail, it delineated areas in which demonstrations were permitted and areas that were off limits. The boundaries had been determined after weeks of negotiating with all the groups that wanted to make statements during the convention.

Burke wore half-spectacles that kept slipping down his nose. He had orange hair, spoke mostly in monosyllables, and looked more like the stereotype of an absentminded professor than like any kind of cop.

Pointing to a section of the map, Burke said, "This will be a frozen area . . ." And everyone jumped on him.

Courtenay: "Don't you know we don't use *frozen* anymore?" He knew perfectly well that he himself used the term all the time, but he enjoyed needling Burke.

"It's like *sweeps*," he said sternly (as in rounding up prostitutes). "We don't use *that* anymore, either."

Sandwiches were brought in, and containers of coffee. Courtenay had been drinking cup after cup.

"At 4 P.M. Monday we button up the taxi-well," he said.

Courtenay glanced at a memo handed to him by Mike Shilensky. "Can we rely on the gays to be responsible?"

Schwartz (from his long experience monitoring demonstrations in the Manhattan South area): "They can be, but sometimes they aren't."

He and Shilensky showed Courtenay on the map where the gay rights demonstrators had been given permission to march.

Courtenay: "We can angle radio cars across a street, if necessary. That will zap them. They'll have to climb over the cars and they're not going to be able to do that too good." (His use of the vernacular was deliberately exaggerated for his own relish.)

At seven o'clock weekend-Chief Cottell arrived. He was entirely sympathetic to Courtenay's need for barriers.

Courtenay to Cottell: "I called Brooklyn North, and they told me they had a total of *nine* barriers in the whole borough."

Cottell: "I knew that's the kind of answer you'd get."

Schwartz: "Sachson hides *his* under trees to camouflage them."

Inspector Burke, of intelligence, who had been brooding over the map, lost in dreams all his own, abruptly entered the conversation. He blinked over the frames of his half-glasses. "The Yippies have no one in Central Park."

Courtenay looked at Burke in puzzlement: "Where *are* they then?"

Schwartz *(facetiously):* "In the Hotel Pierre, where it's more comfortable."

Burke *(another non sequitur):* "The Yippies will go with anyone, just to get bodies."

Courtenay, back to his problem with the gays, straight-faced: "Have we got any gay bosses in the room?"

Hartling made a valiant effort to appear worldly: "Maybe

you'll have some, by the time this is over." His round face crinkled with pure joy at his own wisecrack. (When, a few years later, a police sergeant publicly acknowledged his homosexuality, the NYPD experienced barely a tremor. A great truth had dawned on its members: homosexuals don't really threaten anyone's heterosexuality.)

Chief of Detectives Cottell said to Courtenay soothingly, "We'll get you those barriers, Dan."

Courtenay offered Cottell a tour of the Garden. He had conducted several such tours for members of the headquarters Top Brass during the past months, and had himself walked practically every square foot of the Garden's intricate spaces—not to mention the surrounding streets—many dozen times. He had walked the Garden's miles of corridors and stairways, its basements and subbasements, checking entrances and exits, cubbyholes where an assailant could conceal himself, catwalks from which an assassin could aim a rifle.

Courtenay's team had been on duty since eight in the morning and Schwartz would stay until midnight, when he would turn out a fresh group of patrolmen for the next duty tour. But while Courtenay was looking forward to meeting his Mary for dinner, Schwartz, living alone in a small Manhattan apartment, hadn't much more to look forward to at home than a hot bath. Soaking in a tub after a hard day's work was one of his small indulgences, like good cigars, but they did not compensate for the lack of home life. His teen-aged son and daughter resided in Queens with his estranged wife.

It was Schwartz's habit to carry with him from one command post to another a large framed reproduction of a soulful-looking Bernard Buffet clown. Schwartz regarded the clown as a metaphorical self-portrait, but he hadn't brought it with him to the Garden for his brief tenure there. It hung in his office at the Manhattan South area. Occasionally I would run into Schwartz on the opening night of a Broadway musical, the kind of show attended by celebrities, that attracted huge crowds and television cameras. Schwartz would be walking the streets in civilian clothes, checking on the dispersal of his mounted, motorized, and ambulatory troops and on the presence of properly placed police barriers. A theatergoer himself, he felt at home on Broadway. Area commanders and their aides quickly developed a possessive attitude toward their territorial enclaves.

Schwartz was twenty-four when he joined the police in 1951—four years later than Courtenay—and like both Courtenay and Jim Hannon he'd served in the Navy. Schwartz had been a lieutenant in the Detective Bureau, a captain in the intelligence division, and had just received his master's degree from John Jay College of Criminal Justice at the age of forty-nine. Five years earlier he'd been valedictorian (and summa cum laude) of his graduating class at John Jay. He had wanted to return to college ever since quitting New York University School of Business in his early twenties.

"My breadth of thinking was no wider than a pencil until I went back to college," he once told me. "I went to college for fun."

Schwartz's youth was shadowed by his mother's tragic life. An orphan, abandoned as a child to distant relatives in England and abused by them, she finally made her way to America, arriving illiterate and with hands crippled permanently by arthritis, to marry a widower considerably older than she. Schwartz's father, who had two sons by a former marriage, was fifty when Schwartz was born. A cutter in the garment industry, he did not encourage his youngest son to seek an education. Schwartz's mother died when he was nineteen, and her sad life still haunted him. "She was some kind of saint," he said. Schwartz felt bitter toward his father—"He was the dominant one"—and believed that, had his mother lived, she would have persuaded her husband to send Schwartz to college; clearly, he'd been bright enough to profit from it.

Policing was not a traditional career for urban American Jews, as it was for Irish Catholics. But New York's police department had turned out a surprising number of top-ranking Jewish commanders, including, in recent years, Chief Inspector Sanford D. Garelick and Chief of Detectives Albert A. Seedman (who, in his autobiography, *Chief!*, confessed to having had a problem with his image of himself as a Jewish cop).

In the closed world of the police, the Jewish ghetto-consciousness was heightened, and Jewish cops of Schwartz's generation probably were the most alienated cops of all. Not only were they separated culturally from their fellow cops, they were in opposition to their own American Jewish traditions in having adopted the bellicose calling of law enforcement. Mostly, they kept all this trauma to themselves.

New York's police force was as cosmopolitan as any in the world, and in recent years the police recruited (were obliged to recruit) members of minority groups. They concentrated mainly on blacks, but also swept along mandated quotas of Hispanics (police euphemism for Puerto Ricans) and women. That kind of tokenism, though, was neither sought by Jews nor was it thrust upon them. They were not recruited, nor displayed, nor promoted to express affirmative action. Those Jewish cops who rose into the police hierarchy did so essentially on their merits and in the face of unspoken (mostly) suspicion and hostility. And a trace of dismay lingered, however disguised or suppressed.

Schwartz was, in ways more subtle than Courtenay, a guarded man. Being not only of the wrong ethnic group and religion, he was also in the process of getting divorced. The police department—always behind culturally by a decade or so—was still strongly swayed at the top by rigid taboos (and ponderous tolerances). Heavy drinking was no more than a good man's failing. Fooling around was frowned upon. Divorce was unacceptable.

Yet Mickey Schwartz was personable and self-assured, took great care with his dress, had none of the visible rough edges common to nearly all of the high-ranking Brass. He was as comfortable with command as Courtenay, and as knowledgeable a street cop, if not quite so dominant a presence. He was clear about the goals of policing in the big city and he could, even more articulately than Courtenay, expound on them. And like Courtenay he could work without complaint to the point of exhaustion. Both men were no-nonsense disciplinarians, but both, remembering their own early days in the department, retained a genuine sympathy for the street cops under their command.

At midnight on Saturday, Schwartz turned out his fresh troops and went tiredly home to his hot bath.

Courtenay was back in his Madison Square Garden field headquarters early Sunday morning. He, Inspectors Schwartz and Reed, and Captain Hartling all were in uniform today, ready to patrol the streets. Much to his relief, at 10 A.M. Courtenay got word that all the promised "wood" had at last been delivered and set in place. The authority of the office of the chief of operations, plus renewed efforts by Courtenay's team, had procured the needed 1,000 barriers; some had been wrenched from recalcitrant area commands, some had been unearthed from a previously overlooked storeroom, and a few dozen had been newly built and hastily painted.

The pre-convention demonstrations and rallies and marches were heating up. An aide to Mayor Beame, concerned with the image of a benevolent mayor, wanted the Right to Lifers to switch their rally from the Sheep Meadow in Central Park to the Mall, so that the Yippies could have the larger Meadow. He wanted Courtenay to effect the switch.

The Yippies were scruffy, long-haired, and anti-Establishment. The Right to Lifers were represented by dignified, middle-class women, and they probably reflected Courtenay's (and the majority of the police Brass's) moral stance. Yet it would have been hard to fault Courtenay or his team in the equality and courtesy with which both groups were treated. The commanders didn't even flinch when representatives of the Yippies, evidently anticipating (perhaps *hoping* for) high-handed cop-fascism, insisted on filming and tape-recording the commanders at the Manhattan South area office during a planning session for their demonstrations. Ten years earlier such a procedure would have been unthinkable. (Even more unthinkable: During a similar negotiating session with a gay rights group, one of its members, angered at being denied a particular request, snarled at a deputy chief, "You go take a flying fuck!" The chief, unruffled, answered quietly, "Now who's getting personal?")

The Yippies studied a map showing the available routes for demonstration marches. "Do you anticipate picking up people along your route?" one of the Manhattan South inspectors asked politely.

"Well, we might pick up fifty or so," replied one of the Yippie leaders, well-versed in street protest tactics. "I don't think our march will be a sidewalk march. We should have over five hundred." The police were prepared to close certain streets to car traffic during specified hours, to accommodate large groups of protest marchers. Such groups were expected to provide their own marshals who would maintain contact with the police in the street. "Marshals are no problem," a Yippie leader said, "we're quite experienced at that." They said they wanted to pitch tents and live in Battery Park for the duration of the convention. The police, with the mayor's approval, agreed to that. They said they wanted to gather in Central Park to begin their march. That request, too, was granted. But it was only the first of several meetings.

At a later meeting with Courtenay and Schwartz in Chief Hannon's large conference room at headquarters, also attended by Mike Shilensky, the Yippies made other demands. This time they, too, brought a lawyer.

Courtenay: "Can you give us a time commitment for all your groups? You want to move into the park about July 7 and stay through—when?"

The Yippies' lawyer would not commit himself to a time.

Courtenay: "Do you have any idea, yet, as to numbers?"

Yippies' lawyer: "We expect a great many. We want the Post Office steps for our demonstration on July 12."

Courtenay explained that the Post Office steps were federal property, but that he would permit five hundred demonstrators on the sidewalk at the bottom of the steps.

Yippies' lawyer: "I don't think we're going to be able to work with those limitations."

Courtenay *(very politely):* "I'm sorry. We have to consider the public's safety."

Yippies' lawyer: "Why is the public safety threatened?"

But Courtenay did not wish to discuss the dangers of militant demonstrators storming their barricades (which he knew the Yippies were well aware of).

Schwartz: "Let's go back a step. You said you don't know how many you expect, or if you can control them. You can't promise us to limit your demonstration to a token group."

The Yippies wanted Courtenay to say, try it, if it gets out of hand, we'll stop you. But Courtenay would not chance that sort of confrontation. He looked to Shilensky, who said, "The place for you to test your First Amendment rights is in the courts." The Yippies' lawyer responded, "The place to test them is in the *streets.*"

"In the streets, *everybody* loses," Shilensky said.

Courtenay's patience was being strained and the worry lines on his forehead were deepening. Finally, he agreed to meet with the Yippies again the following week, when they would (they said) have a clearer idea of their numbers; the weather during the convention would be a factor, they said, as would the political events of the next few weeks.

After the meeting Courtenay echoed Shilensky's comment. "They can go any one of three ways: Fight it out at the table, fight it out in court, or fight it out in the street. *They* are the ones who'll decide."

Courtenay picked up the red phone that connected him directly with the DNC's security chief, Cliff Cassidy.

"Hello, Cliff? Those gays who are caucusing here in the Garden—they're not all *delegates*, are they? I *hope* they're

not, or you're in trouble!" Having had his little joke,
Courtenay felt better.

Reed was unhappy with a couple of the captains assigned
to him and asked Courtenay if they could be reassigned.
"You can't reassign a problem," Courtenay said. "Who will
you give them to? You can't give them to another inspector.
The PC approved the list and so did the chief."

"But these two captains are stubborn," Reed insisted.
"They'll make independent judgments out in the street,
you know they will."

Courtenay gave Reed a withering look. *"No they will not,"*
he said, in his most imperious tone.

Chief of Operations Hannon entered the office. He was
wearing civilian clothes. Although it was his weekend off,
he wanted personally to check on Courtenay's operation, to
be absolutely sure it was in good shape and that no contingency arrangement had been overlooked. And besides,
Police Commissioner Codd had said he planned to visit the
Garden later in the morning and Hannon wanted to be
there.

"I thought you were away," Courtenay said.

Hannon merely smiled and seated himself at Shilensky's
desk. Having heard about Courtenay's earlier difficulties,
he needled: "Manhattan North is looking for barriers for
the hospital strike."

"They ain't getting mine!" Courtenay vowed.

At Hannon's suggestion, Courtenay took him on a walk-
around of the Garden's perimeter. In the street all of
Courtenay's troops were on their best behavior. They jaun-
tily saluted Courtenay in the hot sunshine, and those who
recognized the chief of operations out of uniform saluted
Hannon as well. There were the usual Sunday pedestrians
in the street and some placard-bearing demonstrators of
various persuasions behind the barriers, but the police far
outnumbered them.

Back in the boxing office, Hannon said, "You look in

good shape—now that there's no one here but cops. Are you sure you don't have too many men?"

Courtenay: "If we do a good job, it's *because* we had an *adequate* number of police."

Hannon: "I know how to play *that* game."

Courtenay: "Oh, yes, that's right. I forgot, it was *you* told *me* that."

Courtenay and Hannon studied the latest intelligence figures: There were now 2,000 Right to Lifers congregated in the Park. There were only two dozen Yippies visible to the naked eye of Intelligence.

Police Commissioner Codd appeared, accompanied by Chief of Detectives Cottell. They were followed by Mickey Schwartz, who announced that there were five hundred gays at 14th Street and Sixth Avenue. On Schwartz's heels came Inspector Burke of intelligence, who revised the figure to 1,000—a late flash.

Courtenay took Codd on a tour, accompanied by Hannon and Schwartz. The commissioner liked an entourage.

They rode the escalator to the Garden's D Tower where the police had installed a television camera to monitor the crowds outside the Garden. It was unclear whether the American Civil Liberties Union or some other watchdog groups would protest such surveillance, and the camera was a secret—off limits to any but the police.

The assembled Brass looked down at Eighth Avenue. In front of the Post Office, demonstrators for gay rights were being shepherded into the barrier pens. They paced back and forth, holding placards aloft. They were peaceable and orderly, and the cops, densely lined up in front of the barriers, were watching them in a relaxed way.

"That's the first time I've seen a whole line of police *facing* the demonstrators," Hannon said.

Of course Courtenay could not let that pass. "They're afraid to turn their backs," he said. The commissioner chuckled in a restrained way. He was not above making a joke of his own now and then. Earlier, when Courtenay, in the PC's presence, was considering the use of the Garden's bowling alley as a giant press room, someone pointed out that it wasn't really spacious enough, since the pin end of the alley was too low for anyone to stand up in. "We can put Gabe Pressman down at that end," the PC said.

Descending from the tower, Courtenay escorted the PC and Chief Hannon across the Garden floor, where seats were still being installed, bunting being tacked up, the network television booths being fitted with last-minute equipment. Young DNC workers were everywhere. Courtenay, during his months of planning, had become well acquainted with many of them, but they'd never seen him in uniform, and they gaped and mumbled things like, "Wow, Dan, I didn't recognize you!" Courtenay stood and purred.

The PC looked a bit hurt at being, for once, overshadowed. But Hannon, with his usual generosity, beamed at Courtenay, pleased with his popularity. Dan was his boy, after all.

Courtenay was back in his office an hour or so later when a uniformed cop entered, saying that the Right to Lifers were about to be confronted in the street (through someone's error) by a pro-abortion group. Courtenay slapped on his cap, felt for his revolver, and was off with the swiftness of a downhill racer. Mike Shilensky, grabbing his walkie-talkie, dashed out in Courtenay's wake.

Even on a hot summer day the area surrounding the Garden was blowy, and Courtenay leaned into the wind, moving fast. There was in fact no crisis. The pro-abortionists had already been turned by the police into a side street, to await the passing of the Right to Lifers. Once out, though, Courtenay decided to patrol. With Shilensky loping beside him—Courtenay's stride was long—he headed for Seventh Avenue. A medium-sized demonstration was being contained behind barriers in the block above the Statler Hilton. Courtenay spotted a hole in the police line and ordered a sergeant, "Close that up!" But he was too late, and the demonstrators overflowed into the area in front of the Statler Hilton, a space that Courtenay was trying to keep clear for the delegates on their way to and from the Garden across the street. Had the DNC been in session, access to the Garden would have been almost impossible.

"OK, lawyer," Courtenay said, "in view of what just happened, can I freeze the area now?"

Quietly but firmly, Shilensky said no.

Courtenay smiled grimly. "I'm gonna ask you once more. Can I freeze the area?"

Shilensky stood his ground. "No, it was *our* fault."

The general stood advised in the field by his portable attorney, and he paid attention.

Courtenay's gang was assembled in his office in the late afternoon.

"They'll probe until they find a soft spot," he said. What he meant was that some of the more pugnacious of the demonstrating groups would try to challenge the police by bursting their barriers, as they had earlier, or by attempting to push their way into the Garden, or trying to occupy streets by sitting or lying in them; those were some of the traditional strategies of militant demonstrators, and it was the reason Courtenay was keeping in reserve the jackbooted arrest team.

"Today, we came out reasonably clean," Courtenay said.

Hannon, who was still monitoring Courtenay's operation, agreed.

"Tomorrow night will probably be the real test," he said. "I'd like to play it real cool. It will determine, to a large extent, what happens Tuesday, Wednesday, and Thursday."

Courtenay nodded and looked at Schwartz, his field commander. "Don't let your men overreact," he cautioned.

But Schwartz was just as smart as Courtenay in the ways of street demonstrations. "The time to be on guard," he said, "is when a demonstration *dissipates*. That's our most vulnerable time, as we saw today, because that's when the cops relax and another demonstration can build up." He sat on the sofa, his tired legs outstretched, and lit a cigar.

Courtenay sat at his desk, checking last-minute routines for tomorrow's opening session of the DNC. He peered over his reading glasses at Inspector Reed. "We can park the mayor's car in the taxi-well," he said.

Reed, at his own desk, made a note. "What about the governor?"

"Yes, we can park the governor's car there, too. He pays our salary." Courtenay leaned back in his chair, dominating his environment. He stretched, grinning expansively. "I'm going over to the hotel to have a shower, and then have dinner. Is there anything else before I leave, gang?"

Captain Hartling had something. "We have information that there's a group of black female lawyers in the Times Square area, posing as pross, to see if we hassle them."

"They can relax," Schwartz told him. "We're not looking for collars."

There seemed to be no permanent solution to New York's prostitute problem. In the early stages of planning for the DNC, Courtenay had suggested—without much hope—his own scheme: Concentrate on stiff sentences for short periods in different areas of the city, "keep them off balance." But he acknowledged, "You'd need a judge who was bucking for reelection to make it work."

Realistically he cautioned, "Remember, 60 to 65 percent of the delegates have never been to New York before. A lot of them are going to be looking for that kind of action. They think that's what New York is all about." And having delivered himself of that cynical assessment, he departed.

THREE

★ "I was elected in part on my promise to bring the best people available into city government," Edward Koch told a group of invited citizens on November 17, 1977, just nine days after his election. The heavily attended meeting, held in Koch's campaign headquarters, formally launched the mayoral search panels. "With this objective in mind," the mayor continued, "I am asking you to help me conduct a talent search."

He urged his volunteers to consider individuals "who you know are capable, but may not step forward themselves," and he listed some aspects of "general excellence" to be used as a yardstick. Significantly, among his top priorities was "New York background, knowledge of the city, living in the city."

The panel members charged with finding a police commissioner, all busy professionals, were selected for their presumed expertise in the criminal justice system, and they fully believed that they could help Koch find the Perfect Police Commissioner. The co-chairmen of the panel were Franklin Thomas, a former deputy police commissioner (who later became president of the Ford Foundation), and Richard L. Gelb, a longtime police buff, who was board chairman and chief executive officer of Bristol-Myers Company (and not related to me). Panel members included

Gerald Lynch, president of John Jay College, a couple of lawyers, a law school professor, and the president of the Vera Institute of Justice.

I was myself briefly a member of the panel, appointed because the mayor knew of my interest in the police, and I saw that its intentions were high-minded. I withdrew when I was cautioned that I could not write about anything I heard; my observations, in consequence, have been reconstructed from interviews with numerous officials.

On November 28, three days before Chief of Operations Hannon and Assistant Chief Courtenay were summoned to appear before the panel, its members, meeting in the Bristol-Myers offices on Park Avenue, interviewed Patrick Murphy, who wanted his old job back.

Murphy, the son of a New York City cop, had himself come up through the ranks of the NYPD, quit the department as a captain, and gone on to head the police forces of Syracuse, New York; Washington, D.C.; and Detroit. As New York City's PC, beginning in the autumn of 1970, Murphy helped rid the department of organized corruption, and he left it, two and a half years later, shortly before Mayor Lindsay's own departure, a dramatically tidied-up (if not actually a squeaky-clean) police force. Long after his departure, and under three succeeding commissioners— right into 1983, in fact—the NYPD continued to be in many ways Patrick Murphy's police department.

Mild-mannered, diffident, low-voiced, hesitant, of pale complexion and sandy hair, Murphy immediately was nicknamed the Friendly Ghost by his headquarters commanders. But the look and manner were infinitely deceptive. Murphy was that rare bird, an intellectual and visionary cop who had the steel to drive home his reforms. He was brought in to reorganize the New York police as a result of the institutionalized corruption initially exposed by Frank Serpico. An eccentric but dedicated street cop in his early thirties, Serpico was a bearded, long-haired, bead-wearing loner, irresistible to women and honest to the point of evangelical obsession, who had been trying since 1966 to bring his suspicions of widespread and tolerated corruption to the attention of his superiors. Time and again he was ignored or rebuffed. Against all protocol and tradition, he then tried to bring his charges to City Hall. He was snubbed. In desperation Serpico finally went to *The New York Times* police affairs reporter, David Burnham, whose resultant stories, based on Serpico's scandalous allegations, led to the formation of the Knapp Commission. The stories also caused Mayor John Lindsay profound embarrassment, and that was when he brought in Patrick Murphy to cleanse the department and restore its honor.

Policing, Murphy knew, was "almost a clandestine activity" and permitted a system in which entrenched corruption and brutality were tolerated and often covered up by commanders at all levels. Nevertheless, he was flabbergasted by the cynicism of First Deputy Commissioner John Walsh, whom he inherited as his first dep and who, according to Murphy, assumed "that most police officers would be corrupt and that only a small fraction could be counted on to be honest." That, according to Murphy, explained why Walsh "did so little about Serpico's allegations of corruption until they appeared in *The New York Times* exposés."

John Walsh was a phenomenon in the department, "perhaps the single most entrenched police administrator in modern police history . . . surviving police commissioner after commissioner," Murphy wrote in his autobiography. He attributed Walsh's survival to his political friendship with then-Manhattan District Attorney Frank Hogan, who had held office for more than thirty years and was manifestly untouchable. Walsh, from time to time, exposed a token instance of corruption in the department, which Hogan obligingly prosecuted.

But Patrick Murphy believed that police officers "were human beings who had been corrupted by a larger system only partly of the department's making; it wasn't the honest cop who was the freak; it was the failure of administration that had helped produce an atmosphere in which corruption could exist." Murphy, of course, wanted Walsh out, and after some delicate maneuvering, Walsh was persuaded to resign. Murphy also forced out uniformed commanders whom he suspected of laxity, and promoted men known for their integrity and competence—men like Jim Hannon and Dan Courtenay.

Then, acting on his own convictions, Murphy began setting up the machinery to monitor and expose corruption speedily. He let it be known corruption would *not* be tolerated, and he said he would hold commanders at all levels, from headquarters Brass down to precinct captains, accountable for rooting out and reporting all instances of dishonesty. Henceforth *all* the department's bosses would be held responsible and disciplined if they failed to expose any rogue cops under their command, Murphy said.

In issuing its final report, the Knapp Commission noted that although "in past administrations a commander was occasionally relieved of his command, or reduced in rank, or even dismissed from the department, for personal derelictions of duty, it was previously unheard of for such actions to be taken against him *as a result of derelictions by the men under him.*"

The report cited testimony given before the commission by a former police chief who said "he could not think of a single precinct commander who had been shifted for failure to maintain the integrity of his command." Indeed, the report said, "there is little evidence to suggest that such derelictions by subordinates *ever seriously impeded a commander's rise to higher rank.*"

Murphy changed all that, and the commissioners who followed him committed themselves to his policy. The message within the department was clear, from the bottom up. Supervisors were accountable for the integrity of their subordinates, were expected to be ever-vigilant, to pinpoint and report areas of even *potential* corruption; and they would be regarded as derelict in their own duty, would be disciplined, if they failed.

The new attitude was to be instilled into all recruits, as

well as veterans. Rookie cops training at the Police Academy found this paragraph in their curriculum soon after Murphy became commissioner:

> As a practical matter, this is the point in your police career when you should decide what kind of police officer you are going to be. If your decision is, as we hope it is, to be an honest cop, then expect to live on the salary you earn and never start the slow corrosive slide into corruption. A slide that usually starts with a pack of cigarettes or a dollar and ends with disgrace and active criminality. If there is a cynic among you who feels that this hour has been a "snow job," to him we suggest that he become an honest crook. Leave the department and become an honest thief. Before you are caught you will make a great deal more money mugging old men or sticking up shopkeepers than you will as a chiseling cop. And, after you are caught you can expect fair treatment from the other convicts in prison. On the prison social ladder the crooked cop rates just below the child molester.

It was still Murphy's conviction, many years later, that "most cops don't come into the department to be crooked."

"They come in like most human beings into most organizations," he once told me, "and they'll fit into what the values are, what's allowed and what isn't allowed. And if you can keep a climate of integrity for one whole generation, then maybe it will never get as bad again as it was in the past." Thinking back, he added, "Even at the height of the department's worst corruption, it was amazing how many people were trying to do their job in a decent way."

Among Murphy's mechanisms for keeping the department clean was the fearsome Bureau of Inspectional Services and its despised Internal Affairs Division, whose members were contemptuously known as shooflies. The cops assigned to that bureau formed a kind of secret police, charged with both overt and covert spying. Some, called field associates, were recruited right from the Police Academy and put into ostensibly routine assignments from where they spied on their unwitting colleagues. Others shadowed suspect cops or tested the integrity of their fellows at random, by trying to tempt them into corrupt practices. Reporting directly to the commissioner or to his first deputy, the chief of inspectional services was expected to sniff out any efforts at systematic corruption and stop them before they could become entrenched, as was the case prior to 1970.

The spying initially created an atmosphere of suspicion and hostility and increased the sense of alienation among many cops. But the honest cops came to see that the spying was necessary, that in fact it protected them. Often in the past it had been agonizing to defend their honesty in the face of their crooked brothers, to stand fast in an atmosphere of callously condoned corruption. Often they felt that no one knew or cared about their honesty except maybe their wives. That kind of isolation was deadly. Now at last honesty was being made a virtue. Of course, everyone realized that pockets of corruption would continue to form from time to time. But the hierarchy was no longer winking and looking the other way. There was a new, clearly articulated philosophy at the top. The new breed of bosses would at least *strive* for vigilance, for a clean department, for the image of a regenerated, a *varnished* Brass.

Patrick Murphy's philosophy encompassed the reversal of other shortcomings neglected for decades. The college campus riots of the 60s had exposed a shocking lack of restraint among police troops; other instances of police brutality, sometimes racially motivated, had surfaced from time to time. One of Murphy's most significant reforms was directed toward police brutality at its most extreme, the unjustified use of Deadly Force—universal police euphemism for shooting to kill. Unlike the police in other cities, who were officially instructed to shoot first and not ask too many questions afterward, a New York cop was rigidly restricted in his use of Deadly Force. Few people realized that the dictum "Shoot first and ask questions later" originated with Hermann Goering, who thus instructed the Prussian police in 1933, adding, "and if you make mistakes, I will protect you." Murphy took steps to cool down his ranks, telling them, in effect, if you make mistakes, I will *not* protect you.

Scrupulous adherence by the New York police to a policy of nonviolence received little public attention. To watch television was to believe that the New York police had never outgrown the tradition of kicked-in doors and blazing guns. The fact was, though, that the NYPD was now one of the most civilized peacekeeping agencies in the world.

Commissioner Murphy, in 1972, set up an internal watchdog group called the Firearms Discharge Review Board, which met regularly to question every shot fired from a cop's gun. It was virtually impossible for a cop to fire his weapon without the spent bullet turning up, metaphorically speaking, on the desk of the chief of operations, who headed the board. This included not only every shooting of a suspect (whether fatal or slight) but also any cop suicide or uxoricide, any accidental firing that missed its mark, or even the shooting of a distempered animal. Warning shots were forbidden, because a passerby or someone in a building standing near an open window might be hit. Besides, as a top commander explained to me, "shots are considered contagious and other cops in the area, hearing them, might also start shooting."

Some of the cases reviewed by the Firearms Discharge Review Board were grotesque: the case, for instance, of a police officer in Queens who handed his service revolver to a heavy loser in a card game. "Here, kill yourself," the cop said to his friend—presumably as a joke. The man did. The board recommended modified duty without a weapon— assignment to what cops called the "rubber gun brigade"— pending psychiatric evaluation.

Another case heard by the board concerned an officer having an affair with the estranged wife of a man known to have a violent temper. The husband surprised his wife and her lover, jumping out at them—in the words of the report—"from a recessed area" and "reaching into his pocket," presumably for a weapon. The cop fired six shots, two of which hit the husband, killing him. No weapon was found on the dead man. After being placed on modified duty, the cop began drinking and committed a series of minor assaults on civilians in his precinct. He was suspended without pay, and resigned from the department while charges against him were pending.

Still another case concerned a cop's apparent suicide with his service revolver; the detective who investigated was convinced that his wife had killed him, but the evidence was insufficient for prosecution. There was nothing that the review board could do in that instance.

Few of these cases made the newspapers. They came across the desk of the chief of operations daily, and Hannon discussed them with me on the understanding that I would keep confidential anything that might endanger an ongoing investigation. He was so willing to demonstrate the openness of the department and so eager to reveal the complexities of police work, that after a while he permitted me to enter his office at will, even in his absence, and look over anything on his desk, which held a triple-layered box: IN, READING, and OUT. The first layer required his signature or other action; the second was for items the commissioner or one of Hannon's commanders thought noteworthy. All three boxes were always full. (Anything he didn't want me to see he kept locked in a desk drawer.)

On the Firearms Discharge Review Board, in addition to Hannon, were the deputy commissioner for legal matters and the deputy commissioner for community affairs, as well as a couple of firearms experts who taught at the Police Academy. Some of the cases the board reviewed had their comical aspects: the cop, for instance, who used his service revolver instead of his club as a bludgeon. Lieutenant Frank McGee, in charge of the Academy's firearms unit and a member of the board, explained that using a gun that way would get the cylinder out of line. "It's better to jump up and bite the perpetrator on the nose," he quipped.

It sometimes seemed to the cop in the street that his bosses were more concerned with protecting the Bad Guys from getting hurt than with safeguarding the cops. The police High Command was, in fact, very much concerned with its street cops' safety, and the Firearms Discharge Review Board tried to teach cops not to make the kinds of mistakes that could get them into trouble—either by shooting when they shouldn't, or not shooting when they should. A cop often had to make that decision in a split second. It was one of the stresses that went with the job, and more often than not, when a cop overreacted by firing his gun, it was because he was scared, not because he was a sadist or a psychopath.

The majority of cases studied by the review board were unspectacular and concerned cops who were merely careless. But carelessness could cause a cop's death. After I had been visiting Hannon at headquarters for well over a year, and had sat in on several meetings of the board, I spent a day observing the "additional training" of a twenty-five-year-old police officer, Patrick Freeman; he had been assaulted by a burglary suspect while trying to handcuff him on a tenement roof in the Bronx. Freeman had fired two shots at the suspect, both of which missed.

According to the police report:

> Said officer was alone in a very dangerous situation when he fired the first round, and fired the second round in order to halt the escape of a very dangerous criminal who attempted murder in order to retain his freedom and possibly harm another person at some future date. The perpetrator was later arrested in the street and charged with attempted murder on the complaint of P. O. Freeman, and burglary on the complaint of the occupant of Apartment 5F. The perpetrator was interviewed and stated that he is a very nervous person and from fear of the officer's gun pushed said officer and fled.

In his own report, a questionnaire form with boxes to

check, Freeman answered that the weather was "clear," that he did not "have prior knowledge that the situation involved a person with a dangerous weapon," that he did not have his "firearm drawn and ready for use before you needed it," and that he did not have time to aim, that neither he nor his "opponent" was wounded, that he used no "protective cover," and that the distance between himself and his "opponent" when "first shot was fired" was one foot.

P. O. Freeman, Shield Number 31249, of the Four-eight Precinct in the Bronx, had joined the department at twenty-two after a tour with the Marines. "I want to serve humanity," he told me, and I didn't doubt his sincerity. I thought of him as a young Dan Courtenay, an eager, aggressive cop on his way up.

His failure to capture the burglar on the roof, while it could have cost his life, was not regarded by any of his supervisors as a violation of department policy or as requiring disciplinary action. It was due, they all felt, to inexperience and an excess of zeal. Aggressive cops were the ones who grew up to be commanders, perhaps even chiefs. But if Freeman were going to live to be a chief, he needed reminding of the dangers of the street. Hannon and his board recommended that Freeman review the laws and instructions regarding the discharge of firearms and that he receive additional training regarding securing prisoners.

Slim, with short-cropped hair and the build of an athlete, Freeman had a background somewhat more exotic than that of most New York cops, who tended to be city-born and bred. He was born in France, the son of an American serviceman who stayed on after World War II and married a French woman. Young Patrick's parents lived for a time in Morocco and brought him to the United States when he was five.

Freeman reported to the training officer, Frank Schiele, at 9 A.M. on a Tuesday in mid-April. The training was to last all day and took place in the basement shooting range at headquarters. (Everyone, including the chiefs, had to re-qualify as marksmen twice yearly—once indoors at head-quarters, once on the outdoor range in the Bronx.)

Officer Schiele relieved Freeman of his service revolver, a regulation Smith and Wesson .38. In the training exercises a deactivated gun was used, with its firing pin removed and its barrel and backstrap painted red "for maximum vis-ibility in holster and out," Schiele explained. It was the only weapon allowed in the classroom. And the room itself, adjacent to but shut off from, the firing range, was a real classroom with plastic desk-arm chairs, a blackboard, and a television screen. Freeman was the only pupil. Schiele showed several short films of simulated street situations. One was of a cop stopping a suspect car.

Freeman: "The cop stuck his head in the window. That's wrong."

Schiele (approvingly): "Car stops and family disputes are the most common incidents for a cop, the easiest for him to forget and relax and the easiest for him to get hurt. Watch the side-view mirror and the rear-view mirror. The driver can see us very well as we approach. We don't know who's in the car. But he knows who *we* are."

A second training film depicted a family dispute: Four cops respond to a neighbor's report of a violent husband-wife argument. One of the cops pounds on the apartment door, calling "Open up, police!" The door is flung wide by a woman, who hurls a jugful of household chemical con-taining lye into the cop's face (presumably she had intended it for her husband). As the cop gasps and covers his eyes, one of his companions says to another, "Call a bus" (mean-ing an ambulance).

Schiele (instructing): "That cop was too relaxed; he should have stood to the side of the door after knocking. One of the other cops should have helped him flush his face with water from the apartment right away; water is first aid treatment for lye, all cops should know that. And at least one of those cops should have brought along a walkie-talkie in a situation like that."

Schiele, commenting on several other short films:

"When there's a chance of being faced with a shotgun, equalize the situation, if possible. We don't like to face a shotgun with a revolver; shotguns are available to cops.

"In a street situation where the light is bad, or a cop is not in uniform, when a uniformed cop shouts his warning— 'Police, don't move' or 'Freeze'—the out-of-uniform cop should always heed the warning. He must assume the challenge is bona fide. Many cops who ignored the challenge have been shot; they thought the fact of their own identity must be obvious."

After the films Schiele role-played with Freeman. This was specifically designed to address Freeman's foolhardy behavior with the burglar on the roof.

Schiele: "You're gonna frisk me and handcuff me. This is your gun [handing him the deactivated revolver]. Don't be afraid to use it.

"The best way to frisk (if you can) is with your partner covering you. You stop the suspect, frisk him, and then handcuff him, in that order. Go ahead."

Freeman, using the gun as a prod, got Schiele off balance and made him lean against the wall, head first, in a manner as familiar to television viewers of cop movies as it was to the police themselves.

"It's better to use your nightstick than your gun," Schiele instructed, his face against the wall. "Your gun can get in the way." A thorough frisk, said Schiele, could reveal a cleverly concealed weapon.

"Think weird," he instructed. "Look for the razor blade in the hat band. Look for the unusual. Don't settle for finding one weapon; it may be a decoy. Look for a belt-buckle dagger. A car door can be a weapon, it can be rigged with a shotgun with a wire loop activator. Opening the door can aim it at you." Freeman was beginning to feel embarrassed at the way he had conducted his attempted arrest on the roof.

"It's a good thing you had on your helmet," Schiele said. "The handcuffs could have killed you." Later, Freeman told me he was shocked to realize he could have been hurled from the roof by his suspect. "The next day I had to go back to see how far the fall was from the roof. It was five stories. I was all shaken up."

Further instructions from Schiele: "Don't cock your gun in advance, a cocked gun requires less pressure on the trigger. You start thinking—this gun knows me, it'll never shoot *me*, we've been through thick and thin together."

Schiele gave Freeman an hour's break for lunch. "You have to *pound* safety into them," Schiele said, as Freeman left.

After lunch Freeman was turned loose on the shooting range. Using his own revolver, loaded with live ammunition, he fired at a moving paper target.

Schiele cautioned, "Count your shots. I notice you always try for that seventh shot. You should always know when you're empty." Freeman fired sixty rounds before Schiele decided he was proficient. Target practice at the indoor range was restricted to a stance behind a chest-high counter with the emphasis on squeezing off six shots in rapid succession. Other basic techniques were taught at the Police Academy, where rookie cops were instructed always to step to their left and crouch before shooting. Studies had shown that cops most often were hit in the right shoulder, and they were taught to crook their left arms in front of their chests for protection.

Schiele asked me if I wanted to try hitting the target to see for myself how hard it was. I put on the earmuffs and borrowed Freeman's loaded revolver, holding it with both hands, as instructed. (The crack of bullets in an indoor range is ear-splitting.) The target was a life-size black ink outline of a crouching man, with the most vulnerable areas, the head and upper torso, lightly shaded in. The man was pointing a real-looking revolver at me with his right hand and his left was held protectively in a loose fist before his chest. The target moved sideways and forward at the far end of the range, a distance of seven yards from where I stood. The lighting was deliberately dim. I was told to aim at the shaded torso area and to keep firing steadily.

The gun was heavy and it kicked. After the first six shots Schiele reloaded, and I fired another six rounds. When we recovered my paper target I saw that I had placed eleven of my twelve bullets in the chest. Several had been deflected by the hand and wrist, but one had gone straight through the heart. (One shot grazed the shoulder.) Schiele was impressed. After I showed my pockmarked target to Hannon and Courtenay—I couldn't resist gloating a bit—they were more respectful to me. Neither would ever let me accompany him on his own requalifying excursions to the range; I always suspected it was because they both knew their aim was less accurate than mine. Both Hannon and Courtenay, not surprisingly, believed in rigid gun control and disapproved of private gun licensing. They were convinced that only law enforcement officers should carry guns.

At the conclusion of his day's training, Freeman felt both braced and chastened. He said he loved the discipline of police training. In fact, he felt that the police were not disciplined enough, and he regretted the passing of the old standards.

In April of 1981 Freeman, who by then had received twelve citations for his outstanding police work, was transferred into the public morals division of the Organized Crime Control Bureau, the career path to becoming a detective, and in the fall of 1982, still working out of uniform, he was on loan to the Intelligence Bureau, assigned temporarily to duty at the United Nations. He had taken the Civil Service exam for sergeant in 1978 and had missed qualifying by a couple of points. Freeman said he was planning to cram at the Police Academy for the next exam, expected to be given the following year. Meanwhile, he had been recommended for a detective's gold shield.

He relished investigative work and hoped to become a detective commander—his idea of the best of two worlds. But most cops who chose investigative work as their career paths did not, somehow, find the energy to keep studying for Civil Service promotion. The gold shield in itself conveyed a singular status. Few cops who made detective worked their way up to chief, and the chiefs were the first to point that out. It was Dan Courtenay's belief that cops who were aiming to be detectives didn't really take the time to work toward the higher ranks. The detective Brass often was appointed from the uniformed ranks, for it was not necessary to have worked as a detective in the field to qualify as a detective inspector (which Courtenay once was) or as a detective chief. An experienced police manager, Courtenay maintained, could run any kind of unit from patrol through intelligence to investigative. Former Police Commissioner Patrick Murphy, who did not think much of detectives and held that most crimes were solved from information furnished by street cops, would have agreed. He shared the belief of most of the police Brass that detectives were not, ultimately, the material of High Command.

The members of the mayor's search panel knew a good deal about former Commissioner Murphy's views and they held him in high regard. But to suggest reappointing him as PC might have implied that the NYPD needed another extensive cleanup, which it did not. The panel members interviewed him respectfully, but they did not recommend him to the mayor. They did, however, believe that New York's police commissioner should be a cop, and in recent years, more often than not, the commissioner *had* been a former police commander of high rank, sometimes imported from another city.

"The panel wanted me to pick a commissioner only from the uniformed ranks," Mayor Koch later told me, "but I said, don't limit your interviews to cops, include others with law enforcement backgrounds." Koch, supplementing his search panel's efforts, was quietly taking advice from his friend Robert Morgenthau.

Elected by a landslide three years earlier, Morgenthau was the popular Manhattan district attorney. The relationship between the DA's office and the police department had to be more than cordial so that New York's criminal justice system could run smoothly and reflect credit on the mayor.

"The day after his election," Morgenthau recalled, "Ed asked me for suggestions for police commissioner."

"I told the panel to interview John Keenan and Bob McGuire, on Bob Morgenthau's suggestion," Koch said. While Keenan had worked under Morgenthau as chief assistant DA until being named special state prosecutor, Robert J. McGuire had worked under Morgenthau some years earlier, in the federal prosecutor's office, and was currently in private law practice.

The panel members interviewed McGuire on the same day that they met with Patrick Murphy. In addition to his noteworthy political connections, McGuire, who was forty-one, had the advantage of being (like Murphy) the son of a retired New York cop, former Deputy Police Chief James McGuire.

FOUR

★   Chief Courtenay's driver, John Angulat, was fielding telephone calls for his boss. His hand over the mouthpiece of the receiver, he told Courtenay, nervously, "David Durk is on the phone, Boss. He wants passes."

Courtenay did not reply. Instead, he rose from his chair, walked the two steps to his driver and wordlessly pushed down the receiver button, cutting off the call. Then he commented about what Durk could do with his request for passes.

There was a long history of animosity between Durk and the Police Brass. Durk had been Frank Serpico's partner in helping expose corruption in the department in the early 70s. It was not that top commanders like Courtenay were ungrateful for the changes wrought by Serpico's and Durk's efforts. On the contrary, they were relieved and happy to be working in a relatively clean department. But in Courtenay's opinion David Durk, since the Knapp Commission days, had developed delusions of grandeur. Many other commanders agreed that Durk was not a Team Player, was not a Good Soldier. He was a smartass Amherst College graduate, who thought he could go around the chain of command, could circumvent the accepted pecking order. (He was the only cop I ever met who joined the police expressly expecting to become commissioner.) Durk recently had been granted a leave of absence to work on a special assignment for the United Nations. "Our gain and their loss," muttered a headquarters commander. Mavericks did not flourish in the NYPD.

A couple of minutes later Durk called again and this time Shilensky answered, signaling Courtenay who it was. Courtenay growled, "Hang up."

Shilensky knew better than to obey; instead he politely told Durk to call Rocky Pomerance at the Statler Hilton, saying that was where all the passes were being issued. Pomerance, the police chief of Miami Beach, was a special adviser on security to the Democratic National Committee and a practiced public relations man.

Deputy Commissioner Francis J. McLoughlin, overhearing the conversation, asked Courtenay, "Did you know the PC made Durk take out a gun permit and pay the regulation $30 for it, when he took his leave of absence? Durk assumed he could just keep his service revolver."

Frank McLoughlin was there to pick up the credentials promised his colleagues down at headquarters. He was the department's official spokesman, its liaison with the press, and nothing ever ruffled him.

Courtenay sorted through several bulging packets, filled with varicolored cardboard tags—credentials that gave their bearers access to the convention floor, or to the exclusive sky boxes, or to the even more exclusive podium. They were his to distribute with extreme discretion. Courtenay told McLoughlin there were two security credentials giving access to good seats on the Garden floor for each of the five superchiefs, and two for each of the seven deputy commissioners; all this had been worked out with Robert Strauss and was a police department perk.

Courtenay handed McLoughlin the passes. "Please bear in mind," he cautioned, "that I'll have only 50 percent of what I have today, for Wednesday and Thursday—when the real fun begins."

Dressed in a sport shirt and slacks, Courtenay was seated

at his desk, being careful not to cross his legs; he didn't want the revolver strapped to his ankle to show.

Mickey Schwartz entered.

"NBC is on the phone," he announced. "They want traffic stopped between 7 and 9:30 A.M. because the noise interferes with their interviews in the street." Schwartz's voice was edged with resigned sarcasm.

"Aw, that's too bad," Courtenay said.

"Well, I didn't know what commitment you'd made to the *Today Show*," Schwartz said. "OK, I'll tell them no."

"Two cigarette bombs just went off, one in Ohrbach's, one in Macy's," Shilensky called across the room to Courtenay. "No one was hurt."

"Did our bomb truck respond?" Courtenay wanted to know. Shilensky said he'd try to find out.

Courtenay had foresightedly provided himself with the telephone numbers for Macy's and Ohrbach's security chiefs, as well as for the other large department stores in the area; they were pinned to his wall map.

Shilensky said, "I can't find out if the bomb truck responded, but there have been two more bombs, one at Lord & Taylor, one at B. Altman."

"All cigarette bombs?" Courtenay asked, and was told yes. "That's generally the FALN. Reach out for intelligence." The FALN was a terrorist group advocating Puerto Rican independence, whose members long had eluded the New York police. A year and a half earlier, in January 1976, the FALN had bombed the historic Fraunces Tavern just below Wall Street, killing four and injuring forty-four. The cigarette bombs were, for this casually homicidal group, a restrained gesture of protest.

Shilensky reported, "Intelligence says yes, it's FALN."

Courtenay, showing off his political savvy: "You know why FALN has surfaced? It's because the Puerto Rican delegates were not certified."

"The *Daily News* is calling to know how many detectives will be assigned to the DNC in case of an assassination," Shilensky said.

"Tell them one big one," said Courtenay, who wished to keep the numbers vague.

Someone handed Hartling a slip of paper and he announced, "There are now 150 Yippies in the park, and the mayor's office has given them permission to go ahead and put up their tents."

By 3 P.M. there were 500 Yippies in Central Park, and a total of eight cigarette bombs (some unexploded) had been reported in various Manhattan department stores; all bore the FALN signature—a cardboard cigarette box (often Marlboro) containing flashpowder and sulfuric acid. The bombs were placed so as not to injure shoppers, but merely to create a disturbance.

Inspector Herman Reed was talking to an out-of-town security officer who had a problem.

"You got a gun?" Reed asked him. "Then you won't get on the convention floor. I'm sorry, that's our rule. In New York only *we* carry guns." Earlier, permission to carry a gun had been denied to the bodyguard of Mrs. Martin Luther King. The police were asking that all out-of-town guns be checked at the mayor's office.

Courtenay had political instructions to convey to his staff from Clifford Cassidy:

"There are two cars coming through 33rd Street for the opening session," he said. "Let them through." That was one of the "frozen" streets, off limits to normal traffic. "One of the cars is Mayor Daley's, and his car will be coming through every day. The other is Barbara Jordan's; she has a bad leg." Jordan was to be the keynote speaker. The methods of access to the Garden were being decided by the DNC on the basis of political clout; it was Courtenay's job to follow through.

It was also his job, self-imposed, to keep his office looking shipshape, and he strolled through the passageways, checking up. All the doors now had identifying cards affixed, most of them hand-lettered. Intelligence, however, had a *printed* card. And one of Courtenay's sergeants, who had been issued no desk or telephone, had tacked a card with his name—Sergeant Larry Mullins—onto the door of a two-foot-deep supply closet. Courtenay chuckled appreciatively as he passed it.

To the occupants of each room he announced, "Bob Strauss is walking through at 3:30. Shape up the office."

Back at his desk, he was on the white phone, the hot line to Secret Service: "On those incendiaries, eight have surfaced, but there was a message from FALN saying they planted *twelve*. If you get word where the other four are, let me know."

Courtenay told Schwartz and Hartling, "We should fight the Yippies at 59th Street, or it will be too late. We have to keep the lanes clear for the delegates' buses." Only four hours now to the opening session of the DNC at 8 P.M. By "fight" Courtenay simply meant "intercept," unless the Yippies proved to be intractable. They would be diverted from the immediate Garden area and guided to a demonstration site where they could be contained.

On the phone Courtenay listened to a tale of woe about an out-of-town delegate who had driven into the city. "Was his car towed?" he asked. "It was? He wasn't in it, was he? Well, the fastest way to get from the East Side to the West Side is to hide in the trunk of a car while it's being towed away."

Schwartz and Hartling laughed appreciatively. But Courtenay decided to play Captain Queeg. "Don't think it's a joke—until I smile," he snapped.

At 4 P.M. the first dep, James M. Taylor, entered Courtenay's office, just as Schwartz announced that 300 Yippies were now *leaving* Central Park. To Taylor, who was taking in the elaborate electronic equipment and banks of telephones, Schwartz said, "We used to handle this kind of operation from a phone booth with a package of dimes, didn't we?"

At 5 P.M. Commissioner Codd, who was going to attend the opening of the DNC at 8 that evening as the guest of a local Democratic bigwig, dropped in to be briefed. Courtenay obliged, knowing that the PC was looking for anecdotal data with which to entertain his DNC hosts. (Codd always carried with him a three-by-five index card listing current crime statistics, in case of queries.)

"We've had word the hospital workers are planning to rush the Garden after their demonstration outside," Courtenay told Codd. "We'll fatten up our lines."

"What have you got in the way of barrier line, Dan?" Codd had heard about Courtenay's earlier difficulties with barriers.

"Double wood is the heaviest we've got," Courtenay told him, meaning two thicknesses of barriers; the sawhorses were three feet wide at the bottom.

Codd, of course, was as well versed as Courtenay in street tactics. The trouble was, he often slipped back into the role of tactician, forgetting that the commissioner was a policy-maker, not a field general. Courtenay and other of the department's top commanders privately ridiculed this weakness.

Schwartz was in the communications room, speaking into a hand-held microphone to the cops who were manning the closed-circuit television cameras at various viewing points.

"Pull back . . . OK, now turn to the right . . . hold it . . . a little more . . . OK, hold it right there." Absorbed, he didn't notice the ashes dropping from the cigar he held in his free hand.

Courtenay watched over Schwartz's shoulder. "This is the way to fight a war," he said. "You don't get hurt in here."

"You also can't vent any energy," Schwartz said.

"Don't worry, we'll vent plenty of energy in a little while. We'll be out there." On one of the monitors Courtenay spotted some demonstrators marching toward the Statler Hilton. "How the hell did they get in there?" Schwartz quickly spoke into a two-way radio: "Command Post to Factor Two Leader. We don't want them to go north on 33rd."

By 5:45 P.M., Commissioner Codd had been joined by

Chief of Operations Hannon in Courtenay's office, where both men watched the monitors. Hannon was in uniform—not the cooler summer uniform of shirt and pants, but the regulation navy-blue wool blouse that was much too warm for New York's summer. He seemed not to feel it. Good Soldiers don't perspire.

Courtenay explained to his assembled bosses how the breakthrough in the lines had occurred, implying that the fault lay with intelligence's lack of intelligence. He said that intelligence scouts were supposed to be out patrolling in "custom cars," which were police vehicles equipped with computer terminals, but disguised to look like civilian vehicles. "They don't give us the numbers," Courtenay said. "We're in good shape, though."

Hannon, taking over in spite of himself, warned Courtenay, "Don't wait until 8, it may be too late."

Mock-reproachfully, Courtenay told Hannon, "You said I could run this show."

Hannon answered, tartly, "Well, you're running it."

Courtenay didn't realize that Hannon—having, by now, been Top Cop for nearly a year and a half—was being a model of restraint. When he had been in the job only seven months, I had watched him actually take over command, if just for a moment, from an assistant chief in the field. It happened at the end of a tense hostage-negotiating session that began in midafternoon and lasted well into the night, attended by hordes of onlookers, brightly lit by television floodlamps—a frenzied crowd scene in which people could have been trampled.

Hostage-negotiation was yet another concept developed under Commissioner Murphy, and New York's pioneering work became a model for other law enforcement agencies throughout the world. The case that brought Hannon out involved a bank holdup, and at first it seemed to have political implications. Commissioner Codd himself appeared on the scene. Ever since the carnage at the Olympic Games in Munich in September 1972, law enforcement officers everywhere got nervous when an armed man, possibly a terrorist, took hostages. It was, in fact, the Munich episode that had given New York police Inspector Simon Eisdorfer the idea that a special response could and should be marshaled to cope with the emerging crime of hostage-taking.

Detective-Lieutenant Frank Bolz was appointed head of the hostage negotiation team, which consisted of seventy detectives from the five boroughs. All of them worked in other assignments but were on call for hostage emergencies. I saw Bolz for the first time on the evening of October 6, 1975, after driving down to Greenwich Village with Hannon, where the would-be bank robber was barricaded in a branch of the Bankers Trust Company on Sixth Avenue between 12th and 13th streets.

Bolz was leaning on the counter of a small grocery store adjacent to the bank, wearing a navy-blue baseball cap with the insignia DBHNT (Detective Bureau Hostage Negotiation Team). The cap was shoved back from his forehead and he was swigging restorative mouthfuls of milk from a container and trying to reestablish telephone contact with the bank robber next door. Hostage negotiators had to be gregarious, had to be prepared to talk and talk for hours, delivering a flow of soothing platitudes that would distract the hostage-taker, take his mind off shooting his victims. Bolz loved to talk, and he had the born detective's gifts of empathy and persuasion, which made him the ideal hostage-negotiator. He was chunky and ruddy-faced, with blue green eyes and an evangelical bent. He lived and breathed hostage-negotiating. He was wearing a molded, bulletproof vest under his shirt.

"Ray, hey, Ray baby," Bolz was saying into the phone, in his most winning voice. "He's gone," he commented, passing the phone to Detective Joe Mulligan, who was the secondary, or backup, negotiator. Detective Ingeborg Wagner, one of the two female members of the hostage team, was acting as "coach"—the liaison between the negotiators and the uniformed command. Women rarely act as primary negotiators, for male hostage-takers tend to feel sexually threatened by female cops.

It had begun shortly before 3 P.M., when Raymond Olson, a slender, sad-eyed, twenty-three-year-old drifter entered the bank, carrying a sawed-off rifle and a revolver. He ordered the six men and four women he found inside to go to the rear of the bank.

Containment was always the first priority, and this job fell to members of the emergency service, who, wearing body armor and carrying heavy weapons, surrounded the immediate area under siege. It was considered good psychology to let the hostage-taker see that a uniformed force was present, even while the nonuniformed negotiators were talking to him soothingly—a variation of the good guy-bad guy technique.

The emergency service team that turned out in support of the negotiators during a hostage case represented the most extreme example of restraint in the use of Deadly Force. Though the training for these men was totally oriented toward an ability to shoot to kill, they were robotlike in their obedience, and would not move a finger on their triggers, even under fire, unless directed to do so by their commanding officer.

At first Olson had made vague demands for money and hinted at affiliations with terrorist groups. Pressed to be more specific, he asked for the release of Patty Hearst (who was then in jail).

Soon, though, it became obvious that he was reaching for reasons to explain his actions; he was neither bank robber nor terrorist, and he had no interest at all in Patty Hearst. The intelligence gathered from Olson's friends and relayed to Bolz and his colleagues was that Olson tended to confuse fantasy with reality and that he had been impressed by the movie *Dog Day Afternoon*, about a pair of bank robbers who took hostages. He did not know it, but he was imitating art imitating life.

It would have been funny had Olson not had a couple of real guns loaded with real bullets, and if he had not seemed determined to think of *something* to demand, just to test his new-found power. At last, around 6:30 P.M., unable to think of anything else, he asked for beer. Because intelligence reports indicated he was not a heavy or belligerent drinker, the area commander told Bolz it was all right to send in the beer.

It was the kind of maneuver Bolz enjoyed, and for which he was equipped. A box he carried in the trunk of his car contained rope and wooden door wedges. After carefully explaining to Olson what he was going to do, Bolz threw a loop of rope around the bank's front door handle, Olson unlocked the door, and Bolz pulled it open. The beer and some sandwiches were then slid in on a shopping cart and Olson obligingly released a couple of hostages. A detective took them down the block and into a bar for questioning— part of the routine.

Meanwhile, a floor plan of the bank had been obtained and, unknown to Olson, members of the emergency service had entered the cellar through a sidewalk trapdoor and crept up the stairs to a door that led into the rear of the bank. After peering under the doorsill to make sure Olson could not see them, they pushed the door open a crack, secured it with a wedge, and squatted, rifles aimed.

Outside in the street Assistant Chief Carl Ravens was apprised of the situation by one of his inspectors. "We can get a bead on him," the inspector reported. "No," Ravens said. "Delay is in our favor."

As the area commander of Manhattan South, Ravens had the last word about tactics. A dark-haired, craggy-faced man of sixty-one, six times a grandfather, he had already put in a full day's work supervising security for the visiting Emperor Hirohito, when he was summoned to 13th Street. Now here he was, along with Chief of Operations James Hannon and the police commissioner, together with an army of cops, all waiting, forbearingly, on the pleasure of a lunatic drifter who just might decide to start killing people.

At length, as in all previous cases, their patience was rewarded. Olson grew sleepy from the beer and lost heart.

He laid down his weapons, and the officers waiting behind the cellar door rushed him. He looked wan and frail as he was hustled into a squad car and driven away. Because no one had been hurt, the sudden release of tension became a celebration. That was when the crowds surged past the barriers into the street, unruly and potentially dangerous, both to themselves and the glass windows of the shops lining the street. Chief Hannon seized the bullhorn held by Assistant Chief Ravens. He barked commands to his troops and called on the crowd to come to its senses before someone was injured. Standing tall and solid, the Voice of Authority, he finally persuaded the crowd to disperse.

The next day at police headquarters Hannon and Ravens and other commanders who had been at the scene gathered to analyze the operation, as was always done in the wake of a major police turnout. After pointing out some relatively minor tactical mistakes to be corrected in future responses, they agreed that the overall operation had been admirable.

Assistant Chief Dan Courtenay gave Hannon an appraising look and decided he *was* letting him run his own show. He thought it was time to patrol. "Maybe I better take a walk," he told Hannon. Ritual of putting on cap, patting hip for gun.

The sun at 6 P.M. was still bright and hot as Courtenay strode into Eighth Avenue. His long legs were slightly bowed, and his right arm swung outward to accommodate the bulky, holstered service revolver—the familiar swagger of cops and cowboys. His step was wide and measured, authoritative, calculated to inspire confidence among his troops, to dazzle the public, to awe potential provocateurs, rowdies, existentialists.

As he glided past a barricaded, closely patrolled wedge of sidewalk, a young female demonstrator wearing shorts and a halter squealed derisively, "Ooh, a General!"

"You better believe it!" the General replied, breaking his stride to meet and briefly hold the eye of his accoster. The tone was jocular but the glance was steely. The young woman blushed and shrank back.

Courtenay was joined by Rocky Pomerance, the Miami Beach police chief, who also wanted to have a look around. Pomerance, a man of much charm and considerable bulk, was smiling amiably and perspiring freely. He had trouble keeping pace with Courtenay.

Courtenay swung on, reaching a cluster of ranking police officers—a deputy chief, an inspector, a couple of captains—all handpicked for the convention security detail by Courtenay himself during the months of tactical preparation. He flung a genial arm across the inspector's shoulder and, with a broad wink, intoned his signature: "You're doing a helluva job, I've been watching you!"

At an intersection Courtenay suddenly dug in his heels and began directing traffic, waving on buses, holding up cars. Courtenay was a closet traffic cop! And he was lording it over his domain. Under his breath he murmured, "Mine, all mine!" He was indulging in a split second of rare, manic glee.

He politely asked gawking pedestrians to step behind barriers. He *moved* barriers. As a Good Soldier, this was not beneath his dignity. He beckoned a line officer and instructed him; he talked to a street monitor for one of the demonstrating groups and was conciliatory; he pointed out, to a sergeant on the line, a woman who looked as though she might get hurt, out in front of a barrier. "Just move them back, nice and easy," he said.

Because Mike Shilensky was busy elsewhere, Courtenay brought with him as his batsman—the carrier of his walkie-talkie—a sergeant with the piquant name of Lawless. The walkie-talkie, typically, ceased transmitting halfway through Courtenay's fifty-minute walking tour. Suddenly noticing that Rocky Pomerance was no longer with them, Courtenay said to Sergeant Lawless, "How can you lose someone as big as Rocky?"

Courtenay was back in his office, and with him were

Mickey Schwartz and Jim Hannon (Hannon, alone among the Brass, called Schwartz, affectionately, Milty). The DNC would convene promptly at 8.

Courtenay radiated satisfaction. "And what time is it, gang?"

Dutifully, Schwartz answered, "Three minutes to 8."

Everyone and everything was miraculously in place. Demonstrators were demonstrating tidily behind their barriers (a peaceful crowd required less space than an angry one). No streets had been lost. All lines of communication were operating. God was in his Heaven and Commissioner Codd was in his sky box. Dan Courtenay sat back, looking almost smug.

Three hours later, at 11 P.M., Courtenay and Schwartz were buttoning things up when the commissioner stopped in to say goodnight on his way home.

"I felt like I was parting the Red Sea—directing operations from the TV monitor," Schwartz told him.

"Two more, after today," Courtenay said. "I used to do tours that way. I never said to myself, I have five tours. Always, four—after tomorrow." Both Schwartz and Courtenay were ready to drop with fatigue, but they covered their exhaustion. Good Soldiers were never tired.

Mike Shilensky entered, looking rumpled and weary. Commissioner Codd greeted him, remarking, "The trouble with Mike is, he's more of a cop than a lawyer. It's going to be hard for him to simmer down when this is over." Codd had issued his pleasantry for the night. He had remembered Shilensky's first name—and not simply because it was also his own. Codd remembered *everybody's* first name—he knew and always used the first names of the *wives* of all his top commanders. He had a parrot's memory and employed it to great social advantage, having long since discovered that most people felt disproportionately flattered by such trifling tokens of noblesse oblige.

Dan Courtenay liked to point out that he'd survived the terms of twelve police commissioners and expected to sur-

vive several more. He had, of course, done more than survive. He had flourished. He'd long since outdistanced his
two older brothers—one a captain in the police department, one a retired fire department lieutenant. His younger
brother was a patrolman with the NYPD and content at
that level.

What made Courtenay run? He was a devoted family
man, a church-going Catholic—he and Mary often drove
into Manhattan to attend Sunday Mass at St. Thomas
More's Church—morally upright, a little square, and a
chauvinistic New Yorker, as native as the mudflats of
Queens, where he lived and where, at twenty-one, he first
patrolled on foot. Despite his moral rectitude, he had the
wisdom to bend when it came to his children. "My kids live
in *their* culture, not mine," he said.

On the other hand, their father was a cop and therefore
they were in closer touch with violence than other children.
This, too, Courtenay dealt with resolutely. "We're a violent
society," he said, "we always have been; that's how we won
the West and how we won the Revolution." He defused the
menace to his children by familiarizing them with his service revolver. "I let them play with the unloaded gun, and
then told them, 'It's mine, never touch it without my permission.'" They never did. As for Mary Courtenay, "She
wouldn't touch my gun if it were lying on top of a thou-
sand-dollar bill; she'd rather starve to death than move it."
Carrying it always, on duty and off, was, he said, "like
putting my wallet in my pocket."

Courtenay's autocratic manner was derived perhaps from
the German Lutheran side of his family, his mother's side.
The sense of humor, the gift for self-mockery that balanced
the haughtiness, was doubtless his father's contribution—a
mixture of Canadian and Irish.

Courtenay's father worked for Western Union (he died in
1963 when Dan was thirty-seven); but there was an uncle in
the police department, a precedent for Courtenay and his
brothers to follow. Courtenay did not have many career
choices. For a year he attended Queens College, helping to

pay his expenses by working as a floorman for the National
Biscuit Company. But he got restless and volunteered for
the Navy at seventeen. After two years on a destroyer in
the Atlantic he emerged as a quartermaster third class. He
already knew he wanted to be a cop, like his uncle. His
older brother had joined the police in 1943.

"As a kid, I wanted to be a G-man," Courtenay reminisced. "But I pretty much thought all along I wanted to be
a police officer."

Courtenay's horizons when he first joined the force—like
those of most of his narrowly educated young colleagues—
were limited. He simply handed himself over to an organization that would nurture him. Many of the men who
joined the police in the late 1940s and early 1950s were
scarred by their families' battle with the Depression of the
1930s. Putting on a uniform, submitting to a rigid, quasi-
military discipline was like getting into a cage—or, more
accurately, into a goldfish bowl. That was the price you
paid for security.

Once you were in uniform it was like being part of an
extended family, albeit a demanding one of competing
brothers and stern father figures. Most career decisions
were made for you, and it was hard to really grow in a
social and intellectual sense. Studying and taking exams,
year after year—if you had any ambition and wanted to
rise—kept you in a state of constant schoolboy anxiety.

Within their rigidly disciplined routine, most cops
showed off like little boys. They drove their prowl cars as if
they believed they were sheriff's deputies galloping in chase
of Billy the Kid. (I prided myself on being a skilled driver,
having learned at sixteen, but it was only after traveling
with detectives for a couple of years that I began to understand the possibilities of truly creative driving.)

On Jim Hannon's desk one day was this report (rivaling
any chase scene from a movie):

> At 1400 hours somewhere in the Gerritsen Beach
> area a police helicopter piloted by John Rawley ob-

served two male black perps stripping a Lincoln Continental. The two perps observed the copter zeroing in on them and took off in a getaway car with a tire from the Lincoln.

A chase began on the ground by RMPs [Radio Motorized Patrols], going through the 61st, 63rd, 69th, and 75th Precincts. As a result of the chase, numerous cars were damaged in different Precincts, a civilian was injured and an RMP was damaged with three POs [police officers] who sustained minor injuries in the 75th Precinct.

The chase ended at Linden Blvd. and Schenck Ave. Both perps were apprehended. The Lincoln and the getaway car both were stolen vehicles.

That chase took place in 1975, and at least the speeding cops captured a thief. In the second quarter of that year, though, 107 cops were injured in motor vehicles while on what the department described as "routine police duty." Cops were the city's most reckless drivers and there seemed to be little the police hierarchy could do about it. Between 1973 (which was as far back as police department records were available) and the first quarter of 1982, there were 22,365 police vehicles involved in accidents in the city of New York. Of these collisions, 6,354 resulted in injuries to members of the force—which worked out to a rough average of 2,694 damaged RMPs and 765 damaged cops per year.

But, ah! the swagger of those young cops, the appeal of their boyish heroics, their earnestness, their dedication!

Mary O'Hearn had known Dan Courtenay since he was fifteen. She, too, was from Queens, and a year and a half after Courtenay joined the police, Mary married him. A year later their first daughter was born, followed in four years by a son and two years later by another daughter.

Police Officer Courtenay wanted to go up the ladder in his chosen career, but he got a slow start. It was nine years before he made sergeant, having scored 950th out of the 990 who took the Civil Service test with him. Qualifying examinations for sergeant, lieutenant, and captain were given at unspecified intervals, depending on the need to fill job quotas; those scoring highest were appointed to the first vacancies.

By the time he took the lieutenant's test Courtenay had improved to the point of placing 15th out of 960 and he was promoted in 1960, when he was thirty-four. He was made captain in 1965, a month after his thirty-ninth birthday, having passed that exam—the toughest of the three—33rd on the list. A few years later, as a full inspector, he began thinking about a higher education and in 1972, at the age of forty-six, he entered Pace University.

In an essay he wrote for Life Experience credit, Courtenay summarized his early career. "The duties of a patrolman are diverse and challenging," he wrote, "covering a wide spectrum from 'father confessor' to doctor to psychologist." As a patrol sergeant, he supervised, trained, disciplined, investigated, interviewed, inspected, wrote reports about, and commanded the twenty to thirty patrolmen assigned to him in his precinct. As a lieutenant, he served both as patrol supervisor (the same duties, basically, as before, except for a broader area of responsibility) and as a desk officer, with administrative responsibility. He was then assigned to police headquarters in the Bureau of Planning Operations, a unit, Courtenay wrote, "considered as the operating arm of the Chief Inspector." During this time, he modestly continued, "I developed an expertise in emergencies, emergency planning and operational and tactical plans and authored two publications for the Police Department." Both dealt with operational responses to emergencies and disasters, such as the midair plane collision over New York in December 1960 that killed 127 and turned a Brooklyn neighborhood into an inferno.

As a captain, he was given command of the newly formed operations unit, still at headquarters, where he supervised the strategic planning of what he described as "many very sensitive, controversial and demanding operations" that included "the visit of His Holiness Pope Paul VI" and visits of many foreign heads of state; emergency plans to cope with riots and similar situations in all areas of the city; plans to meet flood conditions resulting from hurricanes; transit strikes.

Courtenay was appointed to the rank of deputy inspector in 1969 by Commissioner Howard R. Leary during John Lindsay's first term as mayor; that was the first *political* rank, bestowed at the pleasure of the commissioner. During the next two years, funded by the department and with its blessing, he traveled to other big cities to study aspects of their police systems; acted as liaison with other New York City and State agencies such as the Fire Department, Transit Authority Police, New York State Guard, and the Mayor's Emergency Control Board; and—in anticipation of the NYPD's conversion to computers—journeyed to Omaha to study the equipment used by the Strategic Air Command.

By the time he was promoted to full inspector by Commissioner Patrick Murphy in 1971, Courtenay was one of the most knowledgeable administrators in the department, the sort of headquarters commander who seemed destined for a smooth climb to the top.

The kind of headquarters command Courtenay had lucked into was regarded by the field men of his own rank as desk work, as safe work; headquarters was the breast at which career cops nursed. The field men sneered at the headquarters men, said they were On the Tit. As an inspector, however, Courtenay was weaned and assigned to the command of Bronx detectives.

"I had the ultimate responsibility for the proper investigation of all complaints of crime reported in the borough," he wrote in his Life Experience essay. "On occasion, in the absence of the chief of detectives, it was necessary for me to act in his stead." That planted the seed. Being a detective boss was fun. But he was still two ranks away from aspiring to the goal of detective chief. At the end of 1971, Courtenay was assigned as commander of the elite Tactical Patrol Force, which he described thus:

"A completely mobile, well disciplined group that is used as a supplement to patrol in high crime areas with the potential of immediate mobilization and response to any area of the city, at a moment's notice. . . . It is the Department's first thrust at a disaster, emergency or riot situation." It numbered 609 patrolmen, 48 sergeants, 9 lieutenants, and 3 captains, and its jurisdiction was city-wide. That assignment lasted less than five months. In mid-April of 1972 he was transferred as executive officer to the narcotics division, one of the most sensitive assignments in the police department and traditionally the most corrupt. Commissioner Murphy recently had removed narcotics from the jurisdiction of the Detective Bureau, where the supervision had been appallingly lax, and placed it within the newly formed Organized Crime Control Bureau, operated from police headquarters. "This," wrote Courtenay, "is a city-wide responsibility and requires a firm commitment to the elimination of the narcotics evil."

Patrick Murphy and the Knapp Commission had by then made it a lot easier for an honest police supervisor to do his job. "Elimination of the narcotics evil" was, however, a pipe dream, and Courtenay was waxing rhetorical to impress his professors at Pace.

A mere five months later Courtenay became commanding officer of a section of Manhattan then designated as the Fourth Division, soon to be absorbed into a larger area and renamed Manhattan North. The Fourth Division was composed of four police precincts and 1,100 members of the force. It was largely residential and included the mayor's home, Gracie Mansion; the vast expanse of Central Park into which few New Yorkers ventured after dusk; and Lincoln Center, with its festivals of music and dance and theater and its large but normally well-behaved crowds. The Fourth Division lacked the drama of the area that lay below 59th Street, but still, it gave Inspector Courtenay a taste of what it would be like, five years and two promotions later,

to have command of the plummiest field job in the department, the Manhattan *South* area. Designations such as divi-
sions and areas and zones were merely efforts to slice up a
huge and awesomely complex city into manageable bite-
sized chunks for the police. The smallest and stablest slice
was the precinct, an area of roughly 140 to 150 square
blocks.

After barely seven months with the Fourth Division,
Courtenay was again promoted by Commissioner Murphy.
On April 6, 1973—exactly twenty-five years after being
appointed as a patrolman—Courtenay became a chief.
True, he was only a deputy chief, a one-star chief, but no
one ever wore his first star more proudly than Deputy
Chief Daniel J. Courtenay. He was a couple of months
short of his forty-seventh birthday. That May he was transferred to the field control division of the Organized Crime
Control Bureau, and eight months after that he was made
commander of the narcotics division. His boss was Organized Crime Control Bureau Chief James Hannon and his
exec was Inspector Herman Reed.

Meanwhile he had pursued a variety of self-improvement
courses both within and outside the department, as did
most of New York's ambitious career cops: a ten-session
course in public speaking at the Police Academy; another
ten-session course in disaster management at New York
University; conversational Spanish for fifteen sessions at
Bronx Community College (in order to be culturally sensitive to New York's large and growing Puerto Rican popula-
tion); police community relations, a seven-session course at
the New School for Social Research.

And he had of course joined the various professional so-
cieties that cops joined, including the Captains Endowment
Association and—as soon as he got his star—the International Association of Chiefs of Police.

Courtenay's second star was conferred by Commissioner
Codd in 1975, the same year that Codd also promoted
Hannon from chief of the Organized Crime Control Bureau
to the department's only four-star chiefdom. As an assistant

chief, Courtenay became the executive officer in OCCB under Hannon's successor. And Hannon, in the fall of 1975, asked Commissioner Codd to give him Courtenay for the job of security coordinator for New York's first Democratic National Convention in more than fifty years.

Tuesday, July 13, 1976, was day two of the DNC. (Only two more days to go, after tomorrow, Courtenay told himself.) Blue uniforms were everywhere and so were television and print reporters frantically seeking drama in the streets. There was little enough drama on the convention floor, where delegates waved placards showing a grimacing Jimmy Carter, bouncing their candidate ritualistically higher and higher to a foreordained plateau. And with all their scrounging, the greedy cameras completely missed one of the weirder and more comical mishaps of the street. It was lucky for the police, and especially for Courtenay, that the cameras happened to be looking the other way.

In his office that afternoon Courtenay noticed on one of the closed-circuit monitors that a small group of placard-carrying gays, no more than a dozen, were walking up and down in front of the Statler Hilton. This was in defiance (or possibly ignorance) of the agreements made with the police, who were still attempting to keep the entrance to the hotel clear for arriving and departing delegates.

It was true that Courtenay and his team were trying their best to *avoid* arresting demonstrators. Such arrests were time-consuming and costly and of far greater use to the martyred arrestees than to the police. After many discussions, Courtenay, on Mike Shilensky's advice, had ordered an arrest team into being. Since the team would do nothing else *but* make arrests, it was fitted out somewhat menacingly. And since it looked menacing, it was being kept out of sight—in a cave just off the sunken taxi-well that led into the Garden's side entrance.

The arrest team's orders were to remove any arrestees swiftly to the taxi-well area, where space was reserved for the necessary processing. Courtenay realized that the command post watching the Statler Hilton would automatically alert the arrest team to the illegal demonstration and he feared a possible overreaction. The gays were marching (albeit illegally) without interfering with any passersby, meekly, unmilitantly, minding their own business. Presciently, Courtenay dispatched Inspector Reed and Detective-lawyer Shilensky into the street.

As the two approached the taxi-well, they met a sight that gave them pause. Rhythmically sprinting up the ramp of the well, emerging into the bright sunlight of the street, were ten men led by a sergeant. They were not exactly goose-stepping, but they were lifting their booted feet in precision. Their helmeted heads turned neither right nor left, and they carried their nightsticks like muskets. They were loose on the street, a thunderclap of storm troopers. Unleashed after hours of confinement in their cave, they were a band to strike terror in the heart of any citizen, gay or gloomy.

Reed and Shilensky were appalled, instantly struck by the B-movie possibilities of the situation. This was overkill of the most absurd kind. Sprinting himself, Reed caught up with the helmeted, booted sergeant, who looked bewildered and then frustrated. Reed felt sorry for him, for having to block his moment of possible glory. Sulkily the sergeant led his men back to their dungeon in the taxi-well. No one had observed the incident.

Reed and Shilensky proceeded to the site of the impromptu gay demonstration. The commander of the special operations division (supplier of mounted police, sharpshooters, helicopters)—a deputy chief named Raymond J. McDermott—had thrown a tentative ring of uniformed men around the small, pleased-looking band of gays. Chief McDermott was being assisted by no fewer than two inspectors and four captains. And to whom did this fraternity of Brass look, as one man, for guidance? To Mike Shilensky in his rumpled civilian clothes with his minor rank of third grade detective.

Shilensky recognized one of the demonstrators as Morty

Manford, and took him aside, speaking to him with sweet reason. Manford agreed to move away from the hotel. A confrontation had been avoided. Chief McDermott and his two inspectors and his four captains looked about for other trouble spots.

Back in Courtenay's office Mickey Schwartz relayed a message from headquarters. "The PC says don't keep the cops in blocks of four. It's a waste of manpower."

"Should we put them in twos?" Reed asked.

"What's the matter with *one*?" Courtenay snapped. "If anyone gets lonely, I'll go out and hold his hand."

Reed, who knew that Courtenay's sarcasm was not meant to wound, retorted in kind: "You *would*. As a matter of fact, Morty Manford was asking for you."

"I'm going up to the VIP lounge to socialize a little," Courtenay said. "Let's take a breather till this evening." He looked at Reed, whose face showed fatigue and strain. "Herman can hardly wait to get back to narcotics to rest," he said.

At 9:30 P.M. Courtenay, completing a tour around the Garden's perimeter, was stopped just outside the boxing office by the department's highest-ranking female commander, Inspector Gertrude D. T. Schimmel. Held in affection by most of the male Brass, Gert Schimmel dressed in civilian clothes and carried her revolver in her handbag. (Four years later, handbags for female police officers were outlawed.) She headed Commissioner McLoughlin's public information team, now operating out of a bus parked just outside the boxing office.

Inspector Schimmel told Courtenay that ABC wanted to interview him, together with Rocky Pomerance, about the problems of policing political conventions. Courtenay said no, explaining that the PC was, as he put it, a bit miffed during their walk-through of the Garden Sunday because the television people floating around in search of stories had cast their attention on him, Courtenay.

"The PC told me," Courtenay said, "that an ABC newsman saw him on the floor and sent for his camera crew, but the newsman was given word by his editors that 'we'd rather have Courtenay.' Now the PC told me this with a smile, but . . ."

"OK, we'll tell them no on this one," Gert Schimmel agreed.

Inspector Schimmel was a pioneer. She entered the department in 1940 after graduating Phi Beta Kappa from Hunter College. She had wanted to be a teacher, but there were no jobs. She was the first woman permitted to take the sergeant's examination (after fighting fiercely for the privilege), and she subsequently became the first female lieutenant, captain, deputy inspector, and inspector, and—a little less than two years after the DNC—she became the department's first (and only) female deputy chief. She did all this while raising two sons; she characterized her husband as "a very modern man" who wanted his wife to have an absorbing job.

A phenomenon in the NYPD, Gert Schimmel paved the way for Vittoria Renzullo, who, in 1976, became the first female captain to run a police precinct—one of the department's tests by fire. While Dan Courtenay had never run a precinct, both Mickey Schwartz and Jim Hannon had. Hannon, who called her Vicky, kept an eye on Captain Renzullo. He regarded her as a highly qualified police supervisor and had wanted to give her a precinct command even earlier, when she was forty-two, but she demurred; she was studying medicine and at the time she felt the job would be too demanding. Captain Renzullo was subsequently promoted to deputy inspector and—with Chief Schimmel's retirement in 1981—became the NYPD's highest-ranking woman. (It wasn't until the end of 1980 that a woman reached the rank of captain in the Philadelphia police department.)

Women became eligible for patrol assignment on an equal basis with men in 1972, and in the spring of the following year, shortly before Commissioner Patrick Murphy left, the Department announced one of its periodic nomenclatural changes: thenceforth the words *patrolman* and *policewoman* were banished—along with police *force*. In their stead the sexually neutral *police officer* was to be used.

The fact of women on patrol was, of course, initially resisted by male cops. But the headquarters Brass found little fault with women on patrol. They did the job as well as—sometimes better than—men. (It was true that they sometimes *looked* funny, because many of them were so short, but that was just something to get used to.) The Brass liked to cite examples of the courage and nerve of the women under their command.

On December 8, 1981, for instance, a female cop and her male partner responded to a call to a violent dispute in the 46th Precinct in the Bronx. When they arrived at the small apartment—supported by a backup team of two male cops—they found a distraught woman, her ten-year-old son, and the woman's common-law husband, whom she wanted the cops to remove from the apartment. The first priority was to get the child out of harm's way, a job that conventionally would have fallen to the female cop. In this case, though, it was the male partner who removed the child and stood with him in the hall, leaving the female and two backup cops to confront the enraged husband, who suddenly pulled a gun. The female cop and the two back-ups took cover as the husband fired three shots (hitting no one), and then they returned his fire, killing him.

Clearly the female cop had, in this case, played a more aggressive role than her partner. Had it been she who left the scene with the child, her male colleagues in the precinct doubtless would have told derisive stories about how she walked away and left her partner to face an armed assailant.

With women performing the same rugged street duties as men, dress became an issue. In 1979 skirts for female cops were banned; the women were instructed to dress in pants exactly like their male counterparts. The Policewomen's Endowment Association (still so called in spite of the banned word *policewoman*) approved the standardization.

By 1982 the female-police-person issue had come full circle; there was no blinking the one immutable inequality—women cops sometimes became pregnant. When they did, they were immediately removed from street duty and given indoor jobs. The problem was, what could they wear that was comfortable yet looked like a uniform (to distinguish them from the female civilian workers in the precinct houses and the various headquarters units)? A specially designed uniform was commissioned; it was to consist of maternity-style trousers (with an expandable front panel) and the standard blue cotton shirt, but cut full, like a smock. Since the women would be working indoors exclusively, it was felt they did not require a specially cut wool jacket, although a loose-fitting navy blue wool vest was under consideration as the year drew to a close.

By the end of 1982 there were over 1,300 women in the department, and 30 of them had made sergeant. There were also 97 detectives—5 of them with first-grade rank—but there were only 4 lieutenants and no captains.

Detective First Grade Olga Ford, who worked in the special narcotics prosecutor's office of the Manhattan district attorney, was the president of the Policewomen's Endowment Association. "We've made progress," she said, "but it's difficult to make up in ten years for all the early years when there were no opportunities for women in the department." The PEA was not a labor organization; female cops were represented by the PBA or the unions of their rank. The women's group had begun as a fraternal organization but, as Detective Ford explained, "It became more militant with the rise of women's liberation. It is now a watchdog group for women in the department, making sure our women police officers are treated fairly."

In Courtenay's office at 10:30 P.M. the color television was on, showing Coretta King speaking on the convention floor; the sound was low, a background for the usual bustle of the office.

Shilensky to Courtenay: "The gays have asked permission to use the *street* to march in on their parade up Seventh Avenue."

Courtenay: "How many are there?"

Shilensky: "One hundred fifty."

Courtenay shook his head no. "Keep them on the *sidewalk*. They'll impact traffic."

Shilensky: "They have a parade permit from us." (A parade permit meant police-protected marching privileges in the *street*.)

Courtenay smiled ruefully, thought a second, glanced at his watch.

"OK, if they can get there before the buses start loading delegates to take them back to their hotels. Otherwise, no."

A little later, on the bank of closed-circuit monitors a large group of marching gays could be seen in the street walking behind a police radio car, which was setting the pace for them.

Courtenay watched, scowling: "They're going to get here just the wrong time," he fretted.

"Let's see if we can slow them down a little," Shilensky volunteered. He turned to Schwartz, also watching the monitors. "Can we send a message to the radio car to slow down?"

"Yes," Schwartz said, and gave instructions. "But they probably have their own radio monitoring the convention. They *want* to arrive here just when it breaks."

Shilensky was more optimistic. "I think they'll probably cooperate." They did.

By 11:30 the session was over without incident, and Courtenay was locking into his metal clothes closet the bundle of passes for tomorrow's session, to be distributed to police Brass. Hannon, Codd, and McLoughlin had all stopped in.

McLoughlin told Hannon: "The press got wind of the fact that we're slightly reducing our forces tomorrow." Hannon had decided there was too much police presence, and 300 troops were taken off the DNC security detail.

"What did you tell them?" Hannon asked.

"I denied it," said McLoughlin.

*　　*　　*

Courtenay's team was chuckling over a joke on Herman Reed Wednesday morning—the third day of the DNC. Things were that relaxed, everything running smoothly. Reed, the most circumspect of police commanders, was quiet, thoughtful, devoted to the job at hand. Late the night before, he began scurrying from room to room in the office complex searching for his missing beeper. He asked everyone to help him find it, and one waggish colleague put out a message that was received by Fat Nelly computers in police offices all over Manhattan. "A police beeper was turned in by a prostitute, who said she got it off a gray-haired john named Reed, who liked a kinky sex act called Golden Shower. Copies to the police commissioner, the first deputy, and Mrs. Reed."

Reed, who eventually discovered the beeper clipped to his own gun belt, where he had absently placed it, blushed when shown a copy of the message.

Chief Hannon had decided to spend the whole day Wednesday with Courtenay and his team and happened to be seated at Courtenay's desk when a reporter asked for an interview. Courtenay was out to lunch and Hannon acceded. The reporter wanted to know about the cutback in police numbers. Word of the cut was out despite McLoughlin's denial.

Hannon admitted that the convention security detail had been trimmed slightly (he did not give the actual figure of 300). He explained the department's money problems and said that the department initially might have *overstaffed*, to be safe. He asked the reporter to "hold the information for the time being, please," and the reporter agreed, tentatively.

Later in the day Hannon told Courtenay that the Manhattan North area was having trouble with demonstrating hospital workers and was short of uniformed men. There were three hospitals being struck at the moment—St. Luke's, Mt. Sinai, and Columbia–Presbyterian—all in the half of Manhattan that lies above 59th Street.

"I'd like you to send them some of your men," Hannon said. The juggling of troops in an era of fiscal crisis involved a certain amount of sleight of hand. The public's perception of a visible street force had to be balanced against what the department actually considered to be an adequate force. In this instance Hannon decided it would be quicker and simpler for Courtenay to spare some of his men to the Manhattan North area than to call in off-duty men and pay them overtime.

"But I don't want to impact you too heavy here," Hannon added. "Let's make sure the men are all back here by 8 P.M. when the session begins." He frowned. "One day I'm going to regret being cost-conscious," he said.

At 5 P.M. Courtenay and Hannon walked the Garden perimeter. Hannon spotted a Greek-speaking cop named Missilaides and told Courtenay to tap him as an infiltrator for a Greek demonstration planned for tomorrow, the final day of the DNC.

"Good thinking, Boss," Courtenay said.

Entering the Garden's convention area, Courtenay spotted an unlocked elevator door near the emergency generator room. "I could swear we locked this up Monday morning," he said to Hannon. He called for a bomb-sniffing dog and handler.

While waiting he crawled behind the generator to search for a bomb. He found nothing and when the dog and handler came *they* found nothing. Courtenay locked the door.

Back in his office, Courtenay was on the phone with Inspector Robert J. Johnston, Jr., borrowed for the convention from the Detective Bureau and the guardian of the taxi-well. "Cliff Cassidy says that Governor Jerry Brown is a has-been, and his car *can't* wait for him in the taxi-well." There was a ramp for VIP cars leading to the fifth floor, where candidates and specially privileged others could be delivered and picked up by their drivers after the session.

Johnston complained that several VIP cars were left in the well without their drivers and that incoming VIPs' cars were getting stacked up. Courtenay said, deadpan, "OK, let the air out of their tires."

The convention ground on. Wednesday, too, ended without major mishap. One more day to go.

Thursday, July 15, 10:30 A.M. In Courtenay's office Shilensky was giving Courtenay and Schwartz a rundown of the day's scheduled demonstrations—where, when, the numbers expected.

"Mike," Courtenay asked, "what happened to the Jews for Jesus? I hear they were claiming you gave them permission to demonstrate from 3 to 8."

"I told them they could demonstrate from 3 A.M. to 8 A.M.," Shilensky replied.

"Did they know there wouldn't be any television cameras around?"

"I'm going out and police the Jews for Jesus myself," Schwartz said. "It's the first problem you're going to have down here."

"Not for long," Courtenay said. "I'm putting on my burnoose and chase all of you."

Couriers for the headquarters commanders wandered in to collect credentials for that evening's final session. "It's like junkies coming in for their daily fix," Shilensky observed.

An inspector from headquarters appeared. "I've come to complain about the lack of arrests and brutality," he joked. His arrival heralded the ceremonial visit of the three-star chief of patrol, Thomas D. Mitchelson. Mitchelson was the department's highest-ranking black commander; all seven of the area commanders—the two for Manhattan, the two for Brooklyn, and the one each for the Bronx, Queens, and Staten Island—reported to him. Mitchelson was accompanied by his exec, Deputy Chief Joseph C. Hoffman.

"Welcome aboard, Joe!" Courtenay winked his broad, exuberant wink. "You're doing a helluva job. I've been watching you!"

The two commanders had encountered each other almost

daily at headquarters while the plans for the DNC were being made. Hoffman virtually ran the chief of patrol's operation for his boss, and most of Courtenay's men for the DNC security force were drawn from the rosters of the chief of patrol.

"What are you going to do for an encore?" Hoffman asked Courtenay, enviously.

Clearly the word around headquarters was that Big Dan had everything under control, that he was doing a first-rate job. The other commanders, depending upon their rank and the degree of their own professional security, were either comradely-proud of him or jealous of him. With Hoffman it was hard to know which. In a way he and Courtenay typified the schism that Patrick Murphy unavoidably left as his legacy to the department, along with his reforms. The Top Brass was divided between two factions: the traditionalists, personified by Mike Codd (their credo was: We've always done it this way and it works; change for change's sake can be dangerous); and the innovators, the now-leaderless opposition who, in the Patrick Murphy image, collected what they believed to be scientific data and recommended change, sometimes usefully, but sometimes prematurely or even arbitrarily. The department was constantly reversing itself in small ways.

Hoffman was an innovator, as were a number of other well-thought-of one-star and two-star chiefs, both at headquarters and in various field commands. Hannon was a traditionalist, as were the headquarters superchiefs, almost to a man. Both factions had their hard-liners and their moderates, and Courtenay could be described as a moderate traditionalist, open on occasion to persuasion by the innovators.

While the Courtenay–Hoffman rivalry was always held to the bantering level (at least in my presence), there were undercurrents, little jealousies. For one thing, Courtenay, as a two-star chief, rated a full-time driver for his department sedan. One-star chiefs like Hoffman often had to drive themselves.

Joe Hoffman, nearing forty-nine, was impatiently awaiting his second star. Dressed in the same blue shirt, black
tie, and navy blue trousers as Courtenay, he looked, as
always, slim, boyish, and deceptively artless. A year and a
half Courtenay's junior, Hoffman had been deputy chief
longer than he thought he should be. All of the department's Top Brass knew of his impatience. Hoffman's career
had flourished during the early 1970s under Commissioner
Murphy. Under Mike Codd it stalled.

Courtenay took Chief Mitchelson on a walk-through of
the Garden, accompanied by Hoffman and Schwartz—a
four-man wedge of powerful Brass.

"Do you know that crime in the city is down 35 percent
since all of you moved in here?" Hoffman joked. "What I'm
wondering is, how were the people selected for this job?"

"I'd like to think on the basis of talent," Courtenay said.

After the tour, as Hoffman prepared to escort Chief
Mitchelson back to headquarters, he said, "So long, Dan.
We have to go run the city."

"The city is here!" Courtenay answered.

FIVE

★ Despite the disinclination of Commissioner Codd to promote Joe Hoffman to assistant chief, Hoffman's name was on the search panel's list of candidates for police commissioner. The panel members called him for an interview on November 30, 1977, two days after they met with former Police Commissioner Patrick Murphy and former Assistant U.S. Attorney Robert McGuire. Hoffman was no longer a cop by then; but his reputation as a shrewd administrator, as an imaginative planner and analyst, was well known to the panel members.

Hoffman quit the department in July 1977 to become a vice president of New York's Health and Hospitals Corporation. He had just passed his twenty-fifth year in the NYPD and at nearly fifty was still a one-star deputy chief. He had been with Health and Hospitals four months when the panel summoned him.

Hoffman, like Courtenay, regarded himself as ideally suited to be the police commissioner of New York. Five years earlier, in 1972, he had followed Courtenay as the inspector in command of the Fourth Division, but after Commissioner Patrick Murphy's resignation in 1973, Hoffman had failed to duplicate Courtenay's subsequent rise. In Hoffman's opinion, Commissioner Codd "was not willing to take chances and rarely would consider a person's willingness to accept greater responsibility as a basis for promotion."

Unlike Courtenay—who claimed to be unpolitical, who was "never the commissioner's man"—Hoffman was known by panel members to have formed his philosophy of policing under Patrick Murphy. He earned a reputation as a brainy headquarters commander, recognized for his managerial ability but mistrusted by some of the traditionalists for his progressive ideas—a reformer manqué, a near-maverick—who, at times, could be bluntly critical of the department.

Like Courtenay and Schwartz he had achieved a college education on the job—had in fact been in the same graduating class of which Schwartz was the valedictorian. He went on to earn his master's degree from John Jay College in 1975, the same year he was promoted to deputy chief by Codd and became the executive officer in the Patrol Bureau—the Police Department's largest unit, comprising 65 percent of the total force. The uniformed personnel of the seventy-three precincts of the five boroughs were the direct responsibility of the Patrol Bureau.

His boss, Superchief Tom Mitchelson, was a well-meaning but not very forceful commander, and Hoffman in effect ran the bureau; Commissioner Codd was well aware of that. Hoffman often represented Chief Mitchelson at, or accompanied him to, the Tuesday morning meetings Hannon held in his office to brief—and be briefed by—his inner circle of headquarters commanders.

These closed-door sessions, cabinet meetings of a sort, were regularly attended by three of the five superchiefs and their aides: Patrol, Detectives, and Personnel; the other two superchiefs—the chief of Inspectional Services, who oversaw the department's integrity, and the chief of Organized Crime Control—reported directly to the first dep, James Taylor. Also at these weekly meetings were the deputy chief in command of the Support Services Bureau and *his* aides. Hannon conveyed to his cabinet the PC's thinking on a variety of current issues and got the feedback that he, in turn, later would take up with the PC.

On one of these Tuesdays Mitchelson and Hoffman were deeply involved in a high-level command decision regarding the fate of one of the department's twenty deputy chiefs. The most serious command decision Hannon had made—about three months after being named chief of operations—was to reduce a deputy inspector to captain for a serious failure of leadership. It concerned a problem in the 103rd Precinct in Queens, where widespread "cooping" had been discovered by the Internal Affairs Division. (Cooping is the practice by cops on duty of sleeping in their parked patrol cars; sometimes they would nap away a substantial part of their eight-hour shifts.)

The captain of the precinct was in trouble, but Deputy Chief William Braunstein was in even worse difficulties. He was burdened with the responsibilities of the Queens area commander, whose exec he was. (The area commander himself was out of town on a leave of absence during the several months of the investigation and could not be held responsible.) Since the area commanders were under the supervision of the chief of patrol, Thomas Mitchelson was the man who was supposed to make the final recommendation in the case to Hannon. And since Deputy Chief Joe Hoffman was, practically speaking, the chief of patrol, it was he who worked most closely with Hannon in settling the problem.

The Internal Affairs Division reported the cooping situation in May of 1975. Returning to follow up in November, the shooflies found no improvement. Hannon explained to me that instead of admitting the situation was wrong and seeking to rectify it, Deputy Chief Braunstein complained that he was being harassed. This was precisely the kind of situation that former PC Patrick Murphy had sought to reverse.

"We have to do this right," Hannon told Joe Hoffman. "We have to be concerned not only with this particular situation, but with the peripheral effect on the rest of the department." Adhering to Murphy's Code of Accountability, Hannon decided to transfer Braunstein out of Queens, where he was comfortable, and send him as executive officer to the Bronx area commander, Assistant Chief Anthony V. Bouza, who was used as a kind of high-level retraining officer; the Bronx was in effect a purgatory for top-level commanders who "screwed up." The captain of the 103rd Precinct had to go, too, Hannon decided. That would send a message about Accountability to all the other precinct captains.

Hoffman often saw Hannon as many as half a dozen times daily for brief consultations, and Hannon treated him (as he did Courtenay) with trustful fondness, relying on him for his resourcefulness and tact. Hannon, in fact, had as much affection for Hoffman as he ever permitted himself to have for a brother police commander.

Hannon did not like yes-men: he welcomed the candid opinions and suggestions of the small circle of headquarters Brass on whom he depended for the hour-by-hour administration of his own office. He indulged Hoffman's candor, laughed at his jokes, admired his cleverness, sympathized with his ambition. Hannon enjoyed arguing a case on its merits—up to a point—and he frequently accepted the advice of a trusted junior commander like Hoffman. "Joe's a tough man," Hannon would sometimes say with a smile after having given in to him on some small matter of policy.

Hoffman, for instance, might point out that the neighborhood police team concept did not work in every area. "We can't treat everyone alike, as they do in Los Angeles, where the police chief says, 'The law is the law, period.' He locks up kids for smoking pot. What a waste of manpower." And Hannon listened attentively when Hoffman had a suggestion. For example, during that era of fiscal crisis Hoffman thought it expedient to bring in to headquarters men who had been in their particular jobs for thirty-six months or more, who felt "stagnant."

"Just talking helps," Hoffman said. "After a talk they stay high again for a couple of months at least." Hannon agreed. And when reports reached Hannon that police officers in some midtown precincts were becoming too friendly with "pross" (calling them by their first names), it was Hoffman on whom Hannon called to issue orders for "a more businesslike approach." (Prostitutes often were a good source of information for detectives but the camaraderie could be carried too far, in Hannon's opinion. As for the basic problem of controlling prostitution, Hannon, like most of his fellow police officials, had no solution. He did not think an isolated red-light district would work because, he said, there was nowhere to put it. "I wouldn't want it in my neighborhood," he said, "but it has to be convenient, or they'll do no business.")

It was Hoffman upon whom Hannon relied in matters that required a certain delicacy. For instance, on Hannon's desk one morning was a report concerning a member of the force who took a drug overdose—a combination of Valium, Darvon, and alcohol. It was at first assumed that he had tried to commit suicide. At Hannon's request Hoffman looked into the circumstances and found that the cop had been trying to treat a "headache" brought on by a hospital visit to his adolescent daughter who was terminally ill. Hoffman told Hannon (who concurred) that the department should accept the cop's explanation; he had agreed to undergo psychiatric counseling and his record otherwise was unblemished.

And Hannon respected Hoffman's academic credentials and his ability to theorize constructively. Hoffman had a deceptively soft, self-deprecating manner, a disarming smile, and, always, a quick rejoinder. His informal manner, however, covered a strong ego and a good, absorptive mind for detail. He had the teacher's and diplomat's instinctive gift for making himself viscerally understood. Hoffman moonlighted as a teacher at Suffolk Community College, where he taught a course in introductory criminal justice. His students were eighteen- and nineteen-year olds.

"It's better than teaching cops, I'll tell you that," he said, reflecting the attitude of his mentor, Patrick Murphy, whose skepticism about the cop intellect was well known. Hoffman habitually told his students, "If you want to get on my right side, read *The New York Times* every day," and he kept a file of criminal justice stories clipped from newspapers. He was an avid reader of biography, admired Gore Vidal, and liked to be regarded as a "radical." He enjoyed movies and was a Woody Allen fan. He once told me he would relish being the chief of police in Boston or Chicago—to be "my own boss, have my own shop." He found police work "very exciting," he said, but he might someday "give it all up for a spot in the academic society."

"We don't owe each other anything—me and the police department," he said.

Hoffman was a chess player and once, describing Patrick Murphy, he said that Murphy "always saw five moves ahead."

"That's what the PC's job is all about," he said. "Codd is a perfectly good administrator, but the dynamism is missing."

It was easy to forget that Hoffman was a cop at all, especially when he was out of uniform. He fancied himself as a theoretician, particularly with regard to budgetary policy. In January of 1976 he submitted a "Memo on Crime" to *The New York Times* (he never received a reply) and then to the New York *Daily News*, which printed it under his by-line.

"In early 1975," wrote Hoffman, "President Ford said: 'Crime is making us fearful of strangers and afraid to go out at night.' It was encouraging to hear a national spokesman comment on the fear of crime, but no action followed. . . . A commitment of responsibility by the President and Congress is urgently needed in the fight against violent crime.

"This means a dramatic federal program to improve the effectiveness of all criminal justice agencies. I would suggest establishing an Office of Criminal Justice Management with a director reporting to the White House. This office would be charged with providing budgeting, organization and management assistance to the nation's law enforcement agencies, and this assistance would be channeled through the states.

"If, in fact, fear of crime is the primary concern of the American people, then a fair share of the federal budget, say one percent or about two billion dollars, should be allotted to crime control nationwide. . . .

"The American obsession for avoiding a national system of justice has successfully insulated the federal government from active participation in the control of crime, and placed the entire burden on our financially besieged municipalities. However, as we enter the third century of our nation, the crisis of its cities is crime. They will not survive, nor will the country, if their inhabitants continue to be fearful of each other."

Did Hoffman regard himself as the leading candidate for director of the Office of Criminal Justice Management? Did he wish to follow in the footsteps of ex-Commissioner Murphy, move into a more global area? Under Hoffman's boyishness, under his disarming, open manner, lay the half-quixotic, half-Napoleonic hankering to rule his own broad kingdom.

But he had the good sense to learn from those more experienced than he, and he valued Jim Hannon for his virtues. "I've learned a lot from Hannon," he said. "He makes me slow down. I'm prone to charge right in; Hannon makes me want to charge—after second thought."

In early March of 1977 Hoffman's boss, Chief Mitchelson, resigned abruptly. He was only fifty-two and as a three-star Bureau chief he was earning $43,683 a year. His pension would be about $27,000. He said he was leaving for health reasons—he'd recently had a thyroid operation. "I'm tired, I had an operation and I'm sick," he told *The New York Times* on March 8. He went on to say that recent personnel cuts had made his job difficult. "We've all had to work harder, morale among the men has dropped. It's often a 24 hour job and I need more rest." Few people were long missed when they left the mammoth New York police department, and Mitchelson was no exception.

Some time after he left I asked Commissioner Codd about his relatively rapid rise to high rank. "I picked Mitchelson because he was not part of the group that was dominant in the department; he was a new face—and, yes—a black face," Codd said, with rare candor. "We needed a black chief. You have to have balance in an organization." He paused and smiled wryly. "He may not be the greatest choice I ever made, but I made it."

Hoffman, expecting now to be thanked for his loyalty and patience with a promotion from deputy to assistant chief, was again disappointed. Codd merely offered Hoffman (through channels, not even personally) the command of the Special Operations Division—a lateral move.

According to Hoffman, Codd did not like to be disagreed with—and seldom was. Being a yes-man was not Hoffman's idea of loyalty. "It's loyal to point out things that are wrong, so they can be corrected," he said. But Hoffman was interested in learning to pilot a helicopter, and he accepted the assignment because SOD included the aviation unit. For some time Hoffman had been privately logging air hours toward a helicopter pilot's license.

But the assignment to SOD was not challenging enough, and Hoffman decided to quit the department. Hannon, sympathetic to the younger commander's disappointment, nevertheless urged Hoffman to stay, to be a Good Soldier. Hoffman was unmoved. As for the commissioner, he appeared to take no notice at all.

"Mike Codd let good people go without any effort to persuade them to stay," Hoffman told me. "He just said, 'Good-bye and good luck.' A commissioner should try to give his good men work that challenges them."

Hoffman was a third-generation American (his family originally was from Germany) and an only child. He was a former Marine master sergeant and a Catholic convert. He worked hard at being lovable. He was, in his own words, "the kind of person who brings home stray dogs and cats," the kind of person who found it difficult ever to hold a grudge. "After two martinis, I love everyone," he liked to say. He also liked to say, "I don't have an enemy in the department"—while at the same time maintaining that "a good administrator can't be a 'good guy.'" (Courtenay agreed with him about that.)

His father drove a beer truck in Brooklyn during the Depression. Hoffman dropped out of high school at seventeen, in 1945, to join the Marines, where he served until 1949. Two years later he was wed to Kitty Grossman, a New Yorker of German Catholic heritage; and the same year—in June 1951—he joined the police. That was the year Mickey Schwartz joined, as well. Hoffman was twenty-three, eight months younger than Schwartz.

There were no cops in either Hoffman's or his wife's family, but Hoffman was advised by relatives and friends to "go on the cops, they're the ones who bought houses during the Depression, they always have jobs." Being "on the cops" was a safe job, that was one of the sacred tenets of New York's working class.

Hoffman made captain at forty-one (as compared with Hannon and Schwartz, both of whom made it at forty-two, and with Courtenay, at thirty-nine). For a while he was a fly captain in Brooklyn, which meant filling in at short notice for an absent precinct commander anywhere in the borough. Hoffman was a captain in the department's planning division—which dealt with his major interest, budget problems—when Patrick Murphy was appointed commissioner in 1970. Hoffman soon became a particular pet of the new PC.

Like many other cop-commanders who preferred to be honest, Hoffman was filled with shame when he recalled the pre-Murphy years. Discussing the corruption issue as it affected him, he once asked, rhetorically, "Did I step forward? Did any of the other honest bosses step forward? No. It took a character like Serpico to do it."

Hoffman was impressed with the way Sidney Cooper, Murphy's trusted chief of inspectional services, viewed the corruption problem: There were the hard-core corrupt, whom Cooper called the meat-eaters; then there were the grass-eaters, those who picked around, not really looking, but taking if there was something loose; and finally there were the birds; they saw the meat-eaters and they saw the grass-eaters, but they kept flying.

"Those birds, like myself," Hoffman said, "always wanted someone to open it up, so we could have pride in the police."

Hoffman's police career was spent almost entirely in uniform, and he regretted that, unlike Courtenay, he'd never had a shot at a command in the Detective Bureau or OCCB.

With Patrick Murphy's departure, Hoffman's edge in the department was blunted. Murphy said he was resigning so as not to become an issue in the mayoral campaign of 1973, and suggested that John Lindsay replace him with forty-three-year-old Donald F. Cawley, then the three-star chief of patrol. That was when Michael Codd, then the four-star chief inspector, quit the department. (Later he denied that he was bitter at having been jumped over. "I wanted to give Murphy's successor a chance to pick his own men," Codd said.) As in the Army, as in corporate life, when you were at or near the top, you spent a lot of your time sticking it to your peers or having it stuck to you.

"Everyone acknowledges Pat Murphy's role in changing the department, even if grudgingly," Hoffman said.

Not long after taking office Commissioner Murphy declared he would promote younger commanders to key positions and that this would symbolize "the kind of change and fresh new leadership needed by the department." In August of 1971 he startled everyone by elevating Donald Cawley—at forty-one the department's youngest inspector—to chief of patrol, an advancement of three ranks, skipping him over seventy-two of the department's higher-ranking officials (including Jim Hannon, then fifty-three and a deputy chief, and Dan Courtenay who was, like Cawley, an inspector). Joe Hoffman, two years older than Cawley and still a captain, worked in the planning division of the commissioner's office. Murphy made him a deputy inspector six months later, but meanwhile Hoffman consoled himself with being Murphy's pet.

"Murphy would see me and keep Cawley waiting, even after he was made chief of patrol," Hoffman once gloated.

Lindsay followed Murphy's advice and appointed Cawley, who became New York's youngest police commissioner in May 1973. (Technically, Theodore Roosevelt held that distinction. He was thirty-six when, in 1895, he became president of the Police Commission, the equivalent of today's commissioner.) Cawley said he would continue to "root out any cancers of corruption that exist."

"We have programs on the drawing board," he said, "that I am going to put into effect and build to a point that what we have done will be irreversible." His first innovation would be a panel to screen out violence-prone police officers.

At his swearing-in he described his four goals for the department: combating street crime, monitoring departmental integrity, improving management, and addressing the traffic problem. When asked by reporters if he would submit his resignation to a new mayor after the election in November—only six months distant—he equivocated.

By June he had decided that one way to combat street crime was to put detectives into precinct work, and he took a substantial number of them out of the Detective Bureau. The detectives, naturally, were resentful and claimed that Cawley was trying—as they believed Murphy before him had tried—to eliminate them altogether.

In July Cawley ordered all police officers to wear nameplates over the right breast pockets of their uniforms as a way of improving community relations. The PBA protested, saying this would subject its members to harassment. (Cawley won.)

In August Cawley eliminated the traditional Police Academy marksmanship award of a revolver and substituted a prize of $100 and a plaque. He then ordered a study made for the redesign of the police badge (the New York police always called it a shield). Also in August he initiated the formal, yearly reevaluation process for all commanders above the rank of captain, saying that commanders were under the false impression that appointment to a higher rank involved tenure; appointment was for one year only, subject to review, he emphasized.

In September he dropped the height requirement for police officers—a minimum of five feet seven inches for men, five feet two inches for women—and ordered that the written exam for entry into the department eliminate questions he regarded as culturally biased; he hoped thereby to encourage more women applicants and more members of minority groups.

In October Cawley won judicial sanction for weeding out his top ranks by asking for the retirement of men he thought were "tired" and had been on the job too long.

In November Cawley was too busy stonewalling to initiate anything. The newly elected Mayor Beame asked him to submit his resignation and agree to get out by January 1, 1974. Cawley refused, saying he had been appointed to complete the five-year term of Patrick V. Murphy and that term did not expire until the beginning of 1976. Beame was angry. "Nobody is going to run the city of New York after January 1, 1974, but the mayor," he said.

In December, predictably, Cawley resigned and Beame announced that former Chief Inspector Michael Codd would come out of retirement to serve as police commissioner. "I was impressed," said Beame, "with his intimate knowledge of all facets of police work, the respect he has earned from the rank and file, and the dedication he has shown to his duties." And Codd, responding to a reporter's suggestion that he might be too old-fashioned to follow in Murphy's and Cawley's innovative ways, replied that he was "of the modern age, inasmuch as I grew up in the last thirty years of the department."

Ex-Commissioner Cawley took a job in private industry—he became a vice president of Chemical Bank, in charge of security. But, like his former boss, Patrick Murphy, he longed for another shot at being New York's PC.

Four years later, the members of Mayor-elect Edward Koch's search panel remembered Cawley as a smart and imaginative police official and placed him prominently on their list of candidates. They met with him and were impressed.

On December 6, 1977, the day before its deadline, the search panel held its final meeting. Former Assistant U.S. Attorney Robert McGuire was called back for a second interview. According to Ed Koch, the panel then submitted to him "a list of several names—four or five—all cops," except for Special State Prosecutor John Keenan and former Assistant U.S. Attorney Robert McGuire. "They said their first choice was Cawley," Koch recalled.

The panel's choice was not unanimous. Some of its members believed that Cawley did not meet all the requirements that they themselves had listed—notably that the new PC be Acceptable to the Rank and File. Cawley had been profoundly unpopular. Moreover, according to many department insiders, he had not been a Good Manager. On the other hand, the panel members realized that Koch's intense dislike for Michael Codd's traditionalism would doubtless apply as well to such department stalwarts as Hannon and Courtenay. Even while both these men had (in the panel's judgment) demonstrated their High Intelligence, their Sensitivity, and their Strong Leadership, they were not known as innovators or visionaries, which was what Koch seemed to want (without having any clear idea how a visionary PC could impose his ideas on what was now a fairly stable and clean department). But the panel had agreed to find someone who, above all, would be Able to Work Well with the Mayor, someone who would suit Koch's own style, to the degree they could decipher it. And when they reviewed the qualifications of ex-Commissioner Donald Cawley, they concluded that he would best suit both the mayor and the police department. Keenan and McGuire were on their list because Koch had insisted the panel consider a civilian PC.

But would McGuire, who had no management experience, be a Good Manager? Was Keenan, an old hand at the politics of the criminal justice system, Conceptual and Innovative?

Koch thanked the panel and said he would make known his decision in a few days. All politicians studied their predecessors, especially those they admired, and Koch's favorite was the three-term Mayor Fiorello H. La Guardia (1934–45). But apparently Koch did not think La Guardia knew how to select a police commissioner, for his first appointment had been a civilian named John F. O'Ryan, who turned out badly. His second PC, on the other hand, was a veteran cop named Lewis J. Valentine, who turned out a great deal better. O'Ryan was a lawyer and a World War I veteran who became a general at forty-two and let it go to his head; as commissioner he behaved as a militarist and a strikebreaker and he resigned under pressure within nine months. Commissioner Valentine—who had served as chief inspector under O'Ryan—lasted eleven years, until the end of La Guardia's term—and that was longer than any police commissioner before or since.

"I personally saw everyone on Dick Gelb's and Frank Thomas's list," Koch said. (The panel members and Koch himself were reluctant to mention the names of the other contenders, all "good men.")

"I liked McGuire's freshness, his sense of challenge, his exuberance," Koch said. "He had my outlook. He had a good law enforcement background and he came from a cop's family. Bob Morgenthau recommended him highly." It was true that McGuire had never been a cop, Koch said, "but I knew he could do the job."

"*I'd* never been a *mayor*," he added, with that mix of innocence and ego that enchanted his admirers and appalled his detractors, "but I knew *I* could do the job." Ed Koch believed he had found his Perfect Police Commissioner.

New York City's first Democratic National Convention since 1924 ran as sturdily as a mountain stream because Dan Courtenay had schooled himself in the swirls and surges, the eddies and rapids of a typical political onrush.

At 3:30 in the afternoon of Thursday July 15 Captain Robert Hartling bluntly summed up. "It's over," he said. "I know that we got out there, and I know what our boys can do. It's all over, and I'm tired."

Courtenay was allowing himself to relax. Responding to a phone call from his elder daughter, Kathleen, he crooned, "Hello, Babe, how're you doing? We're having a lot of fun down here."

At 6:45, shortly before the final ceremonial session, Chief Hannon arrived in uniform. "Who do you think we should mention for commendation, Dan?"

"I'm glad you asked," Courtenay said. "We can either go for a Unit Commendation or a Meritorious for the top guys who busted their chops."

Courtenay's own broad chest already gleamed with tribal tokens—ribbon bars in green and white and blue. But not Hannon's. He found such trappings superfluous and had never troubled to apply for the citations and commendations most of his fellow cops amassed on their way up—testaments to their Meritorious Police Duty, their Excellent Police Duty. By the time they were chiefs, most commanders had several of each. Hannon was just as amply entitled to these ribbons of merit (accompanied by letters that became part of their files) but his well-brushed navy blue tunic was bare except for his gold shield, unique with its four stars. He knew, though, that most commanders needed the tangible reassurance of chest decorations.

At 7 P.M. a French television crew arrived to interview Courtenay. He'd agreed to the interview because it would not be aired locally. This time he sat at his desk—the Perfect Model of the Modern American Police Chief.

Interviewer (speaking with a heavy French accent): "Excuse my bad English."

Courtenay: "Excuse my bad French."

Interviewer: "Ah, you speak French?"

Courtenay: "No."

Interviewer: "But you will try, yes?"

Courtenay: "I will try, no!"

The telephone interrupted. Cliff Cassidy was calling to invite Courtenay to the podium between 8 and 8:30 to be thanked formally by Robert Strauss. Courtenay was surprised and flattered; his grin grew wide and his blue eyes snapped with pleasure. He finished the television interview (in English), then changed carefully out of his summer uniform and into the white shirt and navy blue wool blouse of dress occasions. As he left, he said, "I hope the PC has been asked to be up on the podium, too—for *my* sake."

In Courtenay's office the color television set was tuned to the convention floor; the sound was low. Mickey Schwartz asked Jim Hannon, "Is it true that we're supposed to continue providing all that security for all the candidate hotels?"

Hannon said, dryly, "Yes. The mayor wants it, the commissioner wants it, and I want it."

"That's three good reasons," Schwartz said.

Headquarters Superchief Cornelius Behan came in to observe. The biggest police buffs of all were the police Brass themselves. Schwartz filled him in: "So far, there have been six arrests connected with the convention—for robbery and peddling, and a psycho who bit a cop." That was a fairly common form of injury. "Not one demonstrator has been arrested. That must be some kind of record. This city can absorb 400,000 extra people without even shifting gears." Pride and satisfaction sounded in his voice.

Herman Reed, having been alerted by phone, told Behan and Hannon and Schwartz, "Chief Courtenay is at the back of the podium, and about to come out." He turned up the television's sound. Fritz Mondale was being acclaimed as Jimmy Carter's running mate.

Hartling announced, "Secret Service wants more barriers at the Americana Hotel." That was where Jimmy Carter was staying. "I just haven't got the heart to order my men to load barriers and get them over there. They're all exhausted."

"It has to be done," Schwartz said. "I'll give the order." Schwartz, like all the other commanders, was grateful that the troops had behaved so well during the four days of the DNC. The New York police were unpredictable and the Brass had anticipated some sort of police action to protest the layoffs and other forms of internal belt-tightening begun the summer before. The other uniformed services that suffered layoffs conducted job actions, and at first the cops, too, threatened to demonstrate. But they had rallied for Opsail, when many thousands of visitors jammed the city. And while other disenchanted city workers chose to demonstrate in the media free-for-all of the convention that followed Opsail a week later, the helpful, courteous, well-disciplined police did not.

As Schwartz was leaving to give the order about the barriers, Hartling had a bright idea. "Hey, you can use the arrest team, they're not scheduled to leave until 10:45." Schwartz nodded; the underworked storm troopers finally had a job.

In due course, Chief Courtenay squeezed his way onto the overcrowded podium and was thanked by Robert Strauss for his smooth handling of security. Courtenay looked large and splendid and pleased with himself. He had been asked by the Kansas City police department, which had sent an observer to the DNC, to help plan the security arrangements for the impending Republican National Convention in that city.

At 11 P.M. Courtenay was back in the office, triumphant, a star. Hannon watched him change out of his uniform. When he got down to his shorts and undershirt Hannon asked him, sternly, "Why aren't you wearing your shield?" Hannon, not much given to jokes, was feeling relieved and proud of Courtenay.

Still only partly dressed, Courtenay performed a small ritual. He ripped down a telephone number pinned to his bulletin board. "We don't need the National Guard anymore, do we?"

Mayor Beame had invited Hannon, Courtenay, and other Top Brass to a celebration at the Rainbow Room. Courtenay had been trying to reach his wife in her hotel room, but she was happily wandering around the Garden. Finally he found her and told her about the party.

"Dan," Chief Hannon said, leaving for the party at 11:30, "I have every confidence in you to button it up."

"I'll button it up, Chief," Courtenay assured him.

At 11:45 Courtenay, leaving for the party, said to Schwartz and Reed, "Team, I have every confidence in you to button it up."

"We'll button it up, Chief," they said. They did not finish their chores until 1 A.M.

At 11 on Friday morning Courtenay's team was moving out. The electronic equipment was being dismantled, files were being packed in cartons, desks being removed. Courtenay was in his office, having agreed—now that it was all over—to an interview with the *Times*. He was wearing the trousers of a blue cord suit and a short-sleeved shirt.

"I never took my stick or my helmet out into the street during the entire convention," he said, adding brightly, "I'm a pacifist."

Courtenay had tolerated my almost constant presence during the preceding days, but now I felt he wanted to shake me off, along with all the paraphernalia of the DNC security, and get on with his career, unencumbered. It hadn't been easy to have me trailing after him. Out in the street, supervising some of the demonstrations, he nearly tripped over me once or twice. But he bore the burden— most of the time—graciously.

"Come on, I have to go cash my paycheck," he told me curtly. He was trying to fight the letdown setting in. The weather, so brilliantly sunny and hot during the preceding four days, was now sorry and gray. It suited Courtenay's mood.

We stepped into 33rd Street at Seventh Avenue, empty of demonstrators. I crossed heedlessly because I was with him and felt protected, but we both had momentarily forgotten he was out of uniform. A truck trumpeted angrily at us, nearly running us down, and I clutched at his arm reflexively, something I'd never done when he was in uniform.

A bit embarrassed, he said, "Come on, you were dillying when you should have been dallying," and guided me onto the curb. "They never would have dared blow their horns at us yesterday," he said wistfully.

In the bank Courtenay took his place at the end of the line. I remembered being told that professional bank robbers eschewed holdups on the twice-a-month police paydays. When we returned to the Garden Courtenay's driver, John Angulat, was loading his car. The streets—without their rows of blue-shirted cops, without the long gray lines of barriers, the placard-waving demonstrators, the throngs of gaping delegates—looked naked. Immediately outside the boxing office the sidewalk was piled with office furniture and equipment. The stage set had been struck and Courtenay's starring role was over.

He regarded the jumble in the street, the vans being loaded. It had begun to drizzle and there would be a mess.

"It's better than cleaning blood off the sidewalk, no matter whose," he said with his flair for drama.

He entered the boxing office for a final look around. Most of his papers were packed but on his desk he found a hand-delivered letter from the police commissioner, commending him.

"This one I'll frame," Courtenay said—but without his usual zest. The letter was cool and formal in the commissioner's noncommittal style, and not enough to lift Courtenay's spirits.

The only thing that would have cheered him was a promotion. What Courtenay wanted, what he believed he had earned, was a summons by the commissioner to tell him he would be the next chief of detectives. Like Joe Hoffman, Courtenay felt undervalued.

John Angulat took Courtenay's uniform from the metal locker. There was nothing more to do. Courtenay walked out without a backward look and climbed into the front passenger seat of his car. There were boxes and papers piled on the back seat, and Angulat carefully laid the uniform across them.

"In another two days," Courtenay said in a hoarse voice, "you'll never know there *was* a convention." A police commander's life was full of endings.

SIX

★ It was ironic that New York's police should fall into disgrace only two months after their elegant supervision of the DNC. This time it was not a corruption scandal, nor was it the kind of brutality that periodically plagued the racially tense cities of Miami and Philadelphia and Chicago (and often seemed to be tacitly condoned at the top). New York's police had risen to the occasion of the DNC, showing off for the throngs of out-of-towners, proving that they were indeed New York's Finest.

While other municipal workers demonstrated against layoffs and struck for the higher wages that the hard-pressed city said it could not afford, the police bided their time. But they seethed inwardly over the unthinkable: *cops were being laid off.* It was unprecedented and shocking. The Safe Job was no longer safe and they felt betrayed. What would happen now to the mortgage payments on the house in Queens? But they waited until the convention ended, till the city emptied of visitors and the summer holidays were over. By then, their grievances had festered for more than a year. They were ready to turn ugly.

It all went back to July of 1975 when Commissioner Codd—hating to do it—became the first police commissioner in New York's history to lay off police officers. In a bulletin to the ranks, Codd did his best to convey his distress:

> All of us who remain in the Department can only hope and pray that circumstances will improve and permit your return in the near future. . . . We are grateful for your achievements and we are proud of you . . . don't let this unfortunate turn of events disillusion you or defeat you. Keep alive in your heart the spirit that led you to come to us in the first place.

The department's supervisors braced for protest both from within and without. Added pressure was placed on its thinning ranks by a national increase in violent crime. There were no funds to replace deteriorating equipment, no recruitment or training of new cops; the laid-off cops were, naturally, the ones with least tenure, the younger and fresher ones, the more recently recruited ethnic minorities, the females. There was no way to replace stamina and agility in an aging patrol force, whose average age was pushing thirty-eight. Codd, an upright if limited leader, happened to be police commissioner at a grim moment in the history of the crumbling American city.

Chief of Operations Hannon became in a sense Commissioner Codd's hatchet man—as Codd became Mayor Beame's. It was Hannon's job to oversee the shuffling of the department's depleted manpower, to borrow from Peter to pay Paul to keep street patrol at minimally adequate levels. It was Hannon's responsibility to analyze where operating costs could be cut, to respond to the outrage and anguish of the laid-off cops, to deal with the dismay of the public.

Groups of cop-pickets demonstrated sporadically, and the situation was so unstable from day to day that it was a small miracle the police department continued to function at all.

Precinct houses were closed and sometimes reopened under community pressure. Radio car patrols were cut back. "There has positively been a loss in our capacity to fight crime," Hannon told the press, heralding laments by other police chiefs in similarly hard-pressed cities across the nation.

The Top Brass at headquarters felt the pinch, personally. Hannon lost his secretary; she was reassigned to uniformed street duty to replace a laid-off patrolman. He also sacrificed the telephone console from his conference table (a loss he actually welcomed, as it obliged him to walk back and forth between the table and his desk).

The Patrolmen's Benevolent Association called itself a "line organization," and it was in effect a trade union; like most trade unions, it held the greatest appeal for its lowest common denominator. The PBA was undergoing a period of confused leadership, split by factionalism, and it whipped its members into a fury over the complicated wage and work mandates the city was trying to impose. The cops at the bottom, several thousand strong, staged a series of increasingly rowdy street demonstrations that began with the ritual picketing of their own precinct houses. Their line officers—even up to the rank of deputy inspector—found themselves unable or unwilling to take the disciplinary action that Commissioner Codd (and Mayor Beame) demanded. The public was disgusted at the sight and sound of off-duty but armed cops shouting in the streets, disrupting traffic and disturbing residential neighborhoods, including Commissioner Codd's in Queens. The cops even staged loud protests outside the mayor's residence, Gracie Mansion.

"BEAME LIES," read one of their leaflets. "He says we can get what other unions have. Other unions have received their back monies, WE HAVEN'T. Other unions are not asked for sacrifices of their wives and children, WE ARE. . . . Cop demonstrators are now called Hoodlums— We reach out for your support as we support you when you need US."

Another leaflet, longer and more detailed, read: "Dear Fellow New Yorkers, these are some of the reasons your Police Officers are angry: We were the only union to work 5 extra days without pay to save the jobs of officers. They are still laid-off. . . . Doctors have shown that because of odd hours and job conditions Policemen have a 10 year shorter lifespan. Our divorce rate is the highest in the city. . . .

"This is the contract offer the Mayor gave us: We must give up one full week's pay until we retire. We must give up $100 per year from our health and welfare benefits. We must give up one day off which we now receive when we donate blood, such as when a police officer is shot. . . . We must defer the six percent raise we have won in two courts. . . . We must work ten more days per year without extra compensation. . . .

"How would you feel if you were being treated like this? We think you would be angry too. We need your support. Please contact the Mayor or your Councilman and tell them to stop this unfair treatment of the Police Officers and to negotiate with us in good faith."

Mayor Beame declared himself "very much disturbed by the kind of picketing that has been going on" and said, "We believe the police officers have a right to picket, but they have no right to be disorderly or to act in a lawless manner." The mayor summoned Commissioner Codd back from Florida, where he was attending a law enforcement conference; it was a department joke that the commissioner was out of town more than in.

The mayor and the commissioner announced that unspecified disciplinary action would be taken. And even as they were briefing the press, several hundred off-duty cops out of uniform were tying up traffic in a rainstorm in Times Square. In an editorial, *The New York Times* said that these unruly, off-duty cop-demonstrators "disgraced the fine police force to which they belong" and were "a discredit to their uniforms and themselves."

The police bosses from Jim Hannon on down were caught, on the one hand, between sympathy for the cops' genuine grievances and their right as individual citizens to make a public protest; and on the other hand, by embarrassment at the brutish behavior so many of the cops displayed. They knew those unruly cops must be, somehow, disciplined. But it was one thing to place a thieving or sadistic cop under arrest; it was another to try forcibly to restrain an unruly cop-demonstrator in a sea of solidly resisting fellow officers. Yet this was what the commanders were ordered, on pain of dismissal, to do.

Assistant Chief Charles E. McCarthy, commander of the Manhattan North area, failed to make any arrests, as ordered, during a demonstration at Gracie Mansion that disturbed the mayor and other residents of the area into the morning hours of Sunday, September 27, and that was repeated on Monday. I was at headquarters on Tuesday and heard, in the early afternoon, that Chief McCarthy had been relieved of his command—*flopped*, in Copspeak.

"I don't know if anyone could have controlled that situation," Hannon said, after the fait accompli.

McCarthy and Hannon were long-time colleagues, and Hannon knew McCarthy was a Good Soldier and a Team Player. Mike Shilensky walked into Hannon's office, visibly upset. He had witnessed the action at Gracie Mansion in his capacity as legal adviser.

"McCarthy couldn't possibly have done anything differently," he said. "The off-duty cops climbed all over him when he tried to take someone. He almost went down at one point. It was terrifying."

Hannon nodded glumly. "I know. He's a good man and it wasn't his fault. But we had to make a change. We hope the other area commanders will get the message." He soon saw for himself the futility of that message.

As Shilensky left, he passed the deposed area commander coming in. McCarthy was in civilian clothes and was followed by an aide carrying his uniform and a few file boxes. He looked crushed and almost tearful. Commissioner Codd had assigned him to headquarters, but Hannon did not know yet in what capacity. For the time being, he would hang his uniform and store his boxes in Hannon's bath/dressing room. Hannon nodded to him perfunctorily.

Dan Courtenay later remarked that McCarthy was "sacrificed," and that Mike Codd knew it. Codd, however—when I asked him about it some time later—said, "There was absolutely no pressure from the mayor or anyone else to remove McCarthy. It was done to wake everybody up." Codd was adhering to Patrick Murphy's Code of Accountability. By then, McCarthy had been assigned as the exec to the three-star chief of the Organized Crime Control Bureau, the job held by Dan Courtenay before his assignment to the DNC security job.

September 28, 1976, the day after Chief McCarthy was flopped, was the day of the highly publicized Muhammad Ali–Ken Norton championship fight at Yankee Stadium. Such an event normally would have been policed by the Bronx area commander, subject to the cursory review of his immediate superior, the three-star chief of patrol, Tom Mitchelson. But a large contingent of off-duty police, swelled with their own sense of power—hadn't they just got a two-star chief flopped?—were threatening to demonstrate at (and possibly disrupt) the fight.

Because of the earlier, mutinous behavior of the cop-demonstrators, and mindful of what had happened to Chief McCarthy, Hannon planned personally to monitor the operation at Yankee Stadium. The Ali–Norton fight was likely to prove a serious embarrassment for the proud New York police, and Hannon believed it was an occasion that required the physical presence of a four-star General. Let the unruly troops feel the weight of the department's heaviest Brass! Besides, Hannon had misgivings about the Bronx area commander's approach to a potentially incendiary situation.

The Bronx area commander was Assistant Chief Anthony V. Bouza, to whom the mispronunciation of his name was a source of endless irritation; people tended to rhyme the first syllable with booze or bow (as in bow-wow), but it was pronounced as in the French word, *beau:* *Beau*-za. Chief Bouza was a department phenomenon, an extreme example of allowed individuality. He was an ec-

centric cop who made it close to the top with his eccen-
tricities intact, one of Jim Hannon's rare "free-floating
spirits," a commander whose style evolved under Patrick
V. Murphy.

"Tony Bouza runs his own little police department up in
the Bronx," Hannon told me, "and we let him." Partly that
was because Tony Bouza was the only "Hispanic" chief on
the force and, therefore, like Tom Mitchelson, something
of a sacred cow. He was born in Spain, not Puerto Rico,
arriving in the United States when he was nine. He happened also to be better read and better spoken than many of
his peers, and he had learned to be openly arrogant. But
two-star chief was as far up as he went on New York's
essentially traditional and conservative police force. He was
not a Team Player. Yet, outside the department—at City
Hall, for instance—Bouza was admired by some of the
younger members of the Beame administration for his modern ideas.

During the afternoon of Wednesday, September 28, Dan
Courtenay, on behalf of Chief Hannon, was coordinating
plans to patrol the police demonstrators at Yankee Stadium
that evening. While he still did not have a real job,
Courtenay was being patient. "I'm Chief Hannon's eyes
and ears," he told me cheerfully. I hadn't seen him for a
couple of months, not since the end of the convention. "I
was so depressed and let down after the convention," he
said. "I kept waiting for something to come up, but there
was nothing."

Chief Hannon asked Courtenay and Joe Hoffman to ride
with him to Yankee Stadium that evening. He considered
my request to accompany them but finally said no, judging
it too dangerous.

In the headquarters operations division early that afternoon, Courtenay explained why controlling the protest was
going to be so difficult. The demonstrators, being cops,
were themselves experienced in the crowd-control tactics
that would be practiced on them. The chiefs also were
inhibited in issuing instructions for dealing with the cop-

protesters; if the instructions were sent out over the police radio bands, they could be picked up by the PBA.

"They know what we're going to do," Courtenay said. "It's harder for us emotionally, too. It hurts to be a cop and see cops attacking society, when it's our job to defend society."

Courtenay took a call from Hannon. "You want a captain with each wagon? A walkie-talkie with each captain? OK, Chief."

Although distressed, like most of the Top Brass, by the behavior of the disgruntled troops, he was loving the action. "This is like the old days," he said with a wink, meaning the DNC—"*that's* the old days, now." He even seemed rather pleased to have me back as an observer; he actually made a point of telling me that the small, potted plant I'd given him on his birthday the previous June (in a shameless attempt to curry his favor) was still blooming. Seated before a bank of electronic equipment in the communications room, Courtenay put on his steel-rimmed spectacles to study some figures. The glasses gave him an oddly schoolmaster-ish look. The figures were the latest confidential information: 3,000 to 4,000 cop-demonstrators planned to disrupt the fans' arrival at Yankee Stadium and then go back to Gracie Mansion for more demonstrating. A second communiqué on his desk informed him that a group of cops' wives would stage an action of their own on Thursday.

"We have a way to deal with the women," Courtenay said, back in his old form. "You can't hit them. But the ones who want to get arrested, to make their point—we tell them, your children will have to be taken to a welfare center and you know how bad those centers are, and you may not get them back for several days. And suddenly they don't want to get arrested anymore."

Early that evening Chief Hannon's long, black car swung up the ramp of the headquarters garage, ducked into the access lane at the foot of the Brooklyn Bridge, and, leaving the hodgepodge of Chinatown and Municipaldom behind, rolled smoothly up the East River Drive toward the Bronx.

Pete Cassi was driving and Hannon sat beside him to be able to answer his radio calls. Assistant Chief Courtenay and Deputy Chief Hoffman sat in back. All three were in uniform, a triad of blue-clad, gold-braided Generals not to be trifled with—or so they believed.

Cassi brought the car, with its sprouting antennas, close to the barriers that were meant to contain the demonstrators. It was a nightmarish scene, with jostling fight fans, a swarm of unruly juveniles harassing ticket holders, and hundreds of cops divided into uniformed good guys and out-of-uniform bad guys—who, on the next tour of duty, would switch roles.

Seeing the headquarters car, possibly mistaking it for the commissioner's, the men closest to the barriers pushed them over and lunged at the vehicle. For a moment Pete Cassi thought they would roll the car over. The three chiefs shoved their way out of the car and grabbed at the surging men. Within seconds all three were knocked off their feet; nothing like it had ever happened to any of them and they were stunned.

"I felt like I'd been through a rough football game," Hannon later told me, his voice still incredulous. "I've been through battles before. They were cops, yes, but they weren't. I never went down before."

The side of Hannon's face was scraped and bleeding; he was punched in the ribs, his hand was twisted, and a cherished gold and diamond ring, given him by his wife's father, disappeared. Hoffman was kicked in the ankle, and it began to swell. Courtenay lost his hat and the stars from his right shoulder, but he was uninjured except in his pride. "I got my hat back," he said. "I told a cop to crawl under the car and get it. By then I was on my feet, and *he* was on the ground. It was one of the worst nights I've ever spent."

At the sight of the chiefs on the ground, one of them bleeding, the demonstrators melted away. It all happened so fast that no one could be identified, and it had been impossible, physically, to hold on to anyone. Courtenay felt humiliated at being turned on by his own men, dismayed to find himself a cop among cops-turned-thugs. He was glad to get away from the department for a while. He left town the next day for a long-scheduled vacation in Aruba; he seriously considered putting in his papers on his return.

"Cops always lose prisoners when they're outnumbered like that," Hoffman said with cheerful resignation, reliving the episode the next day. "It's like the scene from *Gunga Din*. Cary Grant goes into a cave where there are 200 Muslims and says, 'I arrest you in the name of the Queen' and they fall on him." He paused, reflecting. "Let's pray this was a once-in-a-lifetime thing."

To the intense relief of all three, there were no television cameras within range, nor did any reporters learn of the episode.

Well after midnight the three returned to headquarters so that Courtenay and Hoffman could pick up their cars. There they heard of a disturbance by cops in Commissioner Codd's neighborhood in Queens, and all three headed for the scene. Arriving at 2 A.M. they found the Queens area commander trying to deal with 200 noisy police demonstrators, watched by almost as many wide-awake, irate residents. Hoffman, giddy with fatigue and emotion, identified the leader and told him that he and Courtenay, together with the Queens area commander and his handful of subordinate officers—eight in all—would take on the demonstrators with their fists. Hannon, who had refused to have his cut treated, did not hear the offer and was in no condition to fight in any case. One angry resident asked him why he did not subdue the demonstrators with water cannons, as did the police in Japan.

"We knew we would get the shit beaten out of us," Hoffman said later, "but by then we were so mad we didn't care."

They were not taken on and a short while later the demonstrators dispersed. Hoffman would never have made such an offer—in outrage or in jest—had the demonstrators not been cops. The highest chiefs had all been foot soldiers

and had shared experiences that only cops could share.
Hannon, Courtenay, and Hoffman all knew that. Even divided, cops were brothers under the skin.

Chief Anthony Bouza was in trouble. Jim Hannon believed that Bouza, in whose turf lay Yankee Stadium, had
failed to utilize his troops and his equipment effectively—
had failed to distribute walkie-talkies, had not contained
the demonstrators but had, rather, "let them roam freely."
  The reaction from the press and the public was irate.
There were reports of packs of teen-agers preying on the
fans, picking pockets, snatching away tickets—while cops
looked the other way. Uniformed police were observed
cheering on their rowdy, off-duty colleagues as they
blocked traffic outside the stadium, and one off-duty cop
was seen by a reporter to urinate on the grill of a police van,
while his uniformed colleagues inside the van looked on,
grinning.
  Even the New York *Daily News*, traditionally pro-cop,
berated the police in an editorial for having "disgracefully
shirked their duty," adding that there were "no doubt thousands of policemen who want to live up to the old traditions, and are thoroughly disgusted and ashamed of the
troublemaking hotheads."
  "Unfortunately," the editorial concluded, "they are
going to suffer, too, if the bad apples persist in their calculated effort to turn the public against the force, and tear
down the city."
  The *Times*, itself frequently pro-cop, asked editorially,
"Who will control the hoodlums and the lawbreakers when
the police officers are seen breaking the laws and allowing
rampaging youths to run wild with the apparent approval
of at least some of the off-duty police?" It called the demonstrators "hotheads who have disgraced their union and their
department," and urged the mayor not to negotiate with
them over their grievances "while the city remains under
the threat of further disorder." Off-duty police promptly
threw up picket lines at both the *News* and the *Times*.

Chief Hannon called Bouza into his office at 8:30 A.M. the day after the Yankee Stadium mutiny, thereby starting a full-scale investigation.

"Tony says he takes full responsibility for everything that happened up there," Hannon told me after their meeting. The bruise on Hannon's head was purple and he said it throbbed. He had ordered Chief of Patrol Mitchelson to prepare a report.

"We're not a quasi-military organization when it comes to something like this," said Joe Hoffman, who would be doing the legwork for Mitchelson. "We're a *military* organization. That's why Chief McCarthy was disciplined. And Bouza will be, too." Hoffman's ankle was swollen and he was limping.

On that same Wednesday, in the evening, Commissioner Codd summoned the top 300 commanders in the department to police headquarters. The mayor was there. Codd lectured his commanders about their duty to arrest their fellow cops, if disorderly. All seven of the area commanders attended, as did most of the headquarters Brass, including Hannon and Hoffman. Courtenay had left town earlier in the day.

"Over the last five days," Codd said, "there have been a number of situations in which commanding officers did not command, in which supervisors did not supervise, in which sworn members of this department did not fulfill the duties they were sworn to fulfill."

Mayor Beame took the occasion to point out that "off-duty police officers are always *on* duty." That was a truth that the New York City police not only accepted but were proud of, and Beame knew it (otherwise, why carry guns, always, in or out of uniform?). But blind outrage had overtaken the ranks.

The Patrolmen's Benevolent Association rejected an agreement its leaders reached with the city. The contract, characterized by the *Times* as "the best possible deal that a near-bankrupt city could offer," provided for the rehiring of 400 laid-off officers. But it failed to meet other demands, and the PBA rank and file vowed to renew their picketing—unintimidated by the mayor's challenge, the commissioner's threats, the dismay and anger of the press and the public.

On the following day—Thursday, September 30—Commissioner Codd said in an interview that the police actions "reflected a rising militancy and disrespect for authority on the part of the police and society in general."

"The police department," he said, "is a slice of contemporary society, and what we are seeing is our society in a microcosm." In other words, we had the police we deserved.

The police pickets called off their job action on Monday, October 4, out of respect for the Jewish holiday of Yom Kippur.

Meanwhile, Chief Anthony Bouza was defending himself publicly, much to the annoyance of the headquarters Brass. Good Soldiers took their medicine quietly, as Chief McCarthy had done. Bouza told a *Times* reporter on September 30 that "most of the complaints arose from white people who attended the fight, which was in a ghetto neighborhood, and who apparently had never seen disorderly black and Hispanic youths.

"The kids," Bouza said, knowing full well how much he was irritating the police hierarchy, "impinged on the consciousness of more prominent Americans. If I failed it's because I didn't continue to make these feral children invisible to middle- and upper-class Americans who aren't used to seeing them."

Chief Bouza's exec, two inspectors, two deputy inspectors, and twenty-seven captains in Bouza's area command were being questioned, along with their boss.

No real progress had been made in contract talks between the PBA and City Hall by Tuesday, October 5, a week after the Yankee Stadium demonstration. The police protests were continuing ever more angrily as public opinion waxed ever more irate.

Meanwhile, the deposed area commander, Chief Charles

McCarthy, was placed in command of a special headquarter unit to "supplement" the resources of both the Manhattan South area commander and the man who had replaced him in Manhattan North.

Jim Hannon was coming down with a cold and still felt pain from his bruised rib cage. "I can't sneeze without it hurting," he said. He'd had a medical checkup and so had Joe Hoffman, who was also catching cold. Hoffman had been told by the police surgeon to stay off his feet, but he limped into Hannon's office on Tuesday morning, bright as usual. Responding to Hannon's query about his injury, Hoffman obligingly removed his shoe and sock to show the black-and-blue swelling. The two clucked over each other's war wounds.

Hannon told me he had heard that Tony Bouza was claiming that he, Hannon, had countermanded some of Bouza's orders at the scene, making Bouza's job difficult and actually wrecking his operation.

In midafternoon Hannon heard from Chief McCarthy that at least one rowdy demonstrator from a protest in Staten Island, where the mayor had attended a political function, had been identified from a photograph and had been given "charges and specifications." But the disorderly demonstrations continued.

On Hannon's desk were the detail sheets for policing various sites announced by the PBA demonstrators. Every unit of 100 patrolmen was lopsidedly being supervised by a complement of 200 sergeants, lieutenants, and captains. But the Brass knew by now that not even the captains could be relied on to discipline police protestors, and so the inspectors and chiefs were working very long hours.

Chief of Patrol Mitchelson strolled into Hannon's office. He reported that he had interviewed forty of Chief Bouza's subordinate officers and was now "putting it all together." He looked tired.

On the evening of Wednesday, October 6, 1,000 off-duty cops, chanting and waving their fists, demonstrated outside Madison Square Garden. Some of them were the same cops, in the same place, who had decorously policed the civilian protestors of the DNC three months earlier. There was a New York Rangers game at the Garden, an event that drew large crowds, and as had become their habit, many of the off-duty cop-demonstrators were behaving lawlessly. This time their superior officers managed to grab four of the demonstrators and hustle them off to the 17th Precinct House across town on 51st Street. Chief McCarthy's new special headquarters unit made the first two arrests.

Incensed, the cop-demonstrators spilled into the streets, threatening to storm the station house. They walked the twenty-five blocks from the Garden to the station house, an unstoppable tide, disrupting traffic. The 400 ranking officers who were patrolling them were helpless. It was the classical example of how the police could lose their streets to demonstrators, and why they always worried. Psychology did not always work when they were outnumbered. In this case, the angry off-duty cops had become a mindless stampede. And there was something in each of the commanders—however high in rank—that identified with the cop-rebels. Having learned to suppress the bad little boy in themselves, they behaved like sentimental daddies, halfheartedly trying to discipline their rebellious children.

At the station house the demonstrators were met by barriers, and they began chanting for the release of the four arrested cops. Dan Courtenay was back from Aruba and monitored the operation for Jim Hannon, but it was nominally under the supervision of Manhattan South Area Commander Carl Ravens. Mickey Schwartz had returned to his pre-DNC job as one of the three inspectors on Ravens's staff. He was on duty Wednesday night and was knocked down by the cop-protesters. Schwartz said that First Deputy James Taylor "had to pull someone off my back." He had never, he said, been so badly treated by cops. "I was embarrassed by the demonstrators; they were led by two or three hundred hard-core crackpots."

Courtenay had decided not to resign from the department, but for once he was not having fun. The morning after the confrontation at the 17th Precinct station house, Thursday, October 7, he was back in his headquarters office. He had stayed at the 17th Precinct until 2 A.M. when the arrested cops were released after being suspended from duty, and the protesters finally dispersed. Another commander—an inspector—had been injured and was in the hospital with a fractured vertebra.

"He got jumped by two of our guys," Courtenay said glumly. "Those cops think they deserve the world. Maybe it's because we keep telling them they're the finest."

Courtenay, in uniform, was gearing up for yet another demonstration, this one scheduled to take place outside Carter's New York State Campaign Headquarters on Fifth Avenue between 56th and 57th streets—Chief Ravens's responsibility.

"The sergeants, lieutenants, and captains just aren't making arrests," Courtenay said, heading for the mobile headquarters van at 56th Street, from where he would monitor the demonstration. "I'd like to order just one captain to make a collar and have him give me a jaundiced look! I'll put him on charges!" He said he was glad Chief Hannon had decided to stay at headquarters.

"I'd rather be here than him. He has a cold and his ribs hurt and he's worn out."

Entering the van, Courtenay spotted a captain from headquarters, who worked in civilian clothes and had not been out in the street in uniform for years. For an instant Courtenay's joviality returned. "I didn't know you had a blue suit like that," he said.

The demonstrators began exploding firecrackers, but it was impossible to pinpoint the origin in the thick lines of off-duty cops. It was Theater of the Absurd. Some of the cops wore masks and others wore bandages, to call attention to what they claimed was "police brutality" on the part of the Brass. The demonstrators marched from Carter's campaign headquarters to Times Square, again snarling traffic, but eventually they dispersed without incident.

Kurt Weill could have set them to bitter music. Red Grooms could have made of them a grotesque fresco.

Friday, October 8, was the day that Assistant Chief Charles McCarthy redeemed his reputation and became a hero. He confronted several hundred angry cops who wanted to march on Wall Street. The cops had their own lawyer with them and McCarthy had a police photographer with *him*, poised to snap evidence of insubordination. This time the cops yielded.

When it was over, McCarthy told me, reflectively: "Three years was a long time to last as area commander in Manhattan North. Still, I don't think Commissioner Codd would have taken the action he did if he had all the facts. But my loyalty to Codd prevented me from publicly complaining, like Bouza—who, incidentally, is smart and articulate, but no street commander."

It was not until eleven months later, in August of 1977, three months before Koch was elected mayor of New York, that the PBA finally ratified a new two-year contract with the city. The cops got a 6 percent increase that brought their base pay to $17,458, and they also were promised lump-sum cost-of-living increases. Other complicated technical concessions were made in the areas of work charts, overtime, and time off, and the city, in return, got the PBA's reluctant agreement to allow the department to experiment on a very limited basis with cost-saving one-man patrol cars. Inevitably, the contract was a compromise that left both sides unhappy. Morale in the ranks continued low and a new cynicism settled like silt over the depleted New York police department. Even Courtenay had difficulty maintaining his optimistic outlook, although he knew that the weather in the department could change suddenly, as often for better as for worse.

News item: In New York, on March 24, 1977, Police Officer Thomas A. Grecco, assigned to the 44th Precinct in the Bronx, was arrested for aiding a woman to engage in prostitution, getting money from her and

using his position as a police officer to help her operate. The six-month investigation that led to his arrest
was prompted by information from a former policeman
laid off because of budget cuts.

"I would fire Tony Bouza," Joe Hoffman said, when I
mentioned that I was planning to visit the controversial
police commander.

"He's Rasputin," Dan Courtenay said.

"If I were the PC," Hoffman said, "I'd hand him a gun
and tell him to do the honorable thing." Hoffman probably
had been seeing too many old movies.

Bouza, when I finally did go to see him in his Bronx
office, proved to be even more theatrical in his manner than
I'd expected. He projected an image of a tough cop, educated somewhat beyond the demands of his job, lonely,
misunderstood, locked in combat with an unyielding, un-
enlightened system.

He seemed half-amused and half-annoyed that I'd been
given access to the inner workings of the department. I
found this puzzling in view of the fact that he had been one
of Patrick Murphy's new-style young commanders—presumably open to outside scrutiny.

Bouza held that Chief McCarthy's removal was wrong,
and that Superchief Mitchelson (who had just completed
his investigation of the possible removal of Chief Bouza)
was double-crossing him.

"If Hannon was on the scene in uniform," Bouza said,
referring to the Yankee Stadium debacle, "he was automatically in command. Mitchelson changed my orders and
screwed everything up."

Bouza had been in line for the top job in several police
departments and had, in fact, been once interviewed by
Commissioner Codd as a candidate for chief of operations;
seeking a man with "rounded and *difficult* command experience," as well as "someone who could work harmoniously
with others," Codd had made the traditional choice—Jim
Hannon.

"I love the department," Bouza said, expressing his irritation at not being regarded as a Team Player. He added that he wanted no personal loyalties, scaled either upward or downward, and that he refused ever "to go along with what's wrong." The police department, he said, was like the Vatican—"We've all known each other twenty years or more; no one comes in at the top."

Then he spoke of "slippage" in the department's integrity since the departure of Commissioner Murphy.

"Three years ago we did not have the kind of problems I see now," he said, describing a detective on a special Bronx team who had "set up a locksmith" in order to commit burglaries, and a second detective who was "sleeping with a broad during working hours." I concluded he was trying to entertain me. Probably he didn't realize that through Hannon I knew of sporadic instances of "slippage" and knew, also, how firmly they were addressed by the headquarters command.

Bouza said that there were more Italians entering the department than Irish, "but so far, the Irish have kept control." Curious to know if he was right, I compiled a list of the thirty-eight one-star to four-star chiefs then in the department and found that—at least at the top—the Irish still greatly outnumbered any other ethnic group. There were nineteen chiefs of Irish descent, including three superchiefs, three assistant chiefs, twelve deputy chiefs, and the chief of operations; there were only two—an assistant and a deputy chief—of Italian origin. The Irish might have done better to worry about being supplanted by the three assistant and five deputy chiefs of German heritage waiting in the wings. There were also four Jewish chiefs—one of them a superchief—and two blacks, one of them a superchief. There was not a WASP in sight, and Bouza was the lone Spanish member of the Top Brass.

In mid-October it was widely rumored that Chief Bouza planned to quit the department he said he loved, and on November 6 he was named deputy chief of the Transit Authority police. Ten days later Commissioner Codd announced that Bouza had been cleared of charges that he mishandled the job at Yankee Stadium on the night of September 28. "We have not found any reason for the initiation of disciplinary action," Codd said. Bouza subsequently became chief of police in Minneapolis.

Dan Courtenay still felt bruised in his heart from the effects of the police mutiny. And since the end of the Democratic National Convention in July, he'd been brooding about what turn his career would take. Near the end of the year he said, "I've been on the job for twenty-nine years and I've found out you have to meet it more than halfway." But Courtenay felt Codd had betrayed him. He could have given him Chief McCarthy's area command, when McCarthy was flopped, but had chosen another two-star headquarters chief. Codd could have promoted Courtenay to Bouza's Bronx area command in November but had given the post, instead, to the Commander of Brooklyn South. And in December of 1976, when Louis Cottell retired, Codd failed to promote Courtenay to the three-star rank of detective chief; instead, Codd shifted the three-star chief of inspectional services to the Detective Bureau, and to replace him Codd promoted yet another two-star headquarters chief.

Chief Hannon kept Courtenay on his own staff, but Hannon didn't need an assistant chief as his exec, and they both knew it. "I'm tired of being a gofer," Courtenay said. Then, when Tom Mitchelson suddenly quit as chief of patrol in March of 1977, Codd appointed Courtenay as *acting* patrol chief without conferring the third star. Codd, confronting the financial squeeze, was trying to fill jobs laterally or temporarily where he could, thus avoiding promotions and saving on salaries.

Like Hoffman, Courtenay was growing fretful. Hoffman, who thought he was getting an ulcer, discovered he required a gall bladder operation instead and took a sick leave in December. Courtenay kept his health, but by July of 1977—a full year after the DNC—he was very nearly ready to join Hoffman in leaving the department to which he had devoted most of his life.

Hannon, always generous toward those under his command, was eager to see Courtenay rise in rank, knowing he merited the promotion. But Hannon seldom could bring himself to do more than make a mild recommendation to his boss. Hannon was not a lobbyist in his own cause or anyone else's. His early training in Good Soldiering and Team Playing had led him into the habit of self-effacement, of silent stoicism.

Commissioner Codd had explained that in moving another superchief into the job of chief of detectives, rather than promoting Courtenay to the rank, he was actually doing Courtenay a favor. Courtenay's career would be better safeguarded, Codd said, if he retained his two-star rank until after the impending mayoral election. For the superchiefs, as every high cop commander knew, were usually purged when a new mayor came to power. Just as a new mayor wanted to pick his own police commissioner, so did a new commissioner want to pick not only his civilian deputies, but also his own chief of operations and the five headquarters superchiefs. Therefore, the PC told Courtenay, he was trying to appoint as superchiefs those men who were closest to retirement, and who would hurt less if and when they fell victim to the sweep of a new mayoral broom. That did not explain, though, why Courtenay had not been given an area command, or why another assistant chief only a year older than Courtenay had been made three-star chief of inspectional services (not that Courtenay really wanted that job). Courtenay felt that the PC was not being straightforward. Discussing the situation with Hannon and Hoffman, Courtenay expressed it a little less elegantly. "I don't believe that bullshit," was how he put it, and Hoffman echoed the sentiment. "Only the PC knows why he makes the decisions he makes," Hoffman said.

That July, Hoffman told Hannon he was leaving to take the job with the Health and Hospitals Corporation. Hannon tried to mollify both Hoffman and Courtenay, making excuses for Commissioner Codd, emphasizing how the fiscal crisis was hampering him. But the two younger men knew all about that. Hannon was truly sorry to see Hoffman go. As for Courtenay, Hannon agreed to talk once again to Codd about giving him an area command, where he could run his own shop, assume the responsibility he craved. Courtenay put off his resignation. Although somewhat more self-assertive than Hannon, he had been too rigidly trained as a Good Soldier not to go on responding as one. Then, a month later (and two months after his fifty-first birthday), Codd gave Courtenay command of Manhattan South—not a promotion in rank, but the most glamorous of all the area commands—and three months after that he found himself being interviewed (albeit unsuccessfully) for the job of police commissioner.

When Mayor-elect Koch announced his choice of Robert J. McGuire as commissioner on December 13, 1977, Jim Hannon's hopes were dashed and Dan Courtenay was disappointed, but almost everyone else was pleased. The Patrolmen's Benevolent Association was happy and McGuire's former boss, District Attorney Robert M. Morgenthau, was very happy indeed. McGuire appealed to the rank and file because he was a cop's son and had, as a lawyer, represented cops in trouble during the Knapp Commission investigation.

McGuire's appointment also delighted the second level of the Top Command—the young tigers, as McGuire characterized them—the deputy chiefs and the inspectors like Mickey Schwartz, because they felt that now they would get a crack at the *first* level.

But the doubt expressed by *The New York Times* in an editorial a week earlier, questioning the advisability of John Keenan's rumored appointment, applied as well to Robert McGuire. Pointing out that the police department was "a billion-dollar enterprise," the *Times* cautioned that "it would take even the most sensitive and tireless outsider months to grasp its intricate institutional texture and folk-ways."

"Can the new mayor afford to appoint a commissioner," the *Times* asked plaintively, "who would have to spend so long a time in on-the-job training?"

McGuire was forty-one (younger even than interim PC Cawley) and he appeared to be dynamic, idealistic, and ardent. He spoke the mayor's language.

"I sought *him* out," Koch later said.

With McGuire, Koch could have it both ways. The new civilian PC, while ostensibly in tune with the civilian mayor, was at the same time sufficiently conversant with the police world to be able to comment, soon after taking office, "Cops are the worst and the best." And it was *his* problem, not Koch's, to penetrate the police mystique. Given McGuire's background and knowledge of the Police Experience, it looked as if he had a fair chance to succeed.

One of the most engaging things about McGuire was his admiration for his father, James, who joined the department in 1928, served under fourteen commissioners, and retired in 1967 with the rank of deputy chief.

"My father is a very bright man," McGuire once boasted. "He was second or third in the sergeant's exam. He strongly advocated education for all four of his children. He would have mortgaged the house to give any one of his kids an education." The admiration was mutual. "The kids' education never cost us a nickel," said James McGuire, who did not want his children to be cops. "I believed the Civil Service was wonderful for *my* time, and for *me*," he said. "But it was limited." He didn't need to discourage his sons from joining the police, for they had plans of their own. And so it came to pass that Bob McGuire grew up to be a lawyer, not a cop.

"I am sensitive to the problems of the police," McGuire said, soon after being appointed commissioner. "I was al-ways aware of the uniform as a target. As a kid I knew there was a chance every day that my father might never come back." He remembered that when he was seven his father, then a sergeant, was dragged off a fire escape and badly injured while interceding in a suicide attempt.

His grandfather also had worked in Civil Service for the parks department, and Robert was service-minded enough through family tradition to sacrifice his job as an assistant U.S. attorney to spend a year in Somalia on a grant, as legal adviser to the commander of that country's police force.

"It's not something I would have done," said McGuire's law partner, Andrew Lawler, who also had worked for U.S. Attorney Robert Morgenthau.

The same sense of commitment motivated McGuire to leave his lucrative law practice when Koch asked him to become police commissioner. "My practice was totally fulfilling for a time," he said, "but we all have to review our lives now and then. The job of police commissioner is something you just can't turn down." The commissioner's salary, then $47,093, was considerably less than McGuire made in his private law practice. (By 1982 the commissioner's salary had risen to $76,000; but it was still $18,500 less than that of Los Angeles's top police official.)

Robert Morgenthau was delighted with the mayor's choice of PC because Bob McGuire would understand and sympathize—and know how to cooperate with—the DA's office in prosecuting crime.

"Bob is a very unusual person," Morgenthau said, with almost fatherly pride, soon after the appointment. "He has a special feeling for the city. He's apolitical, extremely intelligent, and a skillful negotiator. No one has *ever* questioned his integrity. He knows the cops' weaknesses and he will be a foe of cronyism. He has a street sense." Morgenthau added that Mike Codd "hadn't the guts or clout" to face *his* boss, Mayor Beame, "with the correct action in certain situations—with non-panicky action."

Would McGuire be able to face his boss? Could any PC really stand up to the mayor who appointed him? The recent history of the NYPD seemed to argue no.

Ed Koch had, as had every mayor, pledged to keep his hands off the department, to allow his commissioner to pick his own deputies, to promote his own Top Brass. But did he mean it?

His predecessors did not. Both Patrick Murphy and Vincent Broderick complained after leaving office that they had been politically manipulated by Mayor John Lindsay. Broderick claimed that one of Lindsay's top deputies went so far as to send him a list of men he wanted promoted to detective. Broderick, outraged (so he later said), retorted that the police commissioner, not the mayor, should make such decisions.

Broderick was an appointee of the previous mayor, Robert Wagner, and his tenure as commissioner had not expired when Lindsay took office for the first time in 1966. He at first made a test of staying on, but then decided to leave after a few weeks. One reason Lindsay wanted him out was that Broderick was not promoting blacks, and that was not in keeping with Lindsay's liberal image. But police commissioners were damned if they did and damned if they didn't. Codd, who *did* promote blacks, was pushed out by Koch because he wasn't "innovative." The simple truth was that no incoming mayor wanted his predecessor's commissioner.

Patrick Murphy claimed that Lindsay had "either encouraged or condoned blatant interference in the operations of the department by a select group of mayoral aides who became known as the 'Kiddy Corps.'" When Murphy took the job of commissioner, he insisted on running his own department and received from Lindsay the assurance that he could do so. The circumstances of the corruption scandal at the time were such that Lindsay was obliged to comply. As for Michael Codd's relationship with Mayor Beame, it was at times enigmatic but certainly not independent. Beame handed down edicts and Codd implemented them—and took the flak.

On December 14, 1977, Mayor-elect Koch held a press conference at City Hall to present his Perfect Police Commissioner. McGuire's image certainly was not that of your everyday, big-city PC. His look and manner at times evoked ex-cop Joe Hoffman's favorite actor, Woody Allen—a tall Woody Allen. He was wiry, dark, intense, and going bald.

A reporter asked Mayor Koch good-naturedly why he had selected yet another member of the "Irish Mafia" to run the police department. Koch, who was something of a stand-up comic, turned to McGuire. "You told me you were Jewish."

"No," McGuire answered, "I only told you I *looked* Jewish."

The conference was attended by District Attorney Morgenthau and by most of the headquarters Top Brass (out of uniform) as well as by Manhattan South Area Commander Courtenay, in whose jurisdiction lay City Hall. And Courtenay was accompanied by his brand-new exec, Deputy Chief Milton Schwartz. Schwartz had been transferred *out* of the Manhattan South area in March 1977 and had been given the command of the arson and explosion squad, whose first priority was to capture the leaders of the FALN. He had failed to bring any of them to justice, but had nonetheless been promoted to deputy chief four months later, soon after his fiftieth birthday.

Some of Schwartz's colleagues complained that "Chief Schwartz" was a tongue twister and that he therefore should have remained "Inspector Schwartz." But Deputy Chief Schwartz said he'd sooner give up his name than his title, and he almost meant it. To be, at last, a chief! To wear the golden scrambled eggs on the peak of his cap! His Buffet clown now hung on a dirty-cream wall, one flight up in the 13th Precinct house on East 21st Street, where his boss, Big Dan Courtenay, ruled a crowded, dingy suite of offices. Courtenay and Schwartz hadn't worked together since the DNC seventeen months earlier.

Jim Hannon was not present at the December 14 press conference at City Hall. He had gone on his annual vacation to Florida with his wife, Isabel, knowing his presence

in New York would have no effect on the planned departmental changes.

I hadn't seen Courtenay or Schwartz for several months,
although we'd been in touch by telephone. They told me
the latest rumor circulating in the department, whose top
level by now was quaking with suspense, was that McGuire
already had picked his first dep, the man he wanted as his
closest aide and adviser, who would act for him in his absence, the only man in the department (aside from the commissioner himself) whom even the chief of operations called
Boss: ex-Police Commander (and now vice president of the
Health and Hospitals Corporation) Joe Hoffman!

Courtenay was sure that Hannon would be asked to leave
the department along with most if not all of the five bureau
chiefs. He was beginning to believe that Mike Codd had,
after all, done him a favor in delaying his promotion.

"McGuire might keep Hannon on for a month or so," he
said and added that he had heard rumors that he himself
was now a strong contender for chief of detectives. His
closest competitor for the job was the area commander of
Brooklyn South, Assistant Chief James T. Sullivan, who
had a long seasoning as exec to Chief of Detectives Louis
Cottell. But Courtenay, the optimist, could marshal any
number of reasons why he and not Sullivan would get the
job.

"Traditionally, the exec never moves into the chief's
spot," he said. "Traditionally, the chief of detectives has
been someone who was commander of detectives in the
Bronx—which I was, and Sullivan was not," he added.
And he also said, "Sullivan has a reputation for not being
good at community relations."

It was true though that McGuire was wasting no time in
acquainting himself with the characters and achievements
of the assistant chiefs and deputy chiefs from whose ranks
he would draw his new team, his middle-aged young tigers.
Courtenay had been asked to submit a résumé to the new
PC, and the Search Panel's evaluations were made available
to McGuire, at his request.

As commissioner, McGuire was—at least for the moment—considerably more approachable than Codd, as well as more candid. One of the things he told me was that in filling key positions he was not going to worry about certain conventional standards. Mike Codd would have shuddered to hear him say that "neurotics have their effectiveness and I'm not averse to using them."

On the other hand, he was profoundly image-conscious, and particularly anxious not to be mistrusted by the police for being a civilian. Turning down my request to accompany him on his first day in office, he said, "I can't be seen driving to work with a writer."

At the time I saw McGuire as a man of evident integrity, who was insecure about the image he wanted to project. Was the image different from, or in some way better than, what he really was? Perhaps he was more concerned than he would admit about his lack of Police Experience. His father was a cop, but was that enough? Perhaps he fitted Plutarch's withering comment: "A man without one scar to show on his skin, that is smooth and sleek with ease and home-keeping habits, will undertake to define the office and duties of a general."

Steeping himself in the police mystique, McGuire was trying to read the just-published autobiography of a man with scars to show—Patrick V. Murphy's *Commissioner*. A copy was on McGuire's desk when I visited him for the first time in late December 1977, in the law office he was about to leave. The book was without its dust jacket; the new PC explained it had been partly eaten by his infant son. While McGuire said he hadn't yet had time to read more than a few pages, he was already formulating a blueprint for early change, such as Murphy outlined midway in his book:

> Typically, in departments of some size, the top officers corps will be divided in half into two contending factions, perceived by those below as, literally and figuratively, the "good" guys and the "bad" guys.
>
> When a new police administrator comes into power,

it is his immediate task to identify that faction which to the younger, more idealistic, more potentially productive officers in the ranks below appears to include the "good" guys frozen out of the very top positions by the old guard clique. Once this potentially inspirational set of officers is identified, then the administrator must selectively but rapidly begin to move its members up at the expense of the bad clique currently in power. Once it is perceived that the new top police administrator has tilted in the direction of the "good" top 5 percent, then the entire bureaucracy below—the 90 percent—will lean in that direction, so susceptible are those below to the nuances of management change at the top.

McGuire needed a first deputy who could help bridge the gap between him and the police, to guide him to the "inspirational set of officers," the "good guys," and he wanted someone who thought the way he did about police service—someone with whom he could consult very closely about all policy-making decisions. While he was free to bring an outsider to this civilian post—which was not the case with the uniformed Brass—he was pretty sure he wanted a seasoned NYPD cop. Joe Hoffman was summoned from the Health and Hospitals Corporation for an informal chat.

McGuire had never met Hoffman, though he knew his reputation and was aware that Hoffman had been strongly under consideration as commissioner. McGuire decided to talk to Hoffman just to hear his ideas on police management. He never thought Hoffman would consider returning to the department; with his salary from the Hospitals Corporation, plus his pension, Hoffman now was earning more than $70,000 a year (compared with the $45,000 salary of the first dep).

The meeting, in Hoffman's words, resulted in "a mutual exchange of shock."

"I couldn't believe, as an outsider, Bob had such insight

into the management needs of the department," Hoffman said.

"Joe looked like a lawyer, not a cop," McGuire said. "He talked like me, he had a broad point of view, a corporate-management point of view."

Hoffman, however, was unprepared for McGuire's offer. After talking for no more than half an hour McGuire abruptly asked Hoffman to be his first deputy. "It was," McGuire said, "love at first sight."

They talked of introducing new ideas and replacing "tired" commanders—Copspeak for traditional, resistant blockers of progress, Patrick Murphy's "old guard clique," the bad guys. But, again, it largely was a matter of style. If the Michael Codd regime was inclined to proceed strictly by the book and avoid taking risks, as Hoffman maintained, the new regime would experiment and dare to make mistakes, as McGuire proposed.

To Commissioner Codd, Joe Hoffman had been an expendable deputy chief. To Commissioner McGuire, Hoffman was the Perfect First Deputy Police Commissioner. Hoffman was surprised at the offer, felt torn about giving up his new Hospitals job and his sizable income, but allowed McGuire to persuade him. They saw eye to eye on one of Hoffman's pet theories—that seniority and specific career assignments are not "the bottom line" for career advancement.

"Where Codd viewed promotion as strictly a reward for good work done in the traditional sequence, McGuire agreed that promotion should be given on the basis of a person's willingness to accept greater responsibility," Hoffman found. The new commissioner and his first dep would try to hold on to the good commanders. "We'll tell them, we owe you, stay with us," Hoffman vowed. Further, McGuire agreed with Hoffman that genuine loyalty obliged those high up on the commissioner's staff to tell the boss when something was wrong, not simply be yes men. The two men agreed that Hoffman, as first dep, should be the PC's "alter ego."

Joe Hoffman's formal swearing-in at police headquarters as the NYPD's first deputy police commissioner was scheduled for the morning of January 4, 1978, a frosty Wednesday. Jim Hannon, back from his Florida vacation, was in his thirteenth-floor office early that morning as usual. It was now two days since McGuire had moved into his fourteenth-floor office at headquarters, and Hannon, who had been coming to work every day since Monday, had heard nothing from upstairs, had been asked neither to stay nor to leave. It reminded him of the old, cold, inhuman days.

While Hannon acknowledged that there were times when a change at the top was mandatory—as during the corruption scandal of the late 1960s and early 1970s— sometimes a change in commissioners and Top Brass seemed merely arbitrary and a reorganization of systems that was functioning *well* seemed wasteful. "Why reinvent the wheel?" he asked. But he did not know the workings of Joe Hoffman's mind or the degree of his ambition.

Attendance by the chief of operations at all ceremonial functions such as swearings-in and promotions was considered obligatory—like his attendance at the hospital bed of an injured cop and his presence at cops' funerals. But on this day, unsure of his status, embarrassed himself and not wanting to embarrass the new PC, Hannon hesitated to attend the swearing-in of his former protégé, Joe Hoffman.

On most working days Hannon changed into his uniform within moments of his arrival at headquarters at 8:30 A.M. On this day, though, at five before 11, he was still wearing a light brown business suit, the jacket hanging open, revealing a handgun stuck in the waistband of his trousers.

Glancing uncertainly at his wristwatch with its bouncing digital ciphers, he stood in the doorway of his office and asked Frank Rossi, his trusted clerical aide, if there had been any word yet from the PC's office. The strain in his voice was palpable and as always when confronting a problem, Hannon was forming and unforming his mouth into an O. He felt a momentary sense of reprieve when Rossi showed him a message from the PC's office, requesting his presence at the swearing-in ceremony.

A smile flicked over Hannon's face and he hastened to change into one of the two uniforms that hung in his bath/dressing room, the jacket pinned with its gold shield and four stars. Always correct, he substituted his holstered service revolver for his handgun. Then he picked up his white cotton gloves. He was not leaving the building, only going by elevator to the second floor, where he could witness Joe Hoffman's swearing in by the new young commissioner, who wanted to surround himself with young tigers.

★ SEVEN ★

★ Cops who came on the job in the late 1940s, like Jim Hannon and Dan Courtenay, held a dissimilar attitude from cops like Mickey Schwartz and Joe Hoffman, who joined in the early 1950s. Those five or six years made a difference. The department was still dominated by a military rigidity, a narrow rulebook attitude, by racism and male chauvinism and a post-Depression mentality when Hannon and Courtenay became policemen; it began to give way tentatively to a more liberal and enlightened attitude when Schwartz and Hoffman joined. And those who became cops in the 1960s and lived through the civil rights revolution, Vietnam, and the women's liberation upheaval—not to mention the shame of exposed corruption during the Knapp Commission's probe—would be different kinds of chiefs from Schwartz and Hoffman by the time they got there in the 1990s.

The higher Hannon climbed, the less time there seemed to be for anything but policing. The time left from his job belonged to Isabel. When I met him, he had been married thirty-four years. He was devoted to his only child, Helen, who lived in a Philadelphia suburb with her husband and three young children. Isabel was often in ill health—the reason she had been able to have only one child—but she was a courageous woman, determinedly supportive of her husband's demanding job. The Hannons talked to their daughter several times a week on the phone and the oldest of her children, Joey, sometimes called his grandfather at work. Hannon's social life seemed to center around his family. The chief of operations was never off duty and it was difficult to make plans. Dinner invitations, theatergoing— even vacations—often had to be canceled at the last minute. In addition, Isabel's health recently had deteriorated and she could rarely count on being well enough to go out. Hannon accepted the conditions of his personal life stoically, as he accepted everything.

Pursuing his career from sergeant to lieutenant to captain—1948 to 1960—Hannon watched others steal and knew it was wrong, looked the other way.

"There were no avenues to heroism in combating corruption then," Hannon said. It took a Serpico, a freak, really, to sound the alarm. "Now that there *are* avenues, we can't tolerate any lapses. We've provided the machinery and the incentive for our men not only to stay honest themselves, but to instantly root out anything they see that might taint the department. We tell them, 'If you don't take advantage of the new system, you are doubly damned; look what *we* had to contend with, and stay honest.'"

As part of his anti-corruption plan, Patrick Murphy formed the Organized Crime Control Bureau in 1972. The OCCB was designed primarily to keep tabs on New York's Mafia. But, as Murphy explained, "underneath the obvious logic of consolidating the growth of organized crime, there was an internal goal." And that goal, wrote Murphy, was to root out organized crime *inside* the department, "whether the monthly pad, the entrepreneurial shakedown, or the unsolicited but accepted bribe."

News item: On October 21, 1977, in New York, Police Inspector Robert H. Johnson was indicted on charges of having lied to a special grand jury when he denied that he accepted "any unauthorized or illegal sum of money" from other members of the department. Inspector Johnson is a prominent and respected figure in the Harlem and South Bronx communities in which he has worked.

The grand jury has sought to determine whether officers in Harlem commands systematically collected bribes to overlook gambling enterprises and other illegal activities. The so-called Harlem Investigation has already resulted in departmental charges against more than sixty people, ranging in rank from patrolman to captain.

News item: Five months later Inspector Johnson heard the jury's verdict of not guilty and sobbed with relief on his attorney's shoulder. In May of 1978, however, during a departmental trial, he pleaded no contest to the charge that he failed to take proper police action against illegal gambling activities in Harlem in 1963 and was fined $30,000. Johnson by then was nearly sixty-three and the department permitted him to retire with his pension, out of which he would pay off his fine.

To head OCCB Murphy appointed a retired police chief named William P. McCarthy, and Jim Hannon succeeded him two years later. Hannon immediately issued a policy memo endorsing the words of his predecessor, words that he said "accurately reflect my views."

"They are to be considered as my policies and will be complied with by all members of OCCB," Hannon wrote on March 22, 1974. "I am certain that the idea still, unfortunately, prevails in our department that a police officer is somehow disloyal when he takes investigative action against criminals who happen to be sworn police officers.

"I am certain that superiors, in effect, often tell subordinates such things as 'be careful,' 'don't get caught,' 'I won't cover you,' rather than indicate that surfacing rogue police officers is their own concern and the concern of every honest police officer."

The memo continued with detailed advice about reporting "any matter of which one might reasonably infer that corrupt practices might be engaged in by personnel of this department, whether this information comes to him while on or off duty." Such information could be telephoned to the chief himself, who vowed to "follow every indication of corruption, to prove or disprove its existence, and to follow the trail wherever it may lead."

The memo emphasized that "we all share the shame of corrupt police officers who are arrested, but you and I owe no allegiance to any others who would bring further shame to us."

The top commanders were convinced that *systematic* and *protected* corruption had been stamped out, and instances of individual dishonesty were discovered quickly and dealt with expeditiously.

> News item: On October 10, 1975, in New York, eleven police sergeants and seven lieutenants admitted shaking down businessmen in Astoria, Queens, for more than $25,000 a year and entered guilty pleas to a departmental trial officer. They face charges relating to participation in a "sergeants' club" which could result in fines as high as $12,000 and retirement from the force. The club apparently had been formed in 1968 and involved many sergeants assigned to the precinct up to 1972, when the club died out. The crackdown followed Special State Prosecutor Maurice Nadjari's investigation. During the probe the implicated sergeants remained true to the time-honored "code of silence" by refusing to testify against other cops. But partway through the investigation an unidentified individual came forward to provide information, which led to a breakdown of the code of silence and voluntary confessions by the officers.

Corruption, in Copspeak, was "an integrity problem." Ethical awareness training was carried out relentlessly, even redundantly. A case that Hannon discussed with me one day involved a patrolman who reported that his partner, John X, had taken money from a grateful husband whose domestic dispute John had helped to settle. John had twice refused a $5 bill, but the husband had finally pressed it into John's hand and, telling his partner he was too embarrassed to refuse it again, John had walked away with the money. This pathetic instance of dishonesty received an exhaustive investigation and the officer was disciplined by being fined two days' pay and having the offense entered into his record.

Hannon always made—within his ability—the ethical, the honorable, the moral decision, and also the strictly interpreted police department decision. He was in his heart a compassionate man, but he seldom if ever listened to his heart in matters of policing. He was the absolutely correct, right-down-the-middle-of-the-road paramilitary commander. And while corruption always was a major anxiety for Hannon, there were other ongoing problems— some of them absorbing, others trivial—to which he had to pay close attention in this era of revitalized police integrity.

A sampling of items on Hannon's desk:

A worried message from the PC about a case concerning an EDP (emotionally disturbed person) wielding a knife and a bottle of acid, who was subdued by emergency service cops with tear gas and then placed in a body bag; he died of suffocation. Was tear gas being used carelessly? There also were complaints from medical personnel in the emergency wards of city hospitals about cops coming in with tear gas clinging to their clothes, which affected patients in the ward. Hannon drafted a memo asking for stricter precautions in the use of tear gas.

EDPs were a tricky problem for the police, and with the years more and more mental cases were being left at large (the police handled 21,000 such calls in 1980). Early in 1981 the police somewhat nervously initiated a new method for coping with EDPs: in responding to all calls involving disturbed persons they would henceforth carry a fire extinguisher containing what they described as a harmless bicarbonate-of-soda mixture to spray at the person to slow him down, and then they would capture the individual in a large net.

In announcing the new method, the chief of operations confessed that it might be controversial. "It doesn't look too nice," he explained, "when you see a fellow enveloped in a cloud of smoke and netted, almost like an animal, but all this is an attempt not to hurt these people."

The idea for the net was borrowed from the Los Angeles sheriff's office, which got numerous calls to subdue persons driven berserk by angel dust; the drug gave them the strength of five men. But New York's EDPs were usually found inside four walls, where space was too cramped for use of the net, and in two years, it had never been used.

Other items on Hannon's desk:

A memo (followed by a personal visit) from the captain of a Manhattan precinct who was worried about the irate community reaction to a newly opened methadone center. The captain called the center a "legalized pusher." Hannon concurred but could do no more than tell the captain to keep his men alert.

A confidential note informing Hannon that Alexander Solzhenitsyn was staying at the Americana Hotel in Room 4101 and that the intelligence division recommended a uniformed police officer be assigned to duty outside the room until the novelist's departure on July 14. Hannon approved.

A memo asking if a male police officer could be assigned to guard a female prisoner, in the absence of any available female police officer. Yes.

A request that Hannon recommend to *Parade Magazine* a candidate for "police hero of the year"; one of the names suggested by his staff was Mary A. Glatzle, who had earned the nickname Muggable Mary for her work as a decoy cop. Hannon didn't know whether she had been let go because of the fiscal crisis. "This could be embarrassing," he muttered, telephoning the personnel bureau; personnel said she was now working in uniform in the Two-oh

Precinct, because of recent cutbacks in the street crime unit. Hannon submitted her name.

In between dealing with his paperwork, Hannon disposed of numerous problems by telephone. After receiving requested figures on what it would cost in manpower and money to provide protection for one million people expected to attend a rock concert in Flushing, he phoned the Queens area commander. "I think we should discourage Arlene Wolff from running that thing," he said. Arlene Wolff was the first deputy commissioner of civic affairs and public events, the agency headed by Angier Biddle Duke. "It will cost about $500,000; tell her the PC doesn't want it. I'll send you the figures, but I don't think *she* should get the report, that's in-house. Just say we can't handle it in view of our reductions in staff. You'd never be able to handle the situation in Flushing Meadow Park—it's three miles long." Hanging up, he said, "We'll probably be hearing from the good Mr. Angier Biddle Duke!"

On the phone to another area commander: "What are we doing about Captain W. losing his shield? I know he's a very idealistic guy. Yes, I know he's died 10,000 deaths over losing it. I don't want to break his spirit." Lost shields were a serious problem because of the possibility of impersonation. As with lost guns, the problem might be addressed merely by a reprimand (if the cop, like Captain W., had a good record and there were mitigating circumstances), or by command discipline for negligence—usually the loss of several days' vacation. But if the culprit had a bad record, losing his shield could lead to charges and specifications and a departmental trial. About thirty shields were lost each year and the department maintained a desk that kept track of them; a substitute shield was issued with a different number. Occasionally a shield was recovered with an arrest and was put back into circulation.

On the phone with a member of the fire department of a small town in New Jersey just across the Hudson: he asked if the New York police would "urgently" send over a net to catch a man on a ledge, who was threatening to jump.

Hannon asked that the request be verified by the New Jersey police. "We can't move into your jurisdiction without an official request," he explained. No verifying call came. Ten minutes later Frank Rossi entered Hannon's office to announce, "He jumped. We couldn't have gotten a net there in time, anyway."

The phone calls and paperwork were interspersed with meetings, some of them regularly scheduled—such as Hannon's Tuesday morning sessions with the bureau chiefs and the support services commander—others hastily called, as the gathering of the seven area commanders following the layoffs. Anticipating the area commanders' dismay at the cuts in manpower that Hannon planned to impose on them, he pointed out that he himself was now making do with less than half his office staff. Of his seventy-five clerical workers, forty (including his secretary) had been sent back on the street to replace some of the laid-off patrolmen. "Now we have to bounce these changes off the budget department," Hannon told the glum-looking assistant chiefs.

A leaner department did not necessarily mean a less efficient one with regard to combating crime. "There aren't conceivably enough cops to patrol every block in the city twenty-four hours a day," Hannon once explained. "If you have a criminal element, crime will be committed—if not in a heavily patrolled area, then in the neighboring one. Saturation is not possible. The criminals find the places that aren't patrolled."

News item: In Washington, D.C., on July 26, 1981, a major study released by the Police Foundation revealed that police officers walking a beat reduce citizens' fear of crime, but do not reduce crime. The study was conducted in twenty-eight New Jersey cities from February 1978 through January 1979.

The researchers found that residents in beats where foot patrol was added saw the severity of crime problems diminishing in their neighborhoods. But researchers found also that the presence of foot patrols

had no significant effect on crime as measured either
in reports to the police or in interviews with residents
to uncover unreported crime.

Some of Hannon's meetings were ceremonial and in the
nature of community relations. I was astonished, one day,
to find the long table in the conference room of the chief of
operations—the table at which grim-faced precinct captains
sat with Hannon, where the Firearms Discharge Review
Board met, where high-ranking members of other city
agencies and out-of-state law enforcement bureaus came to
confer—covered with a festive pink cloth and set with wine
glasses.

The rabbi of Brooklyn's Hasidic community had come to
present plaques to several detectives and their bosses for
their "relentless pursuit of murders of old people." Photog-
raphers were there and Hannon was in a jovial mood as he
and the detectives and their bosses lined up obligingly for a
picture. "Small men in the rear," Hannon said, drawing
himself up to his own five feet eleven inches. He declined to
make the speech that the rabbi had expected. "I will just say
thank you," he said.

Hanging on the walls of the conference room were
framed photographs of the forty-two men—including
Hannon—who had served as New York police chiefs.
Hannon earlier had postponed having his official portrait
made—the small vanities of saintly men—because he'd
nicked his face shaving and wanted to wait until the wound
healed. When the portrait was made he distributed color
copies to the PC, the first dep, the superchiefs, and the area
commanders, while those below that rank received black-
and-white prints. Hannon's own office wall held a color
photo of Michael Codd. (Joe Hoffman's wall held the obligatory portrait of his boss, Chief Mitchelson, and so on,
down the chain of command.)

Whenever there was a conference concerning the Hasidic
community (I later discovered), it became a party. I sat in
on one such affair, called to safeguard peace in the commu-

nity for Succoth, the seven-day harvest festival. During the holiday, as Hannon knew, the Hasidim moved out of their homes to live in symbolic structures of boughs and garlands, and their homes often were burglarized in their absence.

"Whatever manpower you can spare, Chief, we'd appreciate," said Rabbi Arnold Wolf. "And then we'll ask for more."

The meeting began with Rabbi Wolf reading the Lord's Prayer and delivering a blessing in Hebrew for two cops killed the day before. The table was set with dishes of small cakes and glasses of sweet wine and several more rabbis wearing skullcaps and full beards were seated side by side with a plume of uniformed police: area commanders, lesser chiefs, inspectors and precinct captains. On a green metal hat rack the commanders' gold-braided caps and the rabbis' expensive ceremonial beaver hats were lined up side by side. (The beaver hats, costing between $800 and $1200, were often stolen in the street and their identifying names ripped out.) Hannon and the other cops sipped politely from the thimble-sized glasses, nibbled on the cakes, and took notes as the rabbis explained the ritual of Succoth.

"In the Nine-oh," said one rabbi—they were all police buffs and knew the lingo—"we had two incidents of fur-hat-snatching recently. They stripped the fur and wore it like Indians wear scalps. We saw them in the street."

"We can send you some anti-crime people, as decoys," Hannon offered, "but we can't afford to give them fur hats to disguise them."

Another rabbi explained about the lulab—a palm branch carried and waved in the street. He cautioned the police not to mistake the ceremonial branches for weapons.

The meeting lasted an hour. "Rabbi, I think we've all learned a lot from these sessions," Hannon said. "I want to thank you for taking the time to do this." Later he told me, "This has been an education for me. They really are victimized because of the way they look."

*   *   *

Whenever Hannon thought back on his long and often gratifying career, his most cherished memory was of his year as commander of Manhattan detectives. During those days he occasionally traveled to the scene of a crime, but now that he was chief of operations, it was a rare homicide that took him into the street. Such was the case on September 16, 1975, when Hannon had held the four-star rank for only six months. A little after 9 P.M. he was called at home and told that two cops had been shot in a tough neighborhood on the Lower East Side. The case turned out to be his most stressful episode as chief of operations. Every cop-killing had certain familiar elements that an experienced commander recognized and dreaded. And yet it was the sort of police action that served to unite cops of all levels and assignments. During the investigation of a cop-killing the Brass and troops were as one. In Copspeak such a killing was called, with unconscious irony, an Unusual.

In the Unusual report that lay on Hannon's desk the following morning there were only bare details:

"HOMICIDE TWO POLICE OFFICERS, GUN—NO ARREST. Below named members of the service had commanded a 1967 Plymouth, 2 door red convertible bearing Pennsylvania plates, to pull over to a stop. While attempting an investigation of car and occupants, alleged to be three males and one female, they were suddenly gunned down by one of the occupants. All of the occupants fled the scene." The two victims were Sergeant Frederick Reddy, Shield Number 1258, who was fifty years old and white; and Police Officer Andrew Glover, Shield Number 14007, who was thirty-four and black.

Cops all over the city, every night, commanded cars to pull over and investigated their occupants for one reason or another. All cops were taught the right and wrong way to do that. Even *civilians*, having watched the procedure in countless movies, knew the way it was supposed to be done. But, however careful they were, cops got themselves killed—quite often by the occupants of a suspect car who turned out to be criminals with records, unable to afford another arrest and with very little more to lose.

Glover and Reddy were not wearing bulletproof vests, which had not yet become general issue in the New York police department. Glover was shot twice, once in the head and once in the heart at point-blank range. Reddy was hit under his right arm, the bullet tearing into his lungs.

Attached to the "Unusual Occurrence Report" (the document's full designation) was a supplementary report describing the way Reddy and Glover were found by the first cops responding to a signal 10–13—Police Officer in Trouble. Both were still breathing.

"The officers observed a large crowd," the report said, "and found Sergeant Reddy lying on his back on the roadway with his service revolver in his right hand. They did not observe Police Officer Glover at this time. They immediately removed Sergeant Reddy to Bellevue Hospital." The service revolver in Reddy's hand, a .38 caliber Smith & Wesson police special, contained only "three live rounds."

Two other officers responding seconds later to the 10–13 signal, the report went on, found Andrew Glover "lying unconscious in the street being assisted by civilians in the rear of suspect auto. They immediately removed him to Bellevue Hospital." Glover's service revolver (like Reddy's, a .38 Smith & Wesson) was missing and presumed stolen by his assailant.

Within minutes a dozen more RMPs came screeching to the scene. If cops drove recklessly on *routine* runs, they became crazed at their wheels when responding to a distress call involving another officer. Ruby signal lamps whirling madly, sirens squawking with fury, the cruisers lunged to a stop at curbs, on sidewalks; their drivers parked them any which way, letting their doors hang open, leaving their radios crackling with the bad news, leaping into the street where their brother officers had been felled. Soon there would be close to a thousand cops in the area, including the teams of homicide detectives.

Jim Hannon was finishing a late dinner at home when he was called by current situations, the headquarters communications unit that operated around the clock. I happened to be listening to the radio and heard about the shooting the same time as Hannon.

I called to ask if he was coming into Manhattan and if I could accompany him, and he agreed. He said to meet him at Bellevue Hospital, where the two cops were being taken. As far as Hannon knew, both were still alive.

I had a shorter distance to travel from my home in Manhattan than Hannon had from Queens, and I reached the hospital before he did. I could see him in my mind—taut and silent, sitting beside Richie Bauer, the driver on duty that night, in the front seat of his official limousine. I pictured the car moving very fast, its siren and blinker clearing a path. Bauer would be as shocked as Hannon. If there was one aspect of police work and police life that linked every branch and rank in the department in instant sympathy, it was an attack on a fellow cop. Always that lurching sensation: It could have been me. It could, at one time, have been Hannon.

The police radio in Hannon's car told him, at 9:40 P.M.—about forty-five minutes after the shooting—that Glover and Reddy had arrived at Bellevue. As a high-ranking commander for the past ten years Hannon often had sped to the bedsides of injured or dying cops, sometimes in the Bronx, sometimes in Brooklyn, but more frequently in Manhattan, where much of the city's violent crime occurred.

For Hannon, as for other senior police officials, a cop-shooting had its specific rituals and its rote questions. It was the commander's obligation to find out what, exactly, happened. They had to trace any wrong moves made by the cop, so as to safeguard the lives of other cops, if possible. What would I have done in the dead cop's place? Was there a procedural error made? Did he panic? Would I have panicked in his place? Not easy questions to answer.

When you were as high in command as Hannon, the ritual took on a sense of abstraction. *Chiefs* were not blown away in the street, not, at least, in New York. Once in a while you heard or read about chiefs of tiny police departments who were shot down.

It had been a long time since Hannon had risked his own life. His job, now, was to pick up the pieces, to evaluate, to stay on top of the investigation that had already begun, to brief the commissioner (if necessary, to *shield* the commissioner, who once again happened to be out of town), and to shore up morale in the ranks, simply by being on the scene.

He did feel, though, a genuine sense of pain and loss. He began as a street cop, and though that was thirty-two years ago, tonight he felt that a part of him had been violated along with the two cops to whose bedsides he was speeding. Hannon's car approached Bellevue, its huddle of buildings massed along the East River, fronting on First Avenue. Bellevue was a place familiar to all cops, the place where a cop hurt in Lower Manhattan was likely to be rushed. (It was where a lot of wounded criminals were rushed, too.)

The car swung into Bellevue's emergency entrance. Hannon braced, then strode into the outer waiting room, where members of the Top Brass were already assembled. He absently removed his spectacles and nodded to the uniformed cop posted at the entrance, who was saluting him. Two more cops were stationed at the door to the admitting area. A sergeant, sitting at an improvised communications desk, answered the phone, "Temporary Police Headquarters, Sergeant Smith."

Among the assembled Brass was Chief of Detectives Louis Cottell, who was directing the investigation. Cottell and Hannon understood and respected each other's styles. Both were no-nonsense, steely, old-fashioned, firmly religious men.

Cottell was older than Hannon and would soon have to take his mandatory retirement. He was dour and laconic and had a spare but biting sense of humor and a fierce, parochial loyalty to his detectives (which did not go uncriticized by either his peers or his superiors). Greeting Hannon in the hospital's anteroom, Cottell told him quietly that both Glover and Reddy had died on the operating table minutes after their arrival.

Present also was Lieutenant John J. Yuknes, the detective commander in charge of the homicide zone in which the shootings occurred. Yuknes was a detective boss, one of Manhattan's six homicide squad commanders. He was lean, alert, casual in manner, and, like many homicide detectives, he had a glum, abstracted air—possibly because so many of the city's murders went unsolved.

Yuknes had hurried to Bellevue hoping (vainly, as it turned out) that either or both of the wounded cops could tell him something that would lead to the capture of their assailants. Yuknes informed Hannon that Glover's gun was not recovered at the scene; presumably his killer took it. This fact might ultimately prove helpful, for bad guys tended to hang on to guns, even knowing the weapons could incriminate them.

Hannon was also told that Sergeant Reddy's gun had been fired, and local hospitals were being canvassed for possible gunshot injuries. Detectives of Lieutenant Yuknes's squad were already canvassing the area where the shootings took place, and a forensic team was at the scene.

Hannon glanced at Cottell for confirmation, and then wanted to know if the families of the two cops had been notified. That was the responsibility of the Manhattan South area commander's office. He was told that a department chaplain was on his way to the town in Long Island where Frederick Reddy's wife, Marie, lived. There was a bit of confusion about whom to notify in Andrew Glover's case; he was separated from his wife, Lois. Finally, a chaplain was sent to notify both his mother and his estranged wife.

Frederick Reddy and Andrew Glover were now a pair of statistics—the fifth and the sixth police officers dead in the line of duty, a little more than halfway through the year 1975. They were the last cops killed that year, as it turned out. There had been better years and worse. Policing, after all, was inherently dangerous. The highest death rates in recent years for members of the New York police occurred in 1968, when thirteen cops died in the line of duty, and in 1971, when ten were killed. The year before Reddy and Glover were shot, four cops were killed; the following year, one. (But that year, five cops took their own lives.)

Hannon stood silent, seeming to gather his thoughts and possibly offering a prayer. He instructed his driver to take him to the crime scene. He was grateful at a time like this to be in action, to be doing something that seemed useful.

"I'll see you at the scene," he told Cottell and Yuknes, who were also about to leave. The uniformed cop at the door saluted Hannon again, solemnly, as he headed for his car. It was 10:30, about an hour and a half since the two cops had been attacked. Hannon knew that the quicker an investigation got under way, the fresher the scent, the more likely a solution.

The cop-shootings had been the lead bulletin on local radio stations since 9:15 P.M., and many homeward-bound detectives heard it on their car radios. This was their business and they, too, poured into the street where the murders had occurred, their gold shields hanging from breast pockets.

I watched the detectives converge like a flock of irate birds. You didn't actually see them arrive; they were suddenly just there on this particular mean street at the bottom of Manhattan, picking over its detritus, hunting for crumbs of enlightenment, beady-eyed, prickly, peering about for the why and the how and the who of the case, beating about in dismay and anger and curiosity. "I don't see how this could have happened," one of them said, "how he could have gotten both of them."

Hannon's car pulled up at the intersection of East 5th Street and Avenue B, where patrol cars blocked entry. By now there were fifty or sixty cars, some of them the detectives' unmarked ones, ringing the two-block area that was designated, by yellow placards, as the crime scene; the cards were hung on wooden police barriers that had appeared from nowhere. Hannon pinned his own gold shield to the breast pocket of his blue business suit, lest the fiercely protective cops standing guard should fail to recognize their four-star General out of uniform. He hadn't taken the time to change before leaving Queens.

This was not just another New York homicide—of which the city had well over a thousand each year, a rate that was steadily rising. Here the victims were two *cops*. It was the kind of case pursued with special resourcefulness and great personal effort, the kind of case that got all the Top Brass into the street—with good reason, they felt—for if a dent in that thin blue line of protection were to be left unavenged, the whole line would begin to crumble.

For Hannon, who came to lend his presence, his moral support, this was a continuation of the ritual of his office, the ritual that began with his visit to Bellevue. He moved a bit woodenly, a General suffering slightly from battle fatigue, but still in command, always the Good Soldier.

At 11 P.M. Chief of Detectives Cottell, being dryly supportive of his men, stood in the dimly lit street, noisy with police radios, garish with the popping flashbulbs of the forensic men photographing the crime scene. That, too, was different from the way most homicide investigations were run, for normally there would not be anyone higher than a detective-lieutenant at a crime scene. But in this instance, Detective-Lieutenant John Yuknes of First Homicide was outranked all the way to the top, by Manhattan Detective Commander William J. Averill, Assistant Chief of Detectives James Sullivan, and by the top detective boss, Louis Cottell.

Yuknes's detectives carried notebooks for the tedious process of recording answers from witnesses; in most homicide investigations the answers were imprecise and few turned out to have any bearing on the case. That was the way a big city homicide was investigated, though, and as the detectives were fond of saying, sometimes you got lucky.

The detectives optimistically believed that this case promised a quicker solution than most, because the car's occupants seemed to have some connection with the neighborhood. Actually, a surprising number of witnesses willingly came forward; this didn't happen in most homicide cases in the huge and fragmented city, with its unstable neighborhoods, hostility, and paranoia. But the two slain cops were members of a neighborhood police team and were known and liked by community residents, many of whom were hardworking and frightened of crime. (They were particularly frightened of the drug dealers who occupied dozens of abandoned, city-owned buildings in the area, conducting a business that by 1982 had grown into a multimillion-dollar operation. So entrenched was the narcotics traffic in the area that the city administration announced desperately in the summer of 1982 that it would tear the buildings down as the only way to dislodge the crafty dealers and rid the area of corrosive criminal activity—a promise still unfulfilled in 1983.)

Several neighborhood witnesses described vividly at least two of the men who fled from the red Plymouth after the shooting. As reported in the supplement to the Unusual that Hannon received the next morning, one of the men was "Hispanic, 20 to 25 years, about 5′ 10″, large Afro, wearing a red dashiki" and the other was "Hispanic, about 20 years, thin build with beer belly."

And, too, for clues there were a car and a cop's stolen gun. It was dangerous, though, hunting cop-killers; they had nothing at all to lose.

The red Plymouth from which the fatal gunfire came was being crawled over by members of the forensic team. The window on the driver's side was shattered, presumably from the three bullets Sergeant Reddy had fired before falling. They were sifting through broken glass, bloodstained grime, the car's contents, looking for spent bullets from Sergeant Reddy's gun. They were dusting for fingerprints, vacuuming for hairs. Through it all, the red Plymouth's taillights kept blinking on and off, dully illuminating the clots of dried blood in the street.

Hannon watched, not interfering, letting his commanders do the job they'd all done many times before. They'd done almost the same job not far from this spot a few years earlier, in January of 1972. Two police officers from the same 9th Precinct, another neighborhood team—Gregory P. Foster, who was black, and Rocco Laurie, who was white—were shot to death in the street. Occasionally Hannon exchanged a word or two with Cottell. It was Cottell, as head of the investigation, who would be kept informed of the detectives' ongoing inquiries, of the tests for the bullets removed from Glover's and Reddy's bodies, of the medical examiner's findings. And Cottell would brief Hannon, hour by hour.

When the first dep, James Taylor, arrived on the street, it was protocol for Hannon to brief *him*—as the PC's surrogate. Taylor, an ex-cop of high rank, was old-school courtly, Irish to the bone, wise in the ways of evil. He and Hannon were old friends.

Having satisfied himself that all was being done that should be done, Hannon got back into his car, ready for the next ritualistic step: a visit to the 9th Precinct, home of the two slain cops. The 9th, a few blocks east of the crime scene, was one of the oldest and grimiest of Manhattan's twenty-one precinct houses. It had dirty green walls and rusty ironwork, scuffed floors, ancient plumbing, a faltering heating system, and no air conditioning. Hannon was saluted, gloomily, at the duty desk as he "signed in," a department tradition and courtesy borrowed from the Navy, like much police protocol. Many of the cops standing around had already wrapped bands of black tape across their silver shields. Some felt a need to express their grief and outrage more dramatically. Detective-Lieutenant Yuknes, here to organize the initial stages of the investigation, watched a cop pull off his cap, fling it to the floor, and stamp on it when given the news that his two brother officers had died of their wounds. The display annoyed Yuknes. "I felt it, too," he later told me, "but you get on with your job."

The first job was tracing the car's owner, and detectives

were manning the telephones upstairs in an improvised squad room. Hannon climbed the flight of narrow worn steps to the second floor, entering a cluttered maze of small offices, where Yuknes was setting up space for the questioning of neighborhood witnesses. Hannon commandeered a metal desk and begged a cigarette from a passing detective, who said, "Gee, Chief, I didn't know you smoked."

Hannon smiled mechanically. "I don't," he said.

Puffing nervously, not inhaling, he called Isabel to say simply that he would be awhile yet. A cop came in and rummaged in the drawers of the desk at which Hannon was sitting. "Excuse me, Chief, there's supposed to be a Polaroid in here," he said casually. Hannon helped open drawers and found the camera. It was for taking pictures of the suspects detectives would be bringing to the station house.

At 2 A.M. as Hannon stood up to leave, his driver, Richie Bauer, told him there was a message from the PC, who wanted Hannon to telephone him "forthwith" in Denver. Codd was cutting short his stay, Bauer said, to return early Wednesday afternoon, but he wanted an update right now on the killings. Hannon called Codd and then Bauer drove him the sixteen blocks uptown to the First Homicide offices at 21st Street and Second Avenue. Detective-Lieutenant Yuknes's squad was housed in the same building as the 13th Precinct and the Manhattan South area commander's office. The squad room was on the same floor as the Manhattan detective commander's office, which Hannon, not too long since, had occupied.

Hannon walked the short flight up to "B-Deck" (another naval reminder). A wide, tiled, institutionally drab corridor led into the series of rooms that held the desks and the files, the constantly ringing phones and the constantly dripping coffee of one of the city's most active homicide squads.

Already gathered in Lieutenant Yuknes's office, with the door closed, were all the bosses. Chief of Detectives Cottell sat at Yuknes's desk, while Yuknes slouched against the wall. Hannon perched on a windowsill. Waiting for developments, the bosses pondered the whys of the case.

How could *both* cops have been shot, the bosses asked each other, without having time to wound at least one of their attackers? (No gunshot injuries had been reported by the local hospitals; neighborhood doctors were being canvassed.) None of the commanders could believe that the two cops walked, unknowing, into an ambush; they must have known (or thought they knew) what they were doing when they angled their patrol car across the double-parked red Plymouth.

The procedures for accosting the occupants of a parked car in those circumstances were drilled into all cops—first at the Police Academy, later by repeated lectures and refresher sessions, accompanied by graphic film simulations such as those used in the retraining of Patrick Freeman.

You assumed that the car's occupants could be armed. You were supposed to know how to cover your partner's approach. Your partner was supposed to approach cautiously. Still, one cop could be struck, that could easily happen, everyone realized that. But both? Without being able to stop even one of their attackers? That was one reason that cops (so the PBA said) did not want one-man patrols. Your partner was supposed to be able to save your life, or at least avenge it legitimately, in the street.

All the commanders in the room inevitably experienced some sense of guilt and responsibility for Glover's and Reddy's deaths. Maybe the training was, after all, inadequate. Maybe one or the other of the two cops was under some sort of severe strain that made him vulnerable to such an attack—and that endangered his partner, as well as himself. If so, why wasn't his commanding officer aware of it? Of course, no two cops react the same way under the same circumstances, and there still were too many imponderables in this case. The bosses would have to wait several days before getting their answers.

At 4 A.M. Hannon said goodnight and left for a few hours of rest. He was back in the First Homicide's squad room at 11 o'clock the next morning. He'd shaved and had breakfast but he looked unrested. He had found Isabel ailing again. She was a plucky woman, but a crippled arm from an injury many years earlier made even simple household chores difficult for her.

Lieutenant Yuknes and Deputy Chief Averill briefed Hannon on the past few hours' progress by detectives who had worked through the night.

"We have mug shots and yellow sheets on two guys," Yuknes said. "We may be getting lucky." Not yet. As often happened in the earlier stages of a homicide investigation, the two turned out to be the wrong guys. It would be several more days before detectives finally got the real name of the red Plymouth's owner (the registration had turned out to be a fake name and address).

Hannon knew that Yuknes and his detectives were doing their best. The visit, again, was ceremonial. He could have called Deputy Chief Averill into his own headquarters office or got the information by telephone. But Hannon wanted to boost morale, always low after a cop-killing; he wanted to be *visibly* concerned. He wanted the detectives working on the case to *see* him *caring*. Not too long ago some of these detectives, working directly under his personal command, had solved several of the city's more spectacular homicides, including an earlier cop-killing. On his way out of the squad room he greeted by name a couple of detectives who were bringing in a witness.

Hannon returned to his own desk at headquarters. Lieutenant Rossi strolled into Hannon's office. "Chief Cottell is on the line, Boss." Rossi usually worked in his shirt sleeves, and the gun stuck in his belt was the only sign he was a cop. Commissioner Codd frowned on the practice of headquarters staff walking around the building with guns showing, but few of the cops remembered to keep their jackets on.

"Louis?" Hannon said on the phone, "the first dep is giving the commissioner's driver the current report on the case, to take to the airport. The commissioner will be here about 3 and I'd like you to get back to me by 2:30 with the latest update, so I can brief the commissioner as soon as he arrives in the building."

Rossi informed Hannon, "Andrew Glover's funeral is at oh-ten-hundred Saturday, at the Convent Avenue Baptist Church on 145th Street," and he added that Deputy Chief Joseph Hoffman was waiting to see him.

Hoffman was munching on half a sandwich and Hannon eyed it wistfully. He was forgoing lunch, as he did periodically, to lose weight. At six feet, Hoffman was an inch taller than Hannon, but he looked almost frail standing beside Hannon's solid presence.

"I just wanted you to know about the cop who nearly shot his wife last night," Hoffman said.

Hoffman had been promoted only six months earlier to deputy chief and he believed himself to be on his way to the very top of the NYPD. Disillusionment was still a couple of years away. Having just achieved his first gold star, Joe Hoffman was for the moment content. To attain deputy chiefdom was a giant step in the department.

Hannon riffled through a pile of papers on his desk, among them the Unusual of last night's cop-killing, and found the report dealing with the case Hoffman had just called to his attention.

"Have you made a determination of what happened?" Hannon asked Hoffman, in the somewhat stilted language he sometimes fell into.

"He says he was putting the gun away, when his wife shoved him, and it went off," Hoffman said. His own speech was fluent and entirely grammatical—quite un-coplike. "They began having an argument as soon as he got home. But he wasn't trying to shoot her. He *says*. Maybe *she* was trying to shoot *him*—and he's covering up for her. No one, thank God, got hurt." Hoffman said that he had made arrangements for the police officer to receive psychological counseling.

"The man was drunk, apparently, when the argument began," Hoffman elaborated. "He seems to have acquired a drinking problem recently and there are a lot of mitigating circumstances. One of his children is very sick and he's recently been transferred to a high-crime area. He's had a very good record, though, up to now. He's been on the force nine years. He has to be watched, of course, but I think we should go easy on him, now that he's agreed to counseling."

Hannon nodded his agreement and Hoffman left.

Hannon was on the phone again with Louis Cottell. "The PC called from his car. He's on his way to *you* from the airport. He's not coming straight to headquarters. He wants to know why Glover's and Reddy's addresses were given in the Unusual." He listened a moment. "OK. . . . No, I'll call him myself."

On the phone with the executive officer of the Manhattan South area, Hannon went straight to the point, irritated.

"Marty? Why did you let out those addresses? Of Reddy and Glover? Their families could be subjected to all kinds of problems if this information got in the wrong hands." The Unusual Occurrence Report, as ordained, had been distributed to more than a dozen different offices. "You know that," Hannon went on. "It shouldn't happen." (Subsequently on all copies of the three-page report the addresses were carefully inked out.)

Commissioner Codd held a brief news conference at the 13th Precinct, during which he bewailed the proliferation of unlicensed handguns. "It's time Congress stopped holding hearings and passed legislation," he said. He also voiced his anger at the double homicide. "I think the people of New York should be outraged at the wanton killing of two police officers," he said, admitting, "we don't know who we're looking for."

The homicide investigation never far from his thoughts, Hannon pursued his daily routine on Thursday and Friday. He heard frequently from Chief Cottell, sometimes by phone, sometimes in person. The office of the chief of detectives was at the opposite end from Hannon's, down a long corridor. On Friday—the day before Andrew Glover's funeral—Cottell informed Hannon that the owner of the red Plymouth had been traced. He was a suspected drug dealer with contacts on the Lower East Side. He turned out not to have been on the scene the night of the murder. But by now detectives had the identities of the man with the large Afro and the thin one with the beer belly, who had been described by witnesses, and the case was close to being solved. A witness had provided the information that one of the escaping men—the one with the beer belly—was bleeding from the face; it could have been from a bullet or from the shattered glass of the red Plymouth's window.

Increasingly convinced that their best lead would come from the neighborhood of the crime, detectives redoubled their canvassing. They came up with a reluctant witness who finally conceded he'd been parked in his own car on the corner of the street where the red Plymouth was double-parked at the time of the shooting. The witness, who evidently patronized a drug dealer on the block, said he saw a man he knew as Frankie rush by him, seconds after the shooting. Frankie, it seemed, was also a customer of the drug dealer, and, the witness said, *all* of the dealer's customers, men and women, ran when they heard the shooting—not just the shooter and his accomplice or accomplices. Frankie, the witness said, was Hispanic, looked about twenty, was thin, and had a beer belly. The detectives persisted and finally came up with Frankie's last name—Sagarra.

On Friday morning as he prepared to attend Andrew Glover's funeral, Hannon heard the pertinent details of Frank Sagarra's discovery and arrest. Detectives had found Sagarra barricaded in a Manhattan hotel room with his common-law wife and three-year-old son at 2:30 that morning. According to Detective-Lieutenant Yuknes, Sagarra threw away his gun and offered no resistance.

In the First Homicide's squad room, detectives armed with the knowledge that Sagarra's fingerprints had been found inside the red Plymouth, drew from him the admission that he'd been at the scene of the crime. But Sagarra insisted he did not kill the two cops and the detectives were inclined to believe him. Not that he was incapable of such an act. He admitted that he'd recently taken part in a number of armed robberies, in partnership with the owner of the red Plymouth and with the man who *had* shot Glover and Reddy. The shooter, Sagarra told the detectives, was his companion in the car, the man with the Afro, Luis Velez. Sagarra was inside buying dope when the shooting occurred (so he said).

Frank Sagarra was typical of the career criminals who roam the streets of New York and other big cities, the repeat criminals who are often arrested, but who, somehow, never stay in jail very long. His street names were Crazy Horse and Flacco, and his right hand was tattooed with the word *Love*. He was a slight man with a neat haircut, a small mustache, and a fringe of beard.

Sagarra gave the detectives the name of Luis Velez's girl friend and several addresses in the city where Velez might be hiding out. He also told them that Velez was known variously as Blackie and Angelo (for his middle name, Angel; his mother had been hopeful).

According to Sagarra, this was what happened on the night of the killings: Andrew Glover approached the red Plymouth on the pretext of issuing its occupant a summons for double-parking. He asked Velez, alone in the car, for his license and registration. (Velez must have handed Glover the requested papers—which were false—for they were found in Glover's hand, a detail the detectives withheld at the time.) Then "Angelo" Velez opened the car door and shot to kill. With Glover down, Velez stepped out, grabbed the dying cop's gun and put it to his head. Sergeant Reddy, gun drawn, was rushing to Glover's aid when a neighborhood youth on a bicycle swerved in front of him. Reddy took the time to push the boy aside, giving Velez the chance to take a well-aimed shot and bring Reddy down. (That answered the question of how both cops could be killed by one ruthless criminal. No amount of training could have guarded against the sudden appearance of a boy on a bicycle in the line of fire; Reddy's first instinct, like that of every good cop, was to save the life of an innocent.)

By that time Sagarra was back on the street, having made his drug buy, and he and Velez ran to the corner together and then split up. While reserving the right to charge Sagarra as an accomplice in the cop-killings, the detectives booked him on charges connected with one of his confessed armed bank robberies.

Years before it became his *duty* as a police boss to attend the wounded and dying, Hannon would regularly attend his brother officers' funerals. He'd lost count of how many and he was unconscious of any irony in the oft-repeated, almost unvarying ceremony.

Always, it was an inspector's funeral, the honorable way to inter a hero cop. Every cop killed in the line of duty was a hero cop. An inspector's funeral was a symbolic, posthumous promotion to a rank some of them might possibly have achieved, had they lived.

It was 11 A.M. on Saturday, September 20—four days after Glover and Reddy were shot. On the street outside the Convent Avenue Baptist Church in Upper Manhattan stood Mayor Abe Beame, hand over his heart. Beside him, dwarfing him, stood Commissioner Codd, poker-faced, at home amidst the paramilitary pomp. He wore a small, red apple pin in his lapel. Mayor Beame wore his look of all-purpose woe. The mayor and the police commissioner had come to bury Andrew Glover and to praise him.

There were thousands of mourners, there always were, and many of them came from out of town and out of state. Most of them were uniformed police and they lined the streets outside the modest neighborhood church. Military protocol prevailed.

The Top Brass was liberally represented and on dress display and all its members—except, of course, the cocky *detective* Brass—were in uniform. Jim Hannon stood near the commissioner, his pale eyes expressionless behind his spectacles, his jaw tight. He had arrived as always fifteen minutes early, to facilitate the ceremonial lineup of dignitaries (he was one). He looked his best in uniform. The smart, peaked cap lent definition to his features, concealed his thinning hair. The trimly buttoned, dark blue uniform blouse flattened his midriff bulge. His bleached-white cotton gloves reflected the light, making his hands look bigger than life-size.

Standing a little behind the PC and the chief of operations were the two-star and one-star chiefs, among them Deputy Chief Joseph Hoffman, enjoying the newly earned privilege of wearing gold braid on his cap. Assistant Chief Dan Courtenay was there, too, his mind already at work on plans for policing the forthcoming DNC.

Hannon lifted a white-gloved hand in salute as the flag-draped coffin was carried to the small, stone church. Inside the church the mayor, looking even more woeful, read his tribute.

"I can think of no sadder or more difficult duty for me as a mayor," he said, "than to come and pay final respects to an outstanding law enforcement officer who has been the victim of a brutal and senseless act of violence." The mayor had used these words, or very similar ones, before. He would use them again the day after tomorrow when Frederick Reddy was to be buried. He always sounded sincere.

By nightfall on that Saturday, everyone in New York who read a daily newspaper or watched the news on television knew Luis Velez's name and what he looked like. The sketch drawn by a police artist showed a handsome, mean, twenty-six-year-old face. The detectives of the First Homicide zone were inundated with phone calls from people claiming to have seen him. Hannon felt protective of the detectives and he was worried what would happen if they found Velez. As Detective-Lieutenant Yuknes put it, "The guy's a maniac. He's killed two cops; you can't hang a guy twice."

The detectives hunting Velez were under great stress. Many had been working with little or no sleep, and tired men made mistakes, sometimes dangerous mistakes. As a detective-commander, Hannon occasionally had questioned the wisdom of his men in pushing themselves as they did to follow a trail while it was still fresh. It was a macho thing with detectives to go without sleep, and they bragged about it.

"Detectives never get cold. Detectives never get wet. Detectives never get tired." The voice of Detective-Lieutenant John Yuknes was quietly sarcastic.

But men who were fatigued were men whose judgment might falter at a crucial moment. At what point, Hannon wondered, should you stop? When did you reach the point of diminishing returns? When was your life—even as a dedicated cop—*too* much at risk?

Luis Angel Velez had a bomb. That was the word passed to Yuknes by a street informant on the morning that the detectives thought they knew for sure where Velez was hiding. The informant described the bomb—it was a hand grenade, actually—and the bomb squad said it sounded like "a German type, a potato masher" and that it "could cause death or serious injury." Velez was said to carry it tucked into his belt at all times.

Chief of Detectives Louis Cottell strolled down the corridor to Hannon's headquarters offices on the afternoon of Wednesday, September 24. "We're going to try to take Velez in a few hours," he said. He was on his way to the First Homicide squad room to wait. Hannon decided he would stay in his office until he heard, one way or the other, how the action turned out. He would stay even if he had to nap part of the night on his conference table.

"Angelo" Velez's second victim, Sergeant Frederick Reddy, had been buried two days earlier, on Monday. Marie Reddy and her six children watched as the flag-draped coffin was carried into St. Bernard's Roman Catholic Church in Levittown, Long Island. Rows of white gloves touched gold-braided caps as a piper played a dirge. Among the mourners Hannon recognized the brother of Frederick Reddy's partner, Andrew Glover. A police department chaplain, Monsignor James Dunne, asked for a blessing on the souls of Frederick Reddy, Andrew Glover, "and all the men of the Ninth."

In his office after Cottell left, Jim Hannon telephoned Isabel and told her he might not get home at all that night, but she could reach him here at headquarters. Hannon knew as much about the planned capture of Luis Velez as Cottell did, and Cottell knew *almost* as much as John Yuknes, who—with a small, handpicked group of detectives—would actually confront whatever the circumstances of the capture dictated. It was not like planning a parade; snap decisions would have to be made, snap responses to actions that could never be predicted. They thought they knew where a vicious and wily criminal was hiding. They knew he was smart. Ever since Saturday, when Velez's partner and betrayer, Frank Sagarra, had been arrested, the detectives had been raiding apartments all over the city. They'd been acting on information from Sagarra and from others as they went along.

But Velez seemed to have his *own* informants, warning him of impending heat. At each new location the detectives were too late. In one of the apartments they'd found a fake goatee and two wigs—one of them an Afro. But now, thanks to a scrap of paper found in yet another apartment newly vacated by Velez, the detectives thought they finally had Velez cornered. The scrap of paper had a scribbled telephone number, and the detectives, with the help of the telephone company, managed to trace the number to a converted town house on the Lower West Side. They were sure the house now held Velez, but they did not know to which apartment—there were two on the ground floor and two on the top floor—the phone number belonged. The detective Brass suggested mounting a full-scale operation to take Velez—shotguns, battering rams, the block surrounded, emergency service backup, men on roofs. But Detective-Lieutenant Yuknes hesitated; he was seeking an alternative. He was worried about what he called "the Dillinger syndrome"—the cops mounting a "whacked-out, crazy raid," possibly injuring others in the building, causing Velez (who surely would not surrender meekly, like Sagarra) to become a martyr and a folk hero. But not knowing which of the four apartments Velez was in, the police seemed, for the moment, to have no alternative.

While trying to come up with one, Yuknes and two detective-sergeants were conducting close surveillance of the two-story building. There were men across the street in a facing building and men in undercover vehicles circling the area.

When good detectives bent the rules they sometimes got away with it—if they came up with results. Yuknes knew that Chief Cottell would go out on a limb for him if necessary, and he also knew of Hannon's soft spot for detectives. But sometimes even a good detective-commander got flopped for making a bad mistake and John Yuknes was nervous. He finally came up with an alternative plan that he thought would work, and he was not going to tell his superiors about it until it was over. "It was a field decision," he later explained.

He wanted to employ a ruse that would involve no more than a dozen detectives, each with a specific role to play. For the ruse to work, it was essential that Velez notice no sign of police activity from his presumed hiding place within the staked-out building. The detectives' only hope of success—to capture Velez without bloodshed—rested on complete surprise. Yuknes had once shot and killed a suspect in the line of duty; he was the only police commander I'd met who admitted to that. Maybe it made him more careful.

Yuknes's plan was ingenious, but it was filled with risk to the detectives and he asked them to volunteer. They thought for a minute about the bomb Velez was carrying. And then they all volunteered. Yuknes had managed to obtain a sketch of the building's interior, and several of the detectives were given positions to take up inside. The outside men got their instructions, too.

At a little before nine—exactly eight days after the murders of Frederick Reddy and Andrew Glover—Yuknes rang the bell of the adjoining house and asked for the use of a telephone, explaining quietly that it was police business. In his hand he held the telephone number of Velez's presumed apartment hideout next door.

He dialed the number and it was answered. Yuknes had information that Velez's earlier escapes from the detectives who were hunting him had been tipped by a black colleague called Joe. Using what Yuknes later described as a "black voice," the detective-lieutenant muttered into the mouthpiece, "This is Joe. I don't wanna get involved. The cops are on the way." And a voice Yuknes presumed to be Velez's answered, "Thanks a lot." The detectives watching from across the street saw what they later described as "draped movement" from the front apartment on the ground floor—Velez getting ready to run.

Yuknes quickly joined the three detectives in the building's narrow entranceway—it was only four feet wide. They flattened themselves against the wall outside the apartment they'd pinpointed as Velez's. A very tall and wiry detective named Jim Grant was assigned to take Velez. They waited, all of them thinking about the hand grenade, and it seemed like a very long wait. Perhaps Velez was making phone calls in search of a new hiding place; he seemed to have an endless number on tap.

And then the apartment door snapped open and two men hurried out. The first one was Velez, and Jim Grant threw himself on him, while another detective grabbed Velez's companion. Velez had lost his Afro; his head was shaved. He was carrying a blue hand grenade, and in his belt he wore Andrew Glover's .38 Smith & Wesson police special.

Grant wrestled him to the floor and handcuffed him, and then picked up the grenade. All the detectives were frightened of it, fearing it might explode. Later they described to Hannon and the other bosses how Grant tossed the grenade to a fellow detective, who tossed it to another, until it was finally thrown to one of the detectives out in the street, who had the presence of mind to lower it gingerly into a nearby excavation; then someone called the bomb squad to come and pick it up.

Meanwhile, Yuknes and another detective entered the small apartment, which seemed empty—until they heard a scraping noise from under the bed.

"I'll lift the bed and you pop the guy, if you have to," Yuknes said. As he lifted, a puppy ran out into the hallway and licked the supine Velez on the ear. The tension suddenly broke and the detectives indulged in a brief paroxysm of relieved laughter. Soon they were making wisecracks again. They had bent the rules and they had, for once, got lucky.

They escorted Velez safely to the First Homicide offices, where they were greeted as conquering heroes. Chief Cottell telephoned Chief of Operations Hannon. Hugely relieved, Hannon called Commissioner Codd.

On the following morning Commissioner Codd held a small ceremony in his cavernous office. Hannon and Cottell and other headquarters commanders were present, as was the mayor. Lieutenant Yuknes and his detectives were photographed standing next to the commissioner. They were hollow-eyed from celebrating and lack of sleep, but they had shaved and dressed in clean shirts and pressed suits, and their spirits were high.

The ceremony over, Hannon took aside one of the detective-sergeants, Gerald McQueen, of whom he was especially fond—it was McQueen who had caught the grenade in the street and placed it in the excavation. Jerry McQueen headed the Manhattan Homicide Task Force formed when Hannon was the commander of Manhattan detectives, and Hannon knew he was instrumental with Yuknes in the strategic capture of Velez.

"It was a hard night for me," Hannon confided to McQueen. "The only thing that made it bearable was knowing it was harder for you out there, doing the real work."

A few days later, Hannon found on his desk a formal note from the commissioner:

"Dear Chief Hannon: I wish to commend you, and

through you, the members of the Department who were instrumental in the successful apprehension of the suspect and his associates wanted in connection with the deaths of Sergeant Reddy and Police Officer Glover. . . . I would appreciate it if you would extend my thanks to the officers and their commanders for their commendable performance. . . ." He said he would also write "a personal note of thanks" to the detectives, "commending their performance."

Luis Angel Velez confessed to the murders. He said he was afraid of being arrested on bank robbery charges and had shot Glover and Reddy before they could arrest him. He also claimed the two cops had "hassled" him, called him a Spic. In the all-too-familiar phrase of the violent felon, he said, "If I don't get dignity, I take it." He was unrepentant and he sneered at the judge who sentenced him.

Justice Burton B. Roberts called Velez a "lying, despicable, cowardly, brutal, thieving human being" and on November 22, 1976, sentenced him to twenty-five-years-to-life in prison. A month earlier Justice Roberts had publicly said, "If there were ever reason for a person to be electrocuted for a crime, this would be the kind of case." But the constitutionality of New York's limited death penalty statute was in dispute, and DA Robert Morgenthau believed it expedient to accept Velez's plea of two counts of second-degree murder, rather than embarking on a long and costly trial whose end result—a conviction on first-degree murder (not assured) and a death sentence—might very possibly be struck down by the Supreme Court. Recently, the death penalty statutes of Louisiana and North Carolina had been held unconstitutional by the High Court, and New York's statute was similar.

The New York Times, on its editorial page, agreed with Morgenthau, while acknowledging the public anger his decision had provoked. The *Times* pointed out that a "prosecutor's job is . . . to make balanced judgments in the overall public interest." But the Patrolmen's Benevolent Association was angry at the thought of a confessed murderer of two cops not being made to pay with his life. As for the police commanders, many of them believed that if vio lent crime continued to increase, sooner or later the death penalty—at least for cop-murderers—would be reestablished.

Hannon had given much thought to the best means of policing New York, and he felt, with considerable justification, that the legal system was unhelpful. Long before the recidivist theory became popularly accepted, Hannon understood it. "We keep arresting the same people over and over," he said. Like all the thoughtful police commanders, he knew that the best way to control crime was to make sure that the city's hard core of repeat offenders—career criminals like Luis Velez—not be allowed to plea-bargain, and be taken off the streets for life. There was no way that such criminals could be rehabilitated.

EIGHT

★ On a cold Wednesday in January 1978, Joe Hoffman was sworn in as first deputy police commissioner. Clad in a gray business suit, he stepped to the podium in the headquarters auditorium to receive his gold deputy commissioner's shield. He seemed uncharacteristically tense. In a brief, modest speech he said, among other pleasantries, "We will reduce street crime."

He did not say how. Like all sophisticated police officials, he knew it was not a question of more cops in the street, however reassuring that might be to the public. By 1978 it was clear—or should have been—to law enforcement administrators in all large cities that most of the violent crime was committed by a relatively small core of career criminals. Sometimes through careless police work, sometimes through the self-protectiveness of district attorneys, and frequently through the misguided humanitarian instincts of ignorant or incompetent judges, these repeat offenders were often at liberty to strike again and again. Among the most vicious of these offenders were juveniles, and little by little, state after state was beginning to pass legislation permitting patently unredeemable youths to be tried as adults. New York cops had known for years that a twelve-year-old who committed armed assault likely would continue to do so at fourteen and at sixteen, and sooner or later probably would commit murder. Many police officials believed that reform schools had little effect on such youths, were sentimental and useless and actually dangerous to the public.

In March 1980 the New York police department, conceding that the criminal justice system did not deal adequately with habitual, violent criminals, and acknowledging that a nucleus of criminals was responsible for most of the crime, developed the Felony Augmentation Program with the help of the New York City Police Foundation. Investing several million dollars and considerable time, the department attempted to compile a list of career criminals operating in the city, to build solid cases against them, to expedite their trials, and to ensure that they were given substantial penalties. It was an ambitious program, and while it ran into some technical and political stumbling blocks, it did seem to work. In Manhattan, by year's end, 34 out of every 100 arrests of identified career criminals had resulted in sentences to state prisons, as compared with only 7 out of 100 arrests handled in the normal way. The Felony Augmentation Program was expanded city-wide with even better results: in the first three months of 1982, 47 out of every 100 arrests of identified career criminals resulted in sentences to state prisons.

In an article denouncing a proposal for the creation of a national computerized criminal-history system (in *The New York Times*, July 24, 1981) Professor Kenneth C. Laudon of John Jay College pointed out that "prosecutors estimate that well over 90 percent of violent street crime is committed by local criminals who are already known both to cities' and states' computerized systems." There were, he said, "an estimated one million serious career criminals in the United States with multi-state arrests."

And in October 1982, the Rand Corporation released the findings of a six-year study blithely suggesting what everyone already knew, but that seemed impossible to implement: that crime could be substantially reduced by sentencing repeat criminals to long jail terms (and less

active criminals to shorter terms). The study also acknowledged society's change in thinking with regard to rehabilitation; prevention of crime by keeping active felons in
jail had become the primary goal, rather than criminal rehabilitation. The author of the report, Peter W. Green-
wood, said in an interview that his strategy of "selective
incapacitation" could theoretically reduce crime, while permitting an overall decrease in prison populations.

The new police commissioner said he believed in life
imprisonment without parole for career criminals who committed murder. He said he had seen no evidence that the
death penalty was an effective deterrent—except under
"certain limited conditions," as in the case of a murdered
cop or prison guard. Many thoughtful police officials felt
the same way at that time.

All the chieftains sat at respectful attention in straight-
backed, white-gloved rows, caps neatly in their laps. In the
row behind Hannon sat Dan Courtenay, an ironic glint in
his cool blue eyes; and beside him sat Mickey Schwartz, a
look of expectancy on his craggily handsome face. Both
were hopeful that Hoffman's ascendancy would help their
own careers. Surely the new PC and his new first dep
recognized their qualities, saw that they were exactly the
kind of "young tigers" with whom Commissioner McGuire
wished to surround himself.

Courtenay, knowing that Hoffman was the man who
probably would decide his fate within the next few days,
could not resist muttering to Schwartz, "Joe looks older
already." Along with his chest decorations, Courtenay was
wearing his usual breezy front.

As I watched Hannon and Courtenay congratulate Hoffman, the full irony of their situation struck me. The three,
once comrades-in-arms, were no longer marching to the
same drumbeat. Not quite three years earlier I had watched
Hannon sworn in as the NYPD's Top Cop in a more formal
and indeed better attended ceremony. Now Hannon, the
four-star general, still a robust and commanding figure, was

awaiting the coup de grace. Courtenay, the audacious field marshal, hero of the DNC, was again at a career crossroad. And Hoffman, the self-banished maverick, had triumphantly returned to rule the destinies of his former superiors. Here were the makings of—if not quite a Greek tragedy—at least a jaunty melodrama.

As though nothing had changed or was about to change on this morning of January 4, Hannon, after wishing Hoffman well in his new job, returned to his office. He cast a forlorn look about him as he seated himself behind his desk. There were the usual neat stacks of paper awaiting his attention, but he seemed to have lost his energy. I took my accustomed seat at a corner of his conference table, back in my role as Hannon's shadow. I was at a loss myself, concerned about him. What would happen next?

The telephone line that connected the chief of operations directly to the PC, the line that had rung constantly until Mike Codd's departure, was silent. Hannon would have loved to hear it ring, to be summoned to appear "forthwith" for consultation on some major decision, for a policy discussion, a strategy plan. Codd had leaned on him heavily and Hannon had thrived on that. But the phone had not rung at all in the past two days, not since the new commissioner moved in. Hannon tried not to look at it. If it did ring now it probably would mean bad news.

Having hoped to serve until the retirement age of sixty-three, Hannon could not help but suspect that his police career was over. Technically he could not be forced to leave the department. He could, however, be ordered to step down from his job—could, in fact, be broken back to the top Civil Service rank of captain. High-ranking cops frequently made a point of reminding themselves that they were, in effect, captains serving as inspectors or chiefs at the pleasure of the police commissioner. No high-ranking commander, however, would endure the humiliation of being broken. Inevitably, resignation was the graceful way out—sweetened by a substantial pension and often by a second, well-paying career with another government agency, or in the private sector. Like Michael Codd, Hannon would of course resign if asked to by the new PC.

It looked as though he wouldn't make it to his sixtieth birthday as chief of operations; his birthday was less than two weeks off. Hannon would not find it easy to give up either the duties or the perks of his job.

He sighed. "I knew I was on the line when I took this job," he said, trying to convince himself. "I won't be shocked if I'm asked to go. I'll take a long rest and make up for neglecting my family." He lit a cigarette. He still could not quite believe it was all over.

By rote he reached for the papers in his IN and READING boxes and began going through them, reading aloud now and then an item he thought would interest me, stacking others in the OUT box from where I was free to retrieve and read them before Frank Rossi came to collect them—or Hannon, for the exercise, carried them out to Rossi's desk.

When Hannon sent out memos himself, he usually called in one of his clerical men to take dictation. Once, though, he asked that a typewriter be wheeled into his office. "I want to write something I don't want anyone to see," he told me. "I used to be a good typist." The memo was to the commissioner, recommending that Courtenay and Hoffman be promoted, and suggesting that the department might lose either or both of them if their superior work was not recognized soon.

"Can't you afford a clerical man?" Chief of Detectives Cottell asked, stepping unceremoniously through Hannon's wide-open door. "I came in to ask you for some men for a special job," Cottell said, "and please don't ask what I need them for. It will only be for a few days, so just give them to me." Hannon trusted Cottell and acceded to his request. He rolled his memo out of the typewriter and discovered he'd put the carbon paper in backwards. Giving up, he called in Frank Rossi and asked him to make a photocopy (Hannon wanted the copy for his personal file), saying, "Promise not to read it."

"May my mother turn over in her grave if I read it," Rossi replied.

We followed the ritual that Hannon and I had followed for nearly three years—he doing his job, I observing and questioning, he patiently explaining and elaborating. But today the routine was tinged with melancholy, for I was remembering all the other days and felt sure he was too.

Late afternoon on a day in July a couple of months before the two cops were shot: All the area commanders and their execs—summoned by Hannon—were spilling out of elevators on the thirteenth floor, heading for the big conference room. The hallway was thick with Brass in their summer-blue shirts, their stars, their embellished hats hugged against their ribs. Hannon opening the meeting—"OK, gentlemen, we're here to solve an insoluble problem." (How to make fewer cops look like more.)

Hannon at a radio studio for an interview soon after the 5,000 cops were laid off: He sits before the microphone and folds his hands, but his thumbs twitch nervously; he wriggles his foot. He looks dapper in a tan suit, white shirt, pale gold tie. He answers the interviewer's questions without hesitation.

"We have as many cars running on the streets as before. The average response time is twenty-five minutes throughout the city—and a real emergency gets a response of five to ten minutes. My first concern is for the *safety* of our citizens. My second is to provide for their comfort and welfare. My third concern is to see services rendered with the least possible cost." I am impressed with how thoroughly he knows his stuff, how he cannot be intimidated into saying one word more than he wants to say. On our way back to headquarters from the studio, he tells me, "A lot of people across the country seem to be changing their minds about letting New York sink." (Not President Gerald Ford. That October a *Daily News* headline read FORD TO CITY: DROP DEAD. The story said Ford vowed to "veto any bailout" for New York.)

"I just hope," Hannon said, "that we get enough notice to

do what's necessary. If Washington is just playing a political game—if they decide to pull us out *after* the city falls
apart—that's atrocious."

Hannon on the phone to an area commander, worried
about the pickets during a sanitation department strike. (He
wanted to be sure men were put on glass post—a precau-
tionary measure to protect shop windows from being
smashed by vandals and looters.) He explains to me that
usually he works through the chief of patrol, observes the
conventional pecking order; but this is an emergency. "The
bureau heads get pissed off and I understand their problem.
But sometimes there just isn't the time, I have to get the
message across fast to the area people, I can't go through
channels."

An aide comes in with a report on a new type of bulletproof vest: it is light—weighs only five pounds—but has
ten layers and can stop bullets from a .45 as well as a .38. It
is being tested and Hannon says, "Keep me informed."

A delegation from Chinatown visits Hannon to protest
the announced closing of the 5th Precinct in Lower Manhattan: Hannon spends an hour with the delegates,
soothing them, making them laugh. The captain of the precinct—beloved of the neighborhood—will be transferred to
the 7th Precinct, Hannon says, and will continue to protect
them from there. No one who hasn't lived in a big city can
know the significance to its neighborhood of the precinct
house. Particularly in an ethnic neighborhood, the precinct
house creates the illusion of boundaries, of the stability and
security of a village; the precinct commander takes on the
reassuring aura of a benevolent elder, or priest. Hannon
understands that.

On Hannon's desk, a report: At 2240 hours in the 75th
Precinct an eight-year-old girl was raped. In the words of
the report she "was taken in an auto to an unknown location
and raped by an unidentified male in his 20s; complainant
treated and released from Brookdale Hospital. No arrests."
Hannon shakes his head in dismay.

A ceremony at police headquarters to dedicate a memorial plaque in the lobby: Commissioner Codd, First Deputy Commissioner Taylor, Chief of Operations Hannon are all in attendance, misty-eyed. Thirty cops were killed from the time Commissioner Codd entered the department to when he became chief inspector in 1970, he says, and tells me the story of a cop shot down in 1941. "When they took off his gloves, they found a rosary in his hand." All the assembled Brass nod solemnly, loving their quixotic calling.

A discussion about a letter from the first dep's office stating that a detective was suspended from duty and indicted with two others for an illegal wiretap and the extortion of a drug dealer. "The designation Detective is a position of special trust," the letter notes, "requiring a high degree of integrity and professional qualifications." Hannon is directed to review the case. He initials the report, "duly noted."

Chief Behan and Joe Hoffman in with a couple of personnel problems: They must transfer a Puerto Rican cop to a special area, to replace a black cop.

Behan: "This is the first time we've been asked to do it ethnically."

Hannon: "We react to newspaper editorials, you know that."

Behan: "We now have many Spanish-speaking police who are not Spanish."

Hannon: "If a guy has a skill, he should be in the area where he can use it. It gives us a better capability. Years ago we didn't know from the record if a cop was black or white. It's the ethnic groups themselves that insist on their ethnic identity. They don't *want* to be absorbed."

The second problem was a replacement for a captain of the 19th Precinct.

Hoffman: "The 19th is not a hand-to-hand combat place, but it does test the ability to command. There's the diplomatic community, the singles bars. You have to be good."

They discussed the qualifications of Captain McR.

Behan: "Has he overcome being a nice guy? Will he be tough in discipline?"

Hannon: "He's very tough."

Behan: "He was an instructor in the Academy. He did a lot of role-playing, he's a bit of a ham."

Hoffman: "That's OK, especially as a precinct commander." Hannon told me that there were blocks in the city so bad—where rocks were thrown off roofs at the cops— that the department simply did not send anyone into them; they stationed patrol cars at either end instead.

And one day in late November 1975, Chief William Averill—the Manhattan detective commander when Sergeant Reddy and Police Officer Andrew Glover were killed—came into Hannon's office to say good-bye. It was his final day at work, he had reached the mandatory retirement age, and he was almost in tears. When he left Hannon said to me, "How often have you seen this now? It's always sad."

Shortly after the ceremony that made Joe Hoffman the first deputy, Hannon was joined in his office by Courtenay, Schwartz, and several junior commanders.

The business at hand was to draw up plans for the Empress of Iran's visit on January 12. In view of her recent stormy reception in Washington, the Empress's visit was being treated as potentially very dangerous. It would be another year before she accompanied the deposed Shah into exile, and ten months after that when the U.S. Embassy in Tehran would be seized by militant Iranians—among them possibly some of the very same angry students and agents provocateurs who had confronted the police in Washington—and who planned to picket the Empress in New York.

As Manhattan South area commander, Courtenay was in charge of patrolling the demonstration. He placed a cassette on Hannon's color television set—a series of film clips assembled by the Washington police. He had flown down the day before to be briefed by them, and he wanted Hannon to see just how ferocious the demonstration in the capital had been. Courtenay had no choice but to proceed as though Hannon would still be his boss six days hence. Not a word was said about impending change.

Hannon to Courtenay: "I think, Dan, we should have everything in place by next Monday."

Courtenay: "How about Tuesday, Chief? I was going skiing over the weekend and the wife and I were going to take Monday off, too. I worked New Year's Eve weekend." He spoke without conviction. If Hannon decreed Monday, Courtenay would postpone the skiing weekend; Mary would be upset, but commanders' wives learn to live with such disappointments. Hannon knew he did not have to argue with Courtenay. It was his final command decision.

At 4 that afternoon the new first dep walked down the short flight of fire stairs that served as the most direct route between his fourteenth-floor office and that of the chief of operations. He closeted himself with Hannon. Lieutenant Rossi sat tensely at his desk a few feet beyond the closed door. As the minutes lengthened Rossi began to relax; surely such a long talk boded well. At 4:30 First Deputy Commissioner Hoffman emerged, looking noncommittal, loped through the outer office and headed back upstairs. A few seconds later Hannon came and stood at Rossi's desk.

"I'm out, Frank," he said. "Tomorrow is my last day."

Although Hoffman had put it politely, he had, on behalf of the PC, just fired his former boss.

Hoffman told Hannon that he and Commissioner McGuire did not feel Hannon could undertake the quick changes the commissioner had in mind. He had discussed these changes in general terms, and Hannon, a Good Soldier to the very end, had murmured that he understood. Hoffman added that there was no hurry about his leaving; Hannon should do so at his convenience. Hannon told me later that day that he did not take personally Hoffman's notice of dismissal. "We're all professionals," he said. "I've talked it over with Isabel and we've decided there's no point in prolonging it. I think it's best to go quickly."

Dan Courtenay came to say good-bye, as did Mickey Schwartz. "We all have built-in termination dates," Hannon told them, resignedly. "I knew it was coming," he said.

By three the following afternoon most of Hannon's gear was packed into cardboard cartons—two or three framed photos from his walls, his personal papers and desk accessories, a few reference books.

"I travel light," he said.

His three guns, which he had bought himself, as did all members of the force, had been turned in to the property clerk for resale. His prized four-star shield also went to the property clerk (to be held for his replacement), but he kept the gold stars from his uniform as souvenirs. Both Pete Cassi, who had driven him on the night of the Yankee Stadium fracas, and Richie Bauer, who had driven him the night of the double cop-killing, were helping Hannon to pack. Both looked doleful. They knew they would be reassigned, for Hannon's replacement doubtless would want to pick his own drivers.

Bottles, paper cups, and a sack of ice were set out on a bookcase and various members of the headquarters staff drifted in, toasted Hannon farewell, and drifted out. The superchiefs looked solemn. They knew that any minute it might be their turn to be toasted into involuntary retirement. Assistant Chief William J. Devine, a member of Hannon's headquarters staff, arrived to bid his former boss good-bye. Devine, like Courtenay and Hoffman, had been a favorite of Hannon's—regarded by him as smart, levelheaded, decidedly a Team Player.

Headquarters rustled with rumors that Devine was about to be named Hannon's replacement, the inheritor of the four-star shield. If so, he would be jumping a rank. Devine happened to be one of Hoffman's closest friends in the department. He fit Patrick Murphy's description (at least in Hoffman's opinion) of a Good Guy, a "potentially inspirational" leader. As he shook Hannon's hand, Devine was trying not to look like the cat that swallowed the canary.

Hannon telephoned Isabel to tell her he would be on his way home shortly. She reminded him to bring his window plant, and Pete Cassi lifted it tenderly into a carton. By now it was past six and the outer office was deserted. Accompanied by both Cassi and Bauer, Hannon, without a glance behind, left the chief of operations' office and rode the elevator to the subbasement garage. There his official car took him home for the last time.

Every police officer was given a period of several months' grace during which he continued to draw his full salary before his retirement (on pension) became final. The grace period had a harsh name that sounded like a disease—Terminal Leave—and in the case of forced retirement, it could feel as deadly as any illness. Hannon had no specific plans for the future, but he needed time to unwind and—finally—to devote himself to his ailing wife. He and Isabel headed once again for Florida.

A few days later Joe Hoffman told me it had not been easy for him to fire his former boss, and he explained why he and McGuire wanted Hannon and most of the headquarters superchiefs to leave. It was Hoffman's belief that Hannon and some of the others had grown into mirror images of Commissioner Codd. Hoffman had a high regard for Hannon's character and achievement but was impatient with Hannon's absolute conformity to Codd's strict, traditional approach.

"Jim Hannon was very closely supervised by Codd," Hoffman said. "He grew up in a non-risk-taking atmosphere and had operated too long under one kind of system." In other words he was part of the "old guard clique." In effect the ghost of Hoffman's hero, Patrick Murphy, was running the New York police department. (Much later—when he had less reason to be guarded—Hoffman admitted that Hannon had, in fact, been an ideal chief of operations, just as Michael Codd had served under Patrick Murphy as an ideal chief inspector.)

In his vast office on the fourteenth floor Commissioner McGuire looked solemn.

"These past few days have been the saddest in my life," he said, referring to the bureau chiefs (and the civilian deputy commissioners) whose resignations he had requested. "In their gut they all thought, maybe McGuire will see I'm a quiet star. But we have to put our mark on a department this size. The new people's adrenaline is pumping."

He seemed fragile behind his outsize desk and older than his forty-one years, with his balding head and wide-framed, elongated spectacles. His mouth had a downward pull, giving him the semblance of sorrowful contemplation, and there were two sharp, vertical creases between his bushy eyebrows. "Joe Hoffman looks younger than me," he said in a rueful aside. And it was true. Hoffman, ten years McGuire's senior, still appeared boyish and eager. Seated behind the same desk, Mike Codd, with his military bearing, had seemed to fill the space more densely.

McGuire said he planned to serve as commissioner for the next four years of Koch's term—"but I'm also thinking of the next forty years," he added. While protesting he was not a "reform" commissioner, he was clearly planning to leave his imprint on this most visible and largest of American police departments.

"I will bear the responsibility," he said, "but if things work well, the chief of operations should get the public credit. We live in a fallible society. We cannot eliminate crime. But the service we provide can help *reduce* crime." He sounded sincere and hopeful. Nonetheless, crime continued to rise (nationwide, as well as in New York) during the next four years. His "basic team," he promised, would be in place within the next two weeks. "We'll make mistakes, of course," he added wanly.

Three of the superchiefs were asked to leave, but John Guido, the chief of inspectional services—the bureau that policed the police—was asked to stay on. At fifty-three, he was one of the oldest of McGuire's young tigers.

"I'm keeping him because he's not Codd's or anyone else's man," McGuire told me. "He is totally loyal to the commissioner's office, and I don't want any message being heard that IAD is in any kind of trouble."

The Internal Affairs Division, under Guido, utilized a select group of police officers called "field associates," who turned in corrupt or delinquent cops. His philosophy was simple and direct: to create a sense that any cop's partner might be a field associate.

And the chief of the Patrol Bureau, Henry Morse, was moved laterally into the chief of personnel's slot—a difficult job that Courtenay did not want. (Courtenay enjoyed setting targets for achievement, planning strategy, carrying through a mission, evaluating the accomplishment. The personnel job, while vital, was an endless administrative shuffle, a question of responding to manpower evaluation and allocation without the concrete goals by which Courtenay liked to measure himself.) McGuire was relying heavily on Joe Hoffman's advice and guidance. Cronyism—supposedly eliminated with the appointment of McGuire, the Outsider—was in full operation with McGuire's appointment of Hoffman, the Insider, upon whom McGuire *had* to rely.

Mayor Koch, in a news conference on January 6, declared once again that he would not interfere with his police commissioner's appointments. He said he did not know about Joe Hoffman until McGuire informed him the choice was made.

Predictably, Hoffman was leaning toward the brainy headquarters types, the planners and policy makers, the Generals who had sat with him at the knee of Patrick Murphy, the intellectual cop. It was Hoffman's cronies who advanced.

On Monday, January 9, William Devine was sworn in as chief of operations. McGuire pinned the four-star shield to Devine's uniform, symbolically centered over his heart. He was young for the job, only forty-eight. Jim Hannon had been fifty-seven when he became the city's police chief. "I told Chief Devine he could go out to lunch and take the rest of the day off—as long as he got back at 2 P.M.," Hoffman said jovially, tasting his new power.

Commissioner McGuire was growing daily more confident (he was receiving the benefit of Hoffman's expertise), and he enjoyed fencing with the press. After pinning the four-star shield on Devine, he announced he would soon name a female deputy commissioner.

"Can you tell us her name?" a reporter asked.

McGuire: "No, not at this time."

Reporter: "Why not?"

McGuire: "Because I don't feel like it."

Reporter: "What will her duties be?"

McGuire *(with a straight face):* "Her duties will be those of the job for which she is designated." He got a big laugh.

A few days later he appointed a television reporter, Ellen Fleysher, to the job of deputy commissioner for public information, vacated by Frank McLoughlin. Some observers felt the position had been downgraded, but Courtenay (and Schwartz, too, who dated Fleysher for a while) regarded her as capable and supportive; the job had never been clearly defined, because the police department's attitude toward the press tended to swing between hostility and ambivalence.

As I congratulated Devine after the ceremony he made a reference to the time I'd first met him, as one of the regulars at Hannon's Tuesday morning briefings, when he'd been "the Boss of SSB." But I'd forgotten for the moment what that stood for; there were so many abbreviations and acronyms and they kept changing. Devine looked a little hurt. "Support Services Bureau," he reminded me and added with a grin meant to be disarming, "the oyster that the pearl came from."

Dan Courtenay was, of course, among those who shook Devine's hand. Having crossed off chief of operations, he could still hope for one of the three as yet unfilled super-chiefdoms—patrol, organized crime control, or best of all, detectives. Even Joe Hoffman privately would rather have held the chief of detectives job than any other except the commissionership itself.

"It's the best uniformed job in the department without question," he once said. "You introduce someone to the chief of patrol, you have to explain what that means; it sounds like any low-level security job. You introduce the chief of organized crime control, you have to explain he's not a Mafia boss—although both, like chief of detectives, are three-star ranks.

"Even the four-star chief of operations sounds flat. As for the first deputy commissioner, outside the department no one knows what it means. But *chief of detectives of the New York police department!* Everyone wants to meet him!"

But there were rumors that James Sullivan, who was now, like Courtenay, an area commander—of Brooklyn South—would be named chief of detectives. Courtenay was reluctant to credit those rumors. Hannon felt sure that Courtenay would be named chief of patrol and had told him so the day he left. Courtenay, undaunted, went about his work with his habitual bounce.

I knew Jim Sullivan from his headquarters days when he was the assistant chief of detectives. Two and a half years younger than Courtenay, the son of a retired New York cop, he had joined the police in 1953. A determined student, he took and passed the three Civil Service exams in rapid succession and made captain within the remarkably short span of ten years. It had taken Courtenay and Schwartz eighteen years, Hannon and Hoffman seventeen. Sullivan completed his college education at John Jay and took his master's degree in public administration at C. W. Post. Like most of the Brass, he lived in Queens. He and his wife, Lois, had six children and were, in his words, "basically homebodies."

Dark-haired, trim, and actorly-handsome, Sullivan looked as un-coplike as Joe Hoffman, but he was all cop. He had preceded Dan Courtenay as commanding officer of the Tactical Patrol force in 1969 where, he said, "I took pleasure in getting some order out of chaos." He had felt, immediately on joining the department, that many of his bosses were "unimpressive." "I thought I could do better." Doubtless he did as commanding officer of the Police Academy in 1973. He was a quiet man and he often spent his lunch hour jogging.

Along with Joe Hoffman and Bill Devine, Sullivan frequently attended Chief Hannon's Tuesday morning cabinet meetings. And he had been Louis Cottell's exec at the time of the double cop-killing. Like Courtenay, he had expected to be named chief of detectives a couple of years earlier, when Cottell retired. I asked him if the rumor I'd been hearing was true, and he said that he'd had several talks with McGuire and while he had not been told definitely yes (and please keep it to myself for now), he did think the job would be his. Even without Sullivan's caution I would not have had the heart to repeat that to Courtenay.

On Tuesday, January 10, Courtenay summoned to his area command headquarters all the supervisors of sectors and special units assigned to what the intelligence division had whimsically christened Operation Bluebird.

Having lived day by day with the complex DNC operation, I guessed that Operation Bluebird would be an anticlimax—just another showy display of expert crowd control—and from the public viewpoint that's what it turned out to be. But I was curious to see if Courtenay's style had changed with his new status as area commander. Also, more significantly, he was now under a different sort of psychological pressure: his future was in balance, with a brand-new and relatively inexperienced chief of operations supervising and a new commissioner observing. But Courtenay seemed as self-assured as usual.

He briefed his commanders in the muster room of the 13th Precinct station house. On the following Thursday, January 12, the Empress of Iran would travel from the Waldorf-Astoria on Park Avenue at 50th Street, where she was staying, to a banquet at the Hilton on the Avenue of the Americas (no native New Yorker ever called it anything but Sixth Avenue) between 54th and 55th Streets—a distance of six blocks. Then Courtenay showed the film of the

Washington demonstration that he'd run a few days earlier for Jim Hannon.

"We're not letting the troops see this film," he said. "We don't want to spook them."

Once again the police were gearing up for a disaster—in order to forestall it. Once again they were counting on the fact that the mere sight of their stringent security measures, the impact of a vast physical presence, would be a deterrent to violence. It was always easy for police watchers to say— after the fact—that the department had wasted time and money and manpower. But no one knew what might have erupted had there not been that display of controlled threat, that sense of invincibility for which New York's cops were famous.

At the film's conclusion, Courtenay stepped to a large diagram illustrating the site of the two hotels where the Empress would sleep and dine, her route between the two, and where and how the police troops would be deployed.

"The Shahbanu, as she is called, is coming in tomorrow morning," Courtenay said, pleased with himself for knowing Empress Farah's Iranian title; it was the sort of detail he liked to take the trouble to acquire. "Every sector will be supplied with enough wheels to keep moving. The hotel is going to be covered from the time she hits. Sector 4 is going to be the buffer. The major problem we have is to keep the pro's and anti's separate."

With a sudden loud creak the folding doors at the back of the lecture room flew open and the new chief of operations stood revealed.

"Tenshun!" Courtenay barked and, to a man, the occupants of the room sprang to their feet. For a paramilitary group (many were in civilian clothes) it was a pretty smart display of discipline. Formal gestures of respect to superior officers were no longer routine. The Rank and File of the NYPD were now aggressively unionized and, like other sectors of society, had been strongly affected by the civil-libertarian movement of the 60s. The Brass had become increasingly resigned to the blurring of disciplinary edges.

One day I was standing outside a precinct house in Harlem with Chief Hannon—in uniform—when he was accosted by a patrolman, who proceeded to give Hannon a list of surly complaints about his job; Hannon listened impassively, then shrugged and walked away. But the men Courtenay had assembled were mostly captains or above.

Chief Devine, only one day in his new job, looked startled for a split second—as though he had rubbed a magic lamp and the genie had appeared. He recovered, smiled modestly, and made his way to the front of the room. Devine had a friendly teddy-bear face and sleepy-looking eyes, but he was straight of spine and he moved briskly. He had been in the department since he was twenty-three, had two brothers who were cops, and was—like the new PC—the son of a retired policeman.

"This is a new suit I got at Barney's," he said, getting a laugh. The only time I'd seen him in uniform (aside from his swearing in) was during the days of the Police Mutiny, when all the headquarters Brass was ordered out into the streets to patrol their unruly rank and file.

Then, glancing at the roster of ranking officers handed him by Courtenay's sergeant, Tom Callahan, Devine spotted a familiar name, glanced up to find the matching body, and said, "Hi, Paddy, Happy New Year." He went down the list, mentioning each name, pausing at those he recognized. To one he said, "My dad says to say hello—I think you were his boss years ago—he's still *my* boss." The sally was greeted with warm laughter.

"My future is in your hands," Devine concluded earnestly. "We think there might be trouble here. The police in D.C. seemed to be under some kind of anesthetic. It's important for this woman not to be injured. But please don't start any trouble. It's not our job to kill anyone. Good luck—and please give me a hand." Devine was being the "inspirational leader," the man who would set the Patrick Murphy–inspired tone for "younger, more idealistic, more potentially productive officers in the ranks below."

Chief Devine wanted Courtenay to drive him over the

route the Shahbanu would take from the Waldorf to the Hilton and Courtenay turned the briefing over to Mickey Schwartz, who picked up smoothly where Courtenay had left off. He said that the uniform on Thursday night would be hats and bats; that there would be 2,000 men out— double the number used during the DNC—and that the operation would be monitored, as were most, by members of the Civilian Complaint Review Board and the American Civil Liberties Union. "This is good," he said, and stressed that while he did not want cops to be abused, neither did he want *them* to abuse the demonstrators. "Impress on your men that they have no license to kill," he added.

Concluding the briefing, Schwartz summed up some of the defensive measures the police should take: check anyone seen carrying a length of rolled cardboard—an iron pipe could be concealed within; the troops were being given a quick course in how to combat shield-bearing demonstrators—a technique called "the sweep"—nightstick to the knees, below their hand-held shields. Later, in his office, he said that, in contrast to Courtenay, "I react, more than act ahead. You can't plan that far ahead for everything."

As always, when there was a threat of unruly crowds, someone said, "Pray for rain." Rain was the best cop of all. The next day, Wednesday, Courtenay told me I could not, after all, accompany him during Thursday's street action. Chief of Operations Devine had been upset to see me at Tuesday's briefing, he said. Astonished, I telephoned First Deputy Commissioner Hoffman and asked him how come the new, innovative leadership of the department was being more restrictive than the deposed, rigid leadership. Hoffman laughed uncomfortably and said he'd get back to me. Within half an hour, Devine called to say it was simply a question of his not having been informed of my planned presence, and that yes, it was all right for me to accompany Courtenay.

At 11:30 on Tuesday General Courtenay walked the projected battleground. Wooden barriers were in place; the field headquarters—two long police buses packed with electronic equipment—were parked, one outside the Waldorf, one outside the Hilton.

The weather was below freezing and most of the cops in the street, including the Brass, were wearing layers of sweaters and long johns. Not so Big Dan Courtenay.

"I'm not wearing a sweater," he bragged. "I think about skiing and that keeps me warm." He was chewing gum for exercise.

Striding past the Hilton, accompanied by a lieutenant acting as gunbearer, Courtenay gave instructions to a mounted commander about keeping the Empress's path clear. His eyes ran along doorways, up to rooftops, into alleyways, checking for signs of menace—like a housewife expecting company, checking her home for signs of disorder or dust. At the Waldorf garage, where the PBA had parked a van to dispense coffee and sandwiches to its chilled troops, we ran into ex-Chief of Patrol Tom Mitchelson, who was now working as chief of security for the hotel. He looked rested and healthy.

Courtenay greeted a lieutenant he knew. "I understand," the lieutenant said, "that everyone is instructed to take home an Iranian tonight." Courtenay chortled. The lieutenant was harking back to a joke from the days of the DNC, when someone decided the best way to clean up Times Square was for every cop to "take home a pross."

Courtenay arrived at Headquarters Truck No. 2 and stowed his crash helmet, which he had been carrying in a bag like a bowling ball. Mickey Schwartz's helmet was already there, but Schwartz was out on the street looking for trouble.

Schwartz entered the truck, having found some: a heavy cardboard tube, picked up by one of the cops in the street. Schwartz broke it in half—proving it did not contain an iron pipe. Even so, it was a mean weapon and Schwartz went out to alert his troops to be on the lookout for other tubes.

Sergeant Callahan to Courtenay: "Boss, there's a report

of a planeload of Iranians on their way to Kennedy, with tear gas containers."

Courtenay: "How did they get the tear gas aboard?"

No one knew. But the tear gas was anticipated and cans of water in which to douse the canisters were ready. The water had even been treated with ethyl chloride, to prevent it from freezing. But as it turned out, there were no tear gas canisters on the plane.

Someone brought in a copy of the *New York Post* with a story that purported to list "top secret" police promotions to the coveted headquarters bureaus. Courtenay read the story over someone's shoulder, face impassive: James Sullivan to become chief of detectives; an assistant chief named Joseph F. Veyvoda—like Courtenay an area commander (of Queens) to be chief of organized crime control. Courtenay's expression did not alter even when he saw listed the name of Assistant Chief James B. Meehan, the commander of intelligence during the DNC and more recently the area commander of Staten Island. Meehan, according to the *Post*, was the new chief of patrol, the job that Hannon had been certain Courtenay would get.

Chief Meehan was the same age and rank as Courtenay but had achieved his second star only last summer. He was regarded as one of the department's intellectuals—like Joe Hoffman and William Devine—an egghead more than a street cop. The message from headquarters seemed to be that Courtenay was regarded as strictly a field supervisor, an unreconstructed street cop, not wanted for a headquarters bureau chieftaincy. He'd held his two-star rank for three years, and it had not been pleasant watching newer two-star chiefs sail past him. Had he been too outspoken, too self-assertive in his expectation of promotion? Whether the department was being run by a traditionalist like Codd or by an outsider of still undetermined policy like McGuire (as guided by Hoffman), it seemed that headquarters bridled when a commander got too cocky. The contradictory signals, again. Be aggressive, use initiative, take responsibility, play by the rules. (Whose rules? That depended on who the PC was, which depended on who the mayor was.) But also be a mouse, don't seek promotion, don't blow your own horn, wait for your betters to notice you—in other words, stick your neck out but cover your ass. Courtenay may have sensed that he was being punished.

He was aware that the colleagues who crowded around him in the constricted quarters of the headquarters truck were watching to see how he would take the news of the promotions. He made no comment. For once he seemed to have run out of wisecracks. As yet, none of the appointments was official. Still, he was not having an easy time of it.

By 6 P.M. it was dark and very cold, and the Empress would be leaving the Waldorf shortly to attend the dinner at the Hilton. Courtenay slipped on his helmet, buckled the chin strap, tucked his baton smartly under his arm. He pulled on the wool-lined, gray leather gloves that were NYPD winter issue and strode out into the night. Behind the barriers on Sixth Avenue the two sets of demonstrators, separated by helmeted police, their masked faces grotesquely lit by police floodlights, shouted and shook their fists and circled their sidewalk space. They looked more dispirited than militant. The Empress would be whisked into a side entrance of the hotel, and all seemed as secure as human effort could make it.

Back in the truck Mickey Schwartz told Courtenay his own good news. Chief of Operations Devine had just informed him he would be promoted to two-star chief and be given the command of Brooklyn South vacated by James Sullivan (and seeming to confirm Sullivan's appointment as chief of detectives). Courtenay had lost an exec and gained a rival; Schwartz was now of equal rank with him. In view of the afternoon newspaper leak the PC apparently had decided to make an official announcement. Someone in the headquarters bus copied the list onto a paper napkin and it was handed around.

The names of the new bureau chiefs were the same as

reported in the newspaper, and in addition to Mickey Schwartz, three others were advanced to assistant chief. One of them was Patrick S. Fitzsimons, who entered the truck looking quietly pleased. Fitzsimons, borrowed for the evening by Courtenay from his job as exec in Brooklyn South, was forty-seven. He had become at forty-two one of the youngest chiefs ever made by the NYPD and had been in the department just under twenty years. In 1975 he had followed Jim Sullivan as commanding officer of the Police Academy. Courtenay congratulated Schwartz and Fitzsimons warmly, then warned them not to start bucking for his Manhattan command.

Passed over for promotion to the top jobs, watching younger men come up to his own rank, Courtenay was hanging on to the consolation that his current area command was after all one of the best in the department, if he were allowed to keep it. Not a flicker of disappointment showed. His self-possession was superb, an admirable display of grace under pressure.

At 8 P.M. the brand-new chief of operations popped into field headquarters, beaming. Courtenay briefed him: everything was under control. Devine's visit was ceremonial, and he did not stay long. It was as though Jim Hannon had never existed. Courtenay had no thought for him right now; sentimentality was not an affordable emotion for Generals, and Hannon, in Courtenay's place, would be the same.

Courtenay monitored the television screen that was focused on the demonstrators. "Tell them to belly up to the barriers," he ordered Sergeant Callahan. "Tighten up the police line, it's too loose. If they think we're depleted, they'll get rambunctious. If we lose it now, we'll feel like jackasses."

Like all major street events, Operation Bluebird was a media happening, and now the TV crew came to interview Courtenay: reporter, man with floodlight, and Quasimodo, bent under the hump of his camera. Courtenay stood on the sidewalk, framed against the truck, patiently explaining why so much manpower was necessary when everything seemed so quiet.

Back in the mobile headquarters, he instructed: "We want to put up a wall of blue when she comes out of the hotel—someone got too close to her when she went in."

An inspector from intelligence told Courtenay he was leaving for the night. "Drop around again when you have more time," Courtenay said.

Someone reported that an angry demonstrator had bitten a cop. "Poor guy was hungry," Courtenay said.

A sergeant asked Courtenay what to do with a pile of sticks that had been confiscated from the demonstrators. "We got enough to build a house with?" Courtenay asked. "Just don't give it back to those guys."

10:30 P.M.: "Bluebird is on her way out," came the word from inside the Hilton. The departure itself went without a hitch, although several arrests were made of provocateurs who had, somehow, slipped by the police and Secret Service. Soon after, Courtenay could report to Chief Devine, who was waiting at headquarters, "She's back in the Waldorf. We're sending barriers over there. We have thirteen or fourteen prisoners."

At midnight the operation was over. Considering what might have happened, it had been a splendid success. Whereas the Empress's Washington appearance had created a shambles that the police could not contain and had embarrassed President Jimmy Carter, her New York visit had been controlled with silken emphasis and had reflected glory on the new mayor.

In the headquarters truck Schwartz, his eyes red-rimmed, was yawning. Courtenay probably yearned to be home in his Queens lair, unobserved, where he could lick his wounds. But whatever he was feeling, he looked as crisp and indomitable as when he had begun his day fifteen hours earlier.

NINE

★ "I consider the area commanders as important as the superchiefs," Commissioner McGuire told me at headquarters a few days later when I wondered why he had not given Dan Courtenay a bureau chieftaincy. (Joe Hoffman much later implied that Courtenay was made to wait for promotion to teach him humility. "He was in penance," Hoffman said. "He was perceived as a Codd man, in spite of his protestations.") The attitude McGuire wanted in all of his commanders, he said, changing the subject, was a broad overview of police work and the recognition that all the systems of work were ultimately in support of the street cop.

In *Open Door*, the police bulletin that McGuire continued for a while, but later dropped to save costs, he adopted a reassuring, avuncular tone, not much different from Michael Codd's. Having condoned the presence of neurotics, it behooved him to help them function effectively and he addressed the problem thus:

> One of my major concerns in running the Department continues to be the physical and emotional well-being of members of the Department. All the mechanical and technical resources available to us mean little if our prime resource, manpower, is not healthy and up to par. Tough decisions on the street are diffi-

cult enough to make even when you're at your best.
Given the nature of the job, serious consequences can
result when you are not at a top level of efficiency, and
stress can affect efficiency. I think it's important for
you to know that stress and its symptoms are treatable.

He went on to offer his troops confidential and non-
stigmatizing counseling through his newly appointed police
surgeon—an ex-cop turned psychiatrist—whom McGuire
described as "family." But like a lovable uncle who does not
intend to be taken advantage of, he also put his blue-suited
nephews and nieces on notice:

> SICK LEAVE ABUSE—There seems to be a hell of a lot
> of rumors around claiming that the Department in-
> tends to change or even do away with the unlimited
> sick leave policy currently in operation. Nothing could
> be further from the truth. Everything we are doing is
> designed to insure the continuation of unlimited sick
> leave by reducing the flagrant abuse of that policy by a
> very small number of individuals who are hurting
> everybody else. . . .
>
> The vast majority of members of the service are not
> sick leave abusers. The vast majority are decent, hard-
> working people. I guarantee you that no legitimate
> member will wind up being treated unfairly because I
> will personally review any questionable case and make
> the final decision. There should be little sympathy for
> the abuser of our sick leave policy, especially when
> you consider the fact that you are the ones who ul-
> timately have to pick up the slack.

He ended the bulletin on a chatty note meant to dispel
rumors that he intended to hold the job of commissioner
only briefly:

> Let me just say that I love being Police Commis-
> sioner and I love the Department. I did not take this
> job as a stepping stone to public office or anything else.
> In fact I don't know of any other job in or out of public
> life that compares with being Police Commissioner of

the finest Police Department in the world. So for better or worse, I intend to be with you for as long as the Mayor will have me.

McGuire was in his office with Hoffman. A blizzard was blowing and the police were having their hands full.

"We're trying to reverse a trend," McGuire said. "We want the area commanders and the precinct captains to take more responsibility. We have to let them see they're not going to get hurt if they make their own decisions." (Back to the Patrick V. Murphy days.)

By way of example, he and Hoffman were insisting that the decision all over town of whether to "hold the last platoon" on overtime for snow emergency service be made at the source.

"Only the commanders on the scene can tell if the men are needed," Hoffman said. "It's ridiculous for them to ask headquarters to decide."

Jim Hannon returned from Florida after six weeks, in time to attend the Emerald Society dance in Brooklyn on February 24, one of the highlights of police social life. Isabel was well enough to accompany him. They had bought a house in Florida and were looking forward with the enthusiasm of newlyweds to moving south permanently in May, after selling their house in Queens. Hannon's pension would come to about $32,000, and he had no plans to take a job, at least for the time being. Hannon chatted amiably with Bill Devine, who had replaced him, and with Joe Hoffman, who had fired him. Hannon also chatted with Courtenay, admitting his surprise that Courtenay had not been promoted. "I knew Sullivan and Devine would have to surface," he later told me. "They're both very good men." And he chatted with the PC whom he scarcely knew. They all came with their wives. McGuire and his wife, Joan, had been married only three years.

Hannon looked relaxed. He was greatly relieved to be rid of his gun. "That was always a terrible responsibility," he said, "having to safeguard it at home from children, protect it from theft."

"I hope I never see a gun again," Isabel echoed fervently. On balance Hannon found himself not unhappy to be off The Job. "But I suppose I'll be forever part cop," he said. "It stays in your bloodstream."

In the perception of the public, the New York Police Department under Robert McGuire did not look very different from the NYPD under Michael Codd. (It shrank some more and was down to 22,286 by the beginning of 1981.) In the perception of his boss, Mayor Ed Koch, McGuire was aces. "I used to say he was the best police commissioner since Teddy Roosevelt," Koch told *The New York Times* in the summer of 1980, "but then I found out Teddy Roosevelt was not such a good commissioner. So now I say he's the best police commissioner New York City has ever had."

McGuire took early and firm command of the department. He began by weeding out the misfits. As he had promised, he went after those who chronically abused their sick-leave privileges. And he was particularly severe— much more so than Codd had been—with coopers, imposing stiff fines for sleeping on the job. "I am a disciplinarian," McGuire said. "If someone was cooping at General Motors, they would have been fired." Indeed by the end of 1978 the department had arrested, suspended from duty, or placed on modified assignment 173 police officers—as compared with 139 the previous year. Mayor Koch called McGuire "an intelligent guy who has a soul and a heart but is no softie."

Somewhat alarming was the fact that complaints of wrongdoing against the police rose in 1978 by 22 percent over the previous year. But in 1979 they were down 7 percent—to 2,505, or 107 for every 1,000 members of the force. The charges, among others, involved bribe-taking and narcotics use and sale. Chief of Inspectional Services John Guido commented, "While the 7 percent reduction is encouraging, the substantial number of complaints received clearly indicates a need for us to continue to monitor this hazard." Many of the charges were, as always, unsubstantiated, and that year a total of 35 police officers and detectives were arrested, 96 were suspended, and 22 were placed on modified assignment for a variety of misdeeds.

Among the misdeeds that Guido and his fellow commanders were always on guard against was brutality. There were various kinds of brutal cops, some of them psychotic, and there always were other cops who misguidedly protected them, even lied for them under oath.

"We have a hard core of cops who are too prone to use physical force wrongly and we're trying to correct the situation," First Deputy Commissioner Hoffman said. He could have been thinking of the recent case of Thomas Ryan— one of the most shocking occurrences in the history of the department. The Ryan case, which taught the Brass to be always alert to a brutality cover-up, began in 1975, was still being studied three years later, and did not actually end until 1981.

Here was a case of Bad Guys against Bad Guys, the ultimate example of cops who were as mindlessly vicious as the criminal brutes they were sworn to lock up. Here, also, was a cautionary example of a commander who looked the other way.

From the report of Captain Ralph A. Riccelli, executive officer of the 44th Precinct in the Bronx, dated June 14, 1975, to Thomas D. Mitchelson, the three-star chief of patrol, at headquarters:

"At approximately 2315 hours on Friday, June 13, Police Officer Thomas F. Ryan, Shield #1163, 44th Precinct, while investigating a possible burglary at 1030 Nelson Ave., Apt. 2I, and standing outside the apartment door, a shot was fired through the door by perpetrator inside, missing Police Officer Ryan and one Luis Santiago, whom he had in custody. The perpetrator inside, Israel Rodriguez, was arrested, complained of pain while at the 44th Precinct, was removed to Morrisania Hospital, where he expired at approximately 0345 hours, June 14. No shots fired by Police Officers."

Captain Riccelli's report went on to detail the investigation he undertook after the prisoner Rodriguez's death. It was an involved account, describing the presence at the scene where the arrest took place of several teams of police officers in response to a 10–13 signal after the shot was fired through the door. The account also described the discovery of stolen cash, of guns and of drugs and drug paraphernalia. There was no question that Rodriguez was a Bad Guy and that Ryan's prisoner, Santiago, who had led Ryan to Rodriguez's apartment door—presumably to earn leniency in his own case—was a Bad Guy, too.

"Police Officer Ryan had to use necessary force to subdue and handcuff his prisoner," wrote Captain Riccelli. Other police officers searched the apartment, but the only other occupants were Rodriguez's wife, Maria Ramos, "Female/23, who was pregnant, and their 4-year-old daughter." After the search of the apartment, Riccelli reported, Ryan and several other police officers brought Rodriguez, Santiago, and two associates of Santiago who had been arrested in the street, to the 44th Precinct "for processing." At five minutes before 1 A.M. on June 14, Riccelli elaborated, "Rodriguez complained of pain" from injuries "which he alleges were sustained during his resisting arrest and requested medical treatment. Officer Ryan requested an ambulance."

Riccelli wrote that Luis Santiago and his associates were charged with criminal possession of dangerous weapons and that Santiago, too, was taken to Morrisania Hospital, after a police officer "observed some bleeding from Santiago's mouth."

The captain then went on to give details of the testimony of various witnesses, mostly cops, whom he interviewed at the precinct house and the hospital. The gist of their testimony was that no one saw Thomas Ryan use "unnecessary force" on Rodriguez at any time, or saw anything but superficial evidence of Rodriguez's having been injured. Several witnesses, however, "observed some bleeding from Santiago's mouth" while he was handcuffed to a bannister. Santiago, the report said, had been handcuffed by Officer Ryan to a bannister in the hallway outside Rodriguez's apartment after the shot was fired through the apartment door by Rodriguez. Several police witnesses told Riccelli they saw the bleeding from Santiago's mouth at the station house as well, and one police officer admitted he had observed "some slight abrasions on Rodriguez's face."

Police Officer Ryan was among those interviewed by Captain Riccelli, but he provided himself with an attorney from the Patrolmen's Benevolent Association, who advised him not to make a statement. The attorney, Riccelli wrote, "stated that the reason he advised P.O. Ryan to remain silent is the cause of death of Rodriguez has not been determined, and pending an autopsy it may have no bearing as to the officer."

Riccelli further noted that an assistant DA from the Bronx Homicide Bureau examined the facts of the case and said he would present them to the grand jury on Thursday, June 19. He noted, as well, that the cause of the prisoner's death was "to be determined by the Medical Examiner at the time of autopsy."

Captain Riccelli interviewed Maria Ramos, the pregnant wife of Rodriguez, through an interpreter (a Spanish-speaking cop). He reported that "she saw the police hit her husband while he was fighting them on the floor" of the apartment after the shot, and "at the hospital her husband told her that the police hit him."

A routine preliminary investigation by the district attorney's office revealed that Rodriguez's death had resulted from a beating and that Santiago, too, had been subjected to violent physical abuse (at the hospital he was found to have a compound fracture of the jaw).

Rodriguez's wife was sure that the cops had killed her husband. She testified later that she had heard him begging, "Don't hit me no more, don't hit me no more, please." She said she had seen one or more cops punch, kick, and blackjack her husband into insensibility and that there had been blood all over the stove of the room where the beating took place.

The case was no longer routine and the Bronx district attorney, Mario Merola, took the unusual step of requesting the help of the police department's IAD (Internal Affairs

Division). Most cases of reported police brutality were investigated by the Civilian Complaint Review Board and the chief of patrol's office, and resulted in a departmental trial. But since the medical examiner's report indicated the strong possibility of prolonged physical abuse as the cause of a prisoner's death, and the official report *disclaimed* all use of needless force, it appeared that police witnesses were lying to the grand jury and the IAD seemed called for. No one else had the investigative tools, the ability to uncover an internal cover-up. It had been only a few years since the Knapp Commission investigation, only a few years since Commissioner Murphy had put in place the machinery for persuading cops to speak out against the wrongdoing of their fellow cops.

The IAD, commanded by then-Assistant Chief Guido, took over the investigation on July 21, five weeks after Israel Rodriguez's death. Guido, fifty at the time, had been with the department nearly twenty-nine years. He was a tough, pragmatic cop who had spent most of his career, since becoming a captain, doing internal investigations for the police commissioner. "I've always worked in this area," he said, "the misconduct, corruption-type of thing." Guido was what a friend of mine, a former top-notch police affairs reporter, called "a dese-dem-dose kind of cop, tough-talking, gruff, but smart as hell." He was given command of the Internal Affairs Division by Commissioner Patrick Murphy in 1972.

Ultimately, Chief Guido's investigation revealed misleading information in the original report by Captain Riccelli (who was allowed to retire with his pension less than a year and a half later).

The most comprehensive account of the Thomas Ryan case was prepared several years later by Guido's successor as commanding officer of IAD; by then Guido had been promoted to three-star rank as chief of inspectional services, the bureau under which IAD functioned. Guido's successor, Assistant Chief Robert F. Frawley, prepared the report in an attempt to sum up for his boss what really happened. Its subject was: *Allegation That the Death of Israel*

Rodriguez and the Injury to Luis Santiago Were Caused by Members of This Department.

Unlike most departmental reports, which tended to be written in tortured Copspeak, this one was a model of clarity and vivid detail. Frawley described what actually happened both outside and inside Apartment 2I after Officer Thomas Ryan arrived on the scene and began questioning Luis Santiago. When Santiago led Ryan to the apartment, a shot was indeed fired from within by Rodriguez, a marijuana dealer. Ryan handcuffed Santiago to a nearby bannister and called for assistance from the hall window, and when other police arrived and pounded on the door, "it then opened from the inside and Rodriguez stood there with his empty hands in front of him."

"Ryan rushed into the apartment and tackled Rodriguez," the report said. "Officers [Edwin] Young and [Richard] Duggan went past Ryan to search for accomplices . . . and saw Ryan striking Rodriguez as the two were on the floor. Duggan and Young found Maria Rodriguez in the bedroom of the apartment. As they returned toward the hallway door with her, all three saw Officer Ryan striking Rodriguez's head. At this time Rodriguez's hands were cuffed behind his back. . . . In all, over forty police officers were on the scene. . . .

"A search of the apartment was conducted to recover the weapon that had been used to fire the shot through the door. While this was being done Officer Ryan, according to both civilian and uniformed witnesses, struck and kicked Rodriguez who remained handcuffed."

After a time Ryan turned his attention to Santiago, uncuffing him from the bannister and walking him to the roof of the six-story building.

"Once on the roof," the report continued, "Ryan removed the handcuffs from Santiago and brought him to a fire-escape at the rear of the building. There he punched and kicked him until a scream from a Mrs. Jennie Englada [a tenant in the adjoining building] caused him to stop. Santiago was then brought back onto the roof where he was beaten by Ryan and other unidentified members of the service. It was at this point, according to Santiago, that his jaw was broken.

"Ryan returned with Santiago to Apartment 2I. The search for the gun was still being conducted and two handguns were subsequently found in the bedroom. It was at this time that Sergeant Richard J. Riccio (the only supervisor on the scene) first entered the apartment. He saw Ryan strike Rodriguez in the torso with a blackjack and ordered him to stop. He then directed Police Officers Joseph R. Chinea and Patrick J. Halligan to take Santiago to the 44th Precinct Station House.

"Officer Halligan rode with Santiago in the rear seat of RMP 2614, operated by Police Officer Richard McClintock, with Police Officer Dennis Greene as recorder. . . . Officer McClintock testified that no one struck Santiago in the RMP." Santiago, however, said he was beaten in the car by everyone *but* the driver.

"When they reached the Precinct, Officers Halligan and Greene brought Santiago to the second floor squad room. Testimony indicated that Santiago was beaten as he was brought up the stairs of the Station House and again in the squad room by Halligan, Greene and other unidentified members of the service. . . .

"Rodriguez was brought to the Station House by Ryan and Duggan at Sergeant Riccio's order, where Police Officers Young and [Martin] Roos . . . testified to seeing Ryan strike and kick the prisoner. Additionally, at one point a loud scream was heard coming from the second floor men's room, the only known occupants of which were Ryan and Rodriguez. A foot print was later seen on the T-shirt Rodriguez was wearing. The T-shirt was missing when Rodriguez was brought to the hospital and was never recovered. Santiago and Rodriguez were both placed in the cell. . . .

"Both Rodriguez and Santiago were in obvious need of medical attention and Officer Brown called for an ambulance at about 0100 hours. At 0130 hours they were removed to Morrisania Hospital via ambulance. The Medical Examiner's report attributed the death of Rodriguez to a rupture of the spleen. . . .

"At the outset of this investigation, some members of the service who were prospective witnesses were reluctant to cooperate. They made false or misleading statements or denied having specific knowledge of the incident. However, this protective attitude towards a fellow officer was overcome and several of the previously reluctant officers joined with civilian witnesses in testifying before the grand jury."

As a result of the grand jury's findings, Thomas Ryan and three other police officers were indicted and suspended from the force. Arrested on the morning of October 8, Ryan was charged with murder in the second degree and assault in the first degree, while Greene, Halligan, and one other (who later was exonerated) were charged with assault in the first degree. A day later Sergeant Riccio was arrested and charged with fifteen counts of perjury in the first degree for testifying falsely before the grand jury.

According to Assistant Chief Frawley's account, "This stemmed from his statements to that body that he saw no blood or injuries on either prisoner and was not aware that either was in need of medical assistance." (At Thomas Ryan's trial, Riccio testified that it was common practice in the police department to lie to grand juries to help a fellow officer.)

District Attorney Merola, in announcing the indictments of Ryan, Greene, and Halligan, said they had shown "a depraved indifference to human life." Both Rodriguez and Santiago had been left "moaning and bleeding" on the floor of the precinct house cell until someone—not Ryan—called an ambulance, Merola said, adding that Santiago "was attacked with nightsticks, fists, feet and furniture" and beaten "to the point where his jaw was fractured, exposing the bone through the flesh." The grand jury, Merola said, had heard testimony from sixty witnesses, of whom thirty were police officers. Ryan was released on $7,500 bail.

Newspaper photographs of Ryan showed a solidly built man of twenty-six with a round, cherubic face and dreamy eyes. It was hard to picture him as vicious. He had been a cop for five years and was a star on his precinct football team.

How do you account for the kind of brutality of which Ryan stood accused? Any cop might have responded with initial panic-rage at being nearly killed by an unexpected shot from behind a door. At the trial a police officer testified that he heard Ryan say to Rodriguez, "You'll never shoot at a cop again." You could picture Ryan bursting through the apartment door and violently wrestling his assailant to the ground in a fit of reactive fury (even though the shooter stood in the doorway empty-handed). But after that? Did Ryan believe that would-be cop-killers like Rodriguez never received due justice in the courts? Many cops held that view, but most had the judgment to stop short of casting themselves as malevolent avengers.

"There was a priest called as a character witness at Ryan's trial," Chief Guido remembered, "who said he'd known Ryan a long time and that he was known as Nutsy Ryan."

The Ryan case was a classical example of the consequence of unleashed cop-rage, of the self-protective instinct to close ranks, of the pain and shame that a rogue cop could cause to a proud department—and of the pressure from above that finally prevented a cover-up. In the end, it was the willingness of Ryan's brother officers to bear witness against him that unraveled the case.

The assistant district attorney in charge of the investigation would not say if any of the cops who had seen Ryan abuse his prisoners had actually volunteered information. "There are many decent cops, but few courageous ones," he said. "You're unrealistic if you expect it to be the norm for cops to come forward."

"There's a lot of friction," said an officer in the 44th Precinct, at the time. "If a guy went down to the grand jury he's ostracized. Maybe he talked, maybe he didn't. There's a shadow of doubt over everybody."

District Attorney Merola said, "What happened at the 44th is still rare, but it represents the trend of the future.

You can get policemen to turn in policemen when something like this occurs."

At the trial, which did not take place until October 1977, a detective, John Hennessy, testified that the beating of prisoners by cops was a "not unusual" practice, and he admitted that he had lied under oath when a grand jury questioned him about Ryan's involvement in the death of Israel Rodriguez. Hennessy was asked by Ryan's lawyer how many times he had personally struck prisoners. "I would have to guess three or four times," Hennessy answered.

When Ryan took the stand he said he had not assaulted Rodriguez or Santiago, that he had been busy attending to paperwork at the station house. He also said he had heard "piercing screams" while doing his paperwork, but saw no reason to investigate, nor did he see any reason to summon medical help for his prisoners. He said that it was actually Detective Hennessy and Trenton Brown, one of the police officers who testified against him, who were responsible for the death of Rodriguez. (Brown was the officer who, with his partner, Felix Clarke, had been first on the scene and had arrested Santiago.)

The judge, Lawrence J. Tonetti, told the jury of seven men and five women that a witness was "not entitled to any greater degree of credibility" because he was a police officer. "They're human beings," the judge said, "some good, some bad, some truthful, some untruthful."

On November 5, 1977, Thomas Ryan was found guilty of criminally negligent homicide in the case of Israel Rodriguez—the lightest of all the possible verdicts that could have been handed down, short of acquittal—and faced up to four years in prison. He was subsequently acquitted of the assault charge in the case of Luis Santiago. His attorney, Jacob Evseroff, had earlier won an acquittal for Police Officer Thomas J. Shea, who had shot and killed a ten-year-old boy in Queens; Shea was dismissed from the force after a departmental hearing. And in February of that year another police officer, William Walker, was acquitted in the shooting of a college student in Brooklyn; Walker, too, was dismissed from the force. A third police officer, Robert Torsney, then awaiting trial, was later acquitted, on grounds of insanity, of murdering a fifteen-year-old Brooklyn boy.

But Ryan was the first New York cop ever convicted of committing homicide while on duty. In announcing the verdict, local newspapers made much of the fact that this was the first case in at least fifty years of a prisoner in custody at a New York police station having been fatally beaten. Chief Guido disputed that. "I wouldn't bet on it," he said.

From the report by IAD Commander Robert Frawley, bringing the Ryan case up to date in October 1978:

"Police Officer Thomas Ryan is presently free pending an appeal on his conviction of Criminally Negligent Homicide . . . Officer Ryan was dismissed from this Department on December 27, 1977 as a result of his criminal conviction. When initially questioned, Ryan stated that he had acted according to proper police procedures.

". . . Sergeant Riccio agreed to full cooperation with both the Bronx District Attorney's office and the Internal Affairs Division and was allowed to plead guilty to one count of perjury in the third degree on February 11, 1976. On October 14, 1977, after being advised that Sergeant Riccio had cooperated with this Department and the Bronx District Attorney, the court marked Sergeant Riccio's case adjourned contemplating dismissal. On September 1, 1978, he applied for retirement which will become effective on January 13, 1979. As a result of his cooperation, Department charges pending against Sergeant Riccio were not prosecuted."

Police Officers Dennis Greene and Patrick Halligan were tried for assault in the first degree, but the evidence against them was not specific enough to convince a jury, and they were found not guilty. In February 1978—while still awaiting departmental trials—both were restored to active duty and assigned to precincts in Manhattan. Neither ever stood departmental trials, also for lack of evidence. The officer who had been arrested with them, Joseph Chinea, was completely cleared of all charges, given the pay he lost during the period of his suspension from duty, and—in June 1982, having passed the Civil Service exam—was made a sergeant. Greene and Halligan were permitted to negotiate pleas for minor infractions and were disciplined by losing their pay during the period of their suspensions from October 8 to December 17, 1975.

As for the cops who had lied under oath to the grand jury and later changed their stories, becoming witnesses for the prosecution, no charges were brought against them. It was the old trade-off—the *necessary* trade-off, in the view of most law enforcement officials—of letting little fish go in order to net the big ones. "These are the things you have to do to make a case," Chief Guido said. "Ryan was the bad guy. To get him, we had to give the others immunity."

Ryan remained free on bail, pending an appeal. In October 1978 he was arrested again and indicted on an assault charge—this time for running down a postal worker named Reginald Smith and leaving the scene of the accident. The grand jury, in its charges, said that Ryan had displayed "a depraved indifference to human life." Ryan did not show up on the day he was scheduled to begin serving his four-year prison term for the homicide of Israel Rodriguez, and a bench warrant was issued for his arrest. He finally gave himself up in November 1981, still proclaiming his innocence, but saying that he was tired of being on the run.

The Ryan case heightened the awareness of the Brass to the ever-present danger of extreme instances of brutality. No matter how hard they tried to weed out brutal cops, some always slipped through.

"How does that kind of man get into the police department?" Guido asked rhetorically. "We screen our cops psychologically, of course. But we have thousands of cops. You talk to three psychologists, you get six different opinions. It's impossible to screen out all the psychos."

While it could be difficult to spot a mentally unbalanced cop, sometimes it was even harder for the department's supervisors to discern the difference between a potentially brutal cop and one who possessed the desirable pugnacity. And because of the stringent budget, there was less time for sensitivity training; as a result, some of the newer recruits, as McGuire acknowledged, had not yet "mellowed."

"I don't want to rein in the cops' *justifiable* aggressiveness," McGuire told me. "I don't want them to be social workers." There had been no rise by 1982 in complaints of street brutality, he said, and, as for integrity, it was, on the whole, excellent. "But," he said, "we will always have to watch carefully, treat the problem seriously, and vigorously root out any instances of brutality and corruption we find."

By mid-1980, commanders were expressing concern that inflation could lead to a serious increase in corruption. In a report to Commissioner McGuire, Chief Guido stated that "despite second jobs and working spouses," many police officers were "under considerable financial stress." This was leading to "an ominous atmosphere conducive to demoralization and the rationalization of marginally corrupt activities."

Many commanders, Guido said, saw "an even greater danger that this attitude might spread upward through the ranks." He noted that while institutional corruption on a large scale seemed to be a thing of the past, one disturbing aspect appeared to be that "in the last several years small clusters of officers, assigned to the same command, have been able to engage in conspiratorial acts of misconduct."

One such example occurred in June of 1981. It was a particularly flagrant incident of corruption in the 10th Precinct, where four police officers and the brother of one of them, who worked in the Bronx, were charged with criminal facilitation and bribe-receiving. They were caught by an undercover cop working for the Internal Affairs Division, who posed as a drug dealer, calling himself Arturo.

"Arturo" stumbled on the crooked cops while investigating the owner of an after-hours bar, who allegedly was paying off a police sergeant. Unable to find evidence of illegal payoffs, "Arturo" made a deal with Police Officer Anthony Manzo, a customer in the bar, to provide him with protection on his drug-selling rounds. Manzo brought in four other cops. The indictment said that the five cops "would refrain from the proper performance of their duties in the enforcement of law by not arresting" the man they believed to be a cocaine dealer, and by "protecting him from being arrested by other law enforcement officers, should the necessity arise."

Ultimately the five cops were sentenced to prison terms ranging from one to four years. Even more upsetting from the Brass's viewpoint was the laxity, or worse, on the parts of eight sergeants and three lieutenants from the 10th and the Four-Two in the Bronx. They all stood departmental trials on various specifications, mainly "improper supervision," and were disciplined with forfeitures of pay varying from three to thirty days.

Greatly concerned about the lax supervision that could enable such a flagrant incident of corruption to flourish in the post-Serpico era, Commissioner McGuire, that September, ordered a top-level internal inquiry. "We want to go beyond assessing blame and to autopsy the situation to find out what allowed this to take place and what we should do to prevent it from happening in the future," he said.

Whether accountability should go even higher than the disciplined lieutenants was what the chief of operations and three superchiefs were instructed to investigate. They intended, they said, "to look at all our patrol procedures and supervisory controls," using the 10th Precinct "as a starting point and see what systems are in place and where they broke down." The inquiry would take several months.

Despite the sporadic eruption of "conspiratorial acts of misconduct," Commissioner McGuire still believed, as he had when he took over the department, that the New York police possessed great strengths as well as glaring weaknesses. Both characteristics were dramatically juxtaposed in the way his department responded to the murder of a twenty-five-year-old obstetrics nurse named Bonnie Ann Bush. She was attacked on her way to work at Mount Sinai Hospital in Upper Manhattan, and the case was a striking example to McGuire, early in his tenure, of how New York's police could indeed be both the best and the worst.

Worst: On November 24, 1978, Nurse Bush, evidently forced from her car when she stopped for a red light, was seen being dragged, screaming, through the street. Her attacker pushed her into a derelict building, still struggling and screaming. A witness called the 911 police emergency number but the operator—a civilian working for the police department—confused the information. A sergeant and a patrolman who came to the scene in their radio car failed to question the witness thoroughly and, after a desultory look around, left the scene. Bonnie Ann Bush's body was later found inside the building. She had been shot, stripped of her clothes, and set on fire. (The emergency operator was later found to be incompetent and was transferred. The sergeant and patrolman were placed on modified duty.)

Best: Homicide detectives quickly identified a suspect. He was Nathan Giles, Jr., a convicted murderer out on parole; he had sexually abused and shot to death two other women (one of them nine months pregnant) earlier in the year. He was the prototypical recidivist, the felon whom the police kept catching and locking up, only to be released back onto the street to commit further vicious crimes.

Best *and* worst: A city-wide manhunt for Giles was launched. Six days after the murder Giles commandeered the car of nineteen-year-old Gerald Smith, who was waiting outside a candy store in Upper Manhattan for his brother. Giles ordered Smith at gunpoint to drive him away—"to New Jersey or Philadelphia"—but then changed his mind and demanded first that Smith take him to Brooklyn, then to the Bronx, then back to Manhattan, frequently ordering him to run red lights and turn the wrong way into one-way streets. Gerald Smith, terrified, began to think Giles wanted to get caught, wanted to shoot it out with the police. He prayed that his brother, who had seen him drive off with Giles, would report to the police that he had been kidnapped. Eventually the speeding car caught the notice of the police and several RMPs gave chase. Urged on by Giles and his gun, Smith pushed the car to ninety miles per hour. Finally it slammed into a station wagon in Lower Manhattan and was, in turn, slammed into by one of the pursuing radio cars. Giles leaped from Smith's car, firing wildly, and the police returned his fire bravely; they even managed to hit him as he slipped on the sidewalk, bringing him down with a bullet in the back. Then, however, panic made them behave badly.

From the account in *The New York Times*, which interviewed Gerald Smith soon after the capture of Giles: "When Mr. Giles began to run, an officer leaped to the side of the car and pointed a gun at Mr. Smith's head. Another stood at the fender, aiming at him. They pulled him out of the seat by the neck and threw him up against the car. He started to explain, 'He forced me to drive him. Check it out; it's been reported. My brother would have reported it.' But, he said, one officer hit him in the mouth several times with the heel of his hand, telling him to 'shut the hell up until we ask you.' Mr. Smith said another kicked him in the right shin as he was being put in the car, saying, 'That's for running.'"

Smith was forgiving. "It's one of those situations," he said. "If I had been in their shoes I might have done the same. I was just the guy with the guy who was doing the shooting. They didn't believe me. They wanted to know why I was doing ninety miles an hour. If it was them, they'd be doing ninety, too."

If the police work was in the first instance callous and negligent and in the second instance brutal, how can we characterize the judicial system that permitted a convicted murderer to kill again and again? On December 11 the New York State Division of Parole issued a fourteen-page report declaring that the Giles case might be proof of the "failure of the parole system and the entire criminal justice system in New York." The report described Giles as having had trouble with the police since the age of nine, portraying him as a juvenile criminal who murdered a sixty-year-old woman in her apartment in 1963 when he was sixteen. Although sentenced to twenty years in prison for that crime, he was released on parole after fourteen years. In

May 1977, three months after being paroled, he was arrested for raping and robbing a woman at gunpoint. Giles was permitted to plea-bargain and a judge released him on his own recognizance. He then went on to kill (all with the same gun) Willa Solomon and Cindy Pintos (the pregnant woman) and finally Bonnie Ann Bush. According to the parole division report, he faithfully checked in with his parole officer every week, including a telephone check two days before he killed the young nurse.

Giles was found guilty on March 26, 1980, on twelve counts—covering not only the murder of Bonnie Ann Bush, but the kidnapping of Gerald Smith and the assault on the police officers who captured him. Burton Roberts, the judge who had sentenced Luis Angel Velez for the murders of Sergeant Frederick Reddy and Officer Andrew Glover, sentenced Giles on May 5 to the maximum sentence of sixty-two and a half years to life.

In an astonishing display, the spectators in the courtroom, including three members of the jury that had found Giles guilty, burst into applause. For once, justice seemed to have been done. District Attorney Morgenthau had requested a ruling that Giles was an incorrigible repeat offender, which ostensibly ensured that he could not be paroled until he had served the minimum sixty-two and a half years. Judge Roberts told the prisoner that he wanted it understood that "this court does not ever want you to be released." Calling Giles a "classic sociopath," Judge Roberts—repudiating the death penalty—said, "It isn't necessary to wring your neck," adding that putting him to death would serve only to "show that we, too, have no respect for the dignity of human life." But, he said, "You are going to jail forever. Forever." Unless at some future date the ruling were to be appealed and reversed.

★
TEN
★

★ Mickey Schwartz's professional and personal life had been looking up, ever since the night of the Iranian demonstration when he got his second star. He was happy in the command of the tumultuous Brooklyn South area.

The command was not quite as heady as Dan Courtenay's *Manhattan* South. That was the best field assignment in the department, and Schwartz had his eye on that job; Courtenay had to be moved *sometime*. But meanwhile, Brooklyn South was a splendid assignment for a newly made two-star chief. Schwartz had moved into a comfortable apartment in Lower Manhattan and was recovering from the trauma of his divorce.

He had been in charge of Brooklyn South under Chief of Operations William Devine for eleven months when he was hit by the kind of confrontation between citizens and police that New York's Brass zealously sought to avoid. On a December Saturday in 1978 the 66th Precinct House was invaded, and suddenly Schwartz found himself being looked at hard by his bosses. It was a scrutiny similar to that endured by Area Commanders McCarthy and Bouza during the police mutiny in September 1976. Schwartz, happily, came out far better.

The attack on the station house was a surprise, and the weapons were fists, clubs, and hurled rocks. Seventy persons were injured, a few of them seriously; many of those hurt were police and one civilian died of a heart attack. A local assemblyman claimed he was beaten by cops as he attempted to cool down the infuriated demonstrators. The police said he was, on the contrary, a "principal rabble-rouser."

The rioters were members of the Hasidic community, some of whose representatives had not long ago commended the police in the ceremony at headquarters; according to both the police and community leaders, good relations had always prevailed in the area. Now, however, the Hasidim were irate over the murder of a sixty-five-year-old plumber named Irving Sussman who was stabbed to death about fifteen blocks from the station house soon after midnight on Friday. The community leaders claimed that Sussman's death had gone unresponded-to for forty-five minutes and that detectives did not begin investigating for more than two hours. Seized by an inexplicable surge of mass hysteria, these normally reasonable and peaceful members of the sect stormed the precinct house, shouting for greater protection.

They battled the astonished police inside the house as well as in the street, wrecking furniture and equipment, smashing windows, spilling the contents of filing cabinets and tearing out telephone and computer lines. The police finally regained control, pushing the protestors out into the street, where hundreds continued to demonstrate. First Deputy Joe Hoffman, who arrived at the scene soon after the station house was emptied of protestors, estimated that more than $10,000 damage had been done and that the paperwork pertaining to dozens of cases had been destroyed.

Mayor Koch felt obliged to go in person to the scene and attempt to calm the outraged demonstrators; after viewing what he called "the rape of the police station," he demanded that the culprits be identified and brought to justice, whether or not they were "religious persons." Nobody, he said was "going to get their way in this town by force, nobody."

The commissioner ordered Schwartz to conduct an investigation. Schwartz, fearing further attack, kept a wary eye on the precinct house the day of the murdered plumber's funeral. He assigned extra manpower but found it wasn't needed. The frenzied outburst had subsided as suddenly as it had erupted. "They sent cookies to the station house," Schwartz said. "They didn't say so out loud, but they were obviously ashamed of what they'd done."

The investigation revealed, among other details:

The murdered plumber, Sussman, was found in the street at about 12:50 A.M. by a man who did not speak English and who walked around the neighborhood nearly half an hour looking for someone to place a call for help. The police recorded the call at 1:17 A.M. and were at the scene in thirteen minutes. (McGuire was working on improving the response to emergency calls since the bungling of the Bonnie Ann Bush case.) Moreover, within a few hours of Sussman's stabbing, detectives had in custody the four men who had attacked and robbed him. They were arrested for a series of attempted robberies and non-fatal stabbings that occurred soon after the attack on Sussman, but it took time to connect them to the Sussman homicide.

When the demonstration started outside the 66th Precinct house at 11 A.M. Saturday, there were only four officers present—three behind the desk on the ground floor and a detective on the floor above. About half a dozen others were out on patrol in radio cars. According to the investigation, the four officers—facing about 200 outraged protesters who forced their way into the house—showed "remarkable restraint and courage." Further, the 50 reinforcements that later arrived—rushing through a back door in response to a 10–13 signal, believing their fellow cops' lives were threatened—were also said to have behaved with "remarkable restraint, trying to hold back the remainder of the people from entering." Eventually "75 police officers were attempting to quell a riotous mob of 3,500 people," said the report.

Under Schwartz's supervision a team of detectives studied photographs and television clips of the demonstration and interviewed dozens of witnesses, and on January 8, 1979, Brooklyn Assemblyman Samuel Hirsch—the man earlier accused by the police of being a rabble-rouser—was arrested along with three other men. Hirsch was accused of third-degree assault on Officer Paul Fried, who, ironically, had been mugged twice while working as a decoy in the precinct dressed as a member of the Hasidic sect. Another of the arrested men was accused of second-degree assault on a cop named Joseph Archer, who was said to have been seriously injured. The other two men were accused of assault, obstructing governmental administration, and criminal mischief.

Hirsch said he was falsely accused, expected an acquittal, and would then sue for false arrest. Released on a desk summons returnable in February, he showed reporters photographs of what he said was a police officer on the station house roof throwing bricks at the demonstrators. Commissioner McGuire responded by saying the investigation was still under way and promised there would be no cover-up of police wrongdoing. Ultimately, the charges against the police were dropped for lack of substantiation. In December the charges against Assemblyman Hirsch were conditionally dismissed, with full dismissal promised in six months pending good behavior. Schwartz, who had handled the investigation to the commissioner's satisfaction, had by then moved on to a new and far more visible command.

Soon after the Attack on the 66th Precinct House, Commissioner McGuire lost Joe Hoffman. Early in December Mayor Koch asked Hoffman to head the city's ailing Health and Hospitals Corporation, where Hoffman had served briefly as vice president before returning to the police department. Hoffman and Koch had become friendly during the 66th Precinct attack: "Him and me against the world," in Hoffman's words. It was a challenging assignment, perhaps an impossible one, for the corporation had a history of mismanagement, waste, and political manipulation. Hoffman, however, felt he could have the kind of impact there he could not have as second man in the police department and he took the job.

Not long after, he admitted to me that he had become somewhat disillusioned as first dep. The daring changes he and McGuire had discussed were not possible, Hoffman said. "All the men we promoted have really got the same general mindset as their immediate predecessors. It's a mindset that tends strongly to resist any real change." He particularly had in mind the man he himself had suggested as chief of operations to replace the ousted James Hannon.

"I thought Bill Devine was, like me, a pure advocate of Patrick V. Murphy's style. I wanted to get on with reforms, maybe bypass some of the old traditions. But I discovered Bill was less of a Murphy purist than me. Maybe I was just too management-oriented."

Hoffman added, however, that since Commissioner Murphy's cleanup the department had become "a well-oiled machine." Crowd control, the department's biggest challenge, didn't require a PC. "There's always a group of chiefs who can, interchangeably, take full command," he said. "Pat Murphy used to say, take the job where there's a fire, if you want to have an impact."

The fire in the NYPD had long since been put out. "You just pass through the police department," Hoffman said. "The best you can do these days is nudge it along." But there *was* a fire to fight at the Health and Hospitals Corporation.

Hoffman confirmed something I had long suspected— that a police career would not appeal to someone with a risk-taking personality. (I mean, of course, intellectual, not physical risk; most of the cops I came to know were heroes who would readily give their lives in the line of duty.)

Being a cop-commander was essentially a safe career with well-defined and rigid boundaries. Hoffman had educated himself beyond the job and being a police boss was not enough to satisfy either his imagination or his ambition. He was no longer a cop, anymore than Patrick V. Murphy was still a cop.

A few months into 1982 Mayor Koch, to the disappointment of a great many New Yorkers and especially the police, who loved him, seized the chance to run for governor of New York State rather than finish his second term and try for reelection to a third term as mayor in 1986. He had promised after his second election that he would stay for three terms if the voters would have him; he said it would take that long to get the city back on its feet with many restored services including, of course, a full-strength police department. But no sooner had Governor Hugh Carey announced his intention not to seek reelection, than Koch proclaimed his own candidacy for the job.

Only six months into his second term as mayor, Koch was unofficially electioneering for the job of governor. It was a sunny Saturday in June and the event was heralded as "the biggest anti-nuke rally in the history of the world." At least half a million people were expected to participate in a day-long series of marches, speeches, and musical entertainments, and Koch, who was the most visible glad-hander New York ever had, would not for the world have passed up the opportunity to march a little, proselytize a little, kiss and be kissed and toss out, like boutonnieres, his ingenuous query, "How'm I doin?" (Not all that well, as it happened; a lot of New Yorkers seemed angry at him for wanting to quit being their mayor. And the following month even the cops, who had been among his most vocal fans and had promised to support him for governor, became annoyed with him. Negotiations between City Hall and the PBA over a new work contract had stalled, as they invariably did, and the union's president, Philip Caruso, threatened to withdraw the cops' endorsement.)

Five thousand cops were assigned to the rally and at 8 A.M. on June 12, the new Manhattan South area commander, Asssistant Chief Milton Schwartz, was at United Nations Plaza supervising security arrangements. Schwartz had at last succeeded Dan Courtenay in the most exciting and high-pressured of all the area commands. The job became his in September 1979, about ten months after the 66th Precinct attack.

At the same time, Courtenay finally attained superchiefdom: Commissioner McGuire moved Joseph Veyvoda laterally to fill the vacancy left by Chief of Personnel Henry Morse, who quite the department, and made Courtenay chief of the Organized Crime Control Bureau, the job from which Jim Hannon had succeeded to chief of operations. It wasn't the Detective Bureau and it wasn't the Patrol Bureau, but yet, at fifty-three, Courtenay had achieved his third star. Jim Sullivan was still chief of detectives, and patrol had been given in March 1979 to Assistant Chief William R. Bracey, who had proved himself as area commander of Brooklyn North. Bracey was now the department's highest ranking black commander, but at nearly fifty-nine would be able to serve only another three years.

Once again Courtenay could pursue his earlier vision of eliminating the narcotics evil, and he fell to work with the zeal that had marked all his assignments. He raised the level of training for his investigators by initiating work seminars; he pursued better working relations with other agencies concerned with drug traffic. He held sessions with his men on corruption and carefully monitored the integrity of OCCB at all levels. As a three-star chief, he now felt a new and even deeper pride in the department he had served, through good times and bad, for thirty-two years. Having reached superchiefdom, he could look back without too much pain to the really bad times just seven years earlier, when he was still an inspector, and almost ashamed of being a cop. That was the year the Knapp Commission issued its final report on corruption, when the full scope of police villainy lay revealed.

"There were times when nobody talked to us," he once told me, "when my neighbors looked the other way."

There was no pride, *then*, in being a cop-commander; the guilt of his cynical peers was *his* by association. Those were the days of the tarnished Brass.

After a few months in his new job, Courtenay decided he liked it almost as much as he would have liked being chief of detectives. "I totally run my own shop," he said. "No one tells me who to target, how to place my men. I always report to the commissioner's office about my plans, of course, but I have complete freedom to do what I think needs to be done."

As chief of organized crime control, Courtenay seldom went into the field; his was largely a desk job. On St. Patrick's Day it was no longer Courtenay, but Schwartz, who was out in the street shivering in the March winds, directing security (until the parade passed 59th Street). Courtenay *marched* in the parade, now, tall and proud, shoulder to shoulder with the chief of operations, right behind the commissioner and the first dep, who were usually joined by the mayor. (Schwartz was unimpressed. "I'm just as tall as Dan," he said. "The more promotions I get, the shorter he seems to me.")

William Devine had replaced Joe Hoffman as first dep and had himself been succeeded as chief of operations by Patrick J. Murphy—not to be confused with Patrick V. Murphy—whom I'd known as an inspector when he was in charge of Commissioner Codd's Office of Programs and Policies.

Chief of Operations Pat Murphy decided to personally supervise the anti-nuke rally, because it was expected to be the biggest crowd-control operation in the city's history. Although only forty-nine, Murphy was much in the style of Jim Hannon—perhaps a bit more sophisticated, but just as straightforward, unshowy, serious about his job, judicious in his official relations. He gave his orders quietly but with indisputable authority, and he was as uncomplaining as Hannon. He had a serious, chronic back problem, likely to be aggravated by the nearly twelve straight hours he anticipated spending on his feet this day, and he wore a back brace.

Mickey Schwartz was supervising the downtown part of the rally below Central Park, and I watched with him— along with the cops on their posts—as speakers and entertainers gathered near the United Nations. On a platform built high above the sidewalk, there were preliminary speeches and entertainment for the benefit of the marchers lining up between 45th and 47th Streets. Eventually everyone would gather in Central Park's Great Lawn, supervised by the chief of the Manhattan North area, where there would be more speeches and entertainment.

Schwartz and I watched the actress Colleen Dewhurst being interviewed by a radio reporter for her views on nuclear armament. A great-hearted woman of deep convictions and boundless vitality, she was active in behalf of more causes than anyone could keep track of. Only a couple of months earlier Schwartz had nervously ordered her arrested in the street, along with a group of her fellow actors, playwrights, directors, and producers who were protesting the imminent demolition of a pair of illustrious Broadway playhouses to make way for a new hotel. "I hope I won't have to arrest her again today," Schwartz said uneasily.

At 8:40 A.M. Chief of Operations Murphy, who had been surveying the parade and demonstration areas from a police helicopter, pulled up at 45th Street in his official car. He was in full-dress uniform, wearing the four-star shield that Jim Hannon had been forced to forfeit and that—if Ed Koch became governor—Murphy, in his turn, would doubtless have to yield. Murphy was keeping in close touch via his car telephone with Commissioner McGuire at headquarters. McGuire's instructions, Murphy told me, were to "be flexible." Though a solemn and serious protest against nuclear weapons, the event was intended by all its heterogeneous elements, both local and imported, to be entirely peaceful and law-abiding. It was to be a massive love-in.

At 10:30 a sergeant told Chief Murphy the mayor was on

the scene. "He's giving us a little problem," the sergeant said, pointing out the crowd that was beginning to surround Koch, threatening to hold up the long line of marchers.

"Leave him alone," Murphy said, "he's paying for this." (The rally was costing the city about $700,000.) Koch, beaming, talking nonstop, was in his shirt sleeves, working the crowd, aggressively accessible.

At 11:30 Commissioner McGuire arrived, dressed in jacket and tie. Bella Abzug, in a straw hat, was speaking from the platform. Murphy and McGuire agreed that their goal was "just to get through this without anyone getting hurt." The police had been planning the operation for days, consulting with the leaders of the many diverse groups, coordinating with the staff of the parks commissioner and with union leaders, who were strongly represented among the marchers and the speakers, and who had pledged to keep order.

At 12:30 I rode with Chief Murphy to Central Park. He was accompanied wherever he went by a detective from intelligence named Jack Finnegan, carrying a walkie-talkie. Reporters kept asking Murphy for estimates of the crowd, and he consulted with Deputy Commissioner Alice McGillion, in charge of Public Information. The vast Sheep Meadow, over 840,000 acres, could contain more than 700,000 persons, standing; no one was quite sure how many it could hold sitting, which was what most of the onlookers were doing. There was a lot of movement in and out, which made it even harder to estimate the numbers. The chief of operations and the commissioner for public information agreed on a figure—as of half past twelve—of 160,000. But marchers and viewers were still pouring into the park.

Supported by his back brace, Murphy walked with a somewhat stiff-legged gait toward one of the department's barrier trucks, parked strategically so as to command a sweeping view of the crowds on the Great Lawn, as well as of the large platform that had been erected for the speeches and music. He crouched painfully on the truck's hydraulic lift and was hoisted onto the truck bed, where Chief of Patrol Bracey stood, surveying the scene while munching a sandwich. "I'm starving," Murphy said. Like Jim Hannon, he frequently went without lunch. Unlike Hannon, he smoked steadily whenever he was out of the public view, as now. He was offered a seat on the truck bed but declined, saying, "I don't like to sit down on the job." We gazed down at the Mayor, who, still in shirt sleeves, continued working the crowd.

By 2 o'clock the over-amplified sounds of impassioned speeches and throbbing music had grown deafening. I walked with Murphy (and his faithful shadow, Finnegan) along the aisles between tidy pens defined by snow fences that contained the peaceful onlookers. Many of the cops lining the aisles had cotton stuffed in their ears against the noise and one show-off had stuck bullets into his ears. The blue line seemed to stretch on endlessly.

"You try not to make eye contact," Murphy said, "so they don't feel like they have to salute. In a situation like this they shouldn't take time to salute. But some do, anyway." He patted a cop on the shoulder as he walked by, shook hands with another, returned an occasional salute, spoke a word of greeting now and then. We passed Commissioner McGuire, who told Murphy, "Things look good." He asked Murphy how his back was holding up.

"It's hard to do eight hours on my feet at my age," Murphy said, not really complaining.

"I hope you're wearing your brace," McGuire said.

The area commander of Manhattan North told Murphy, "Mickey Schwartz wants to know if we need any of his men." Murphy said no. To an inquiring reporter, he gave an estimate—it was now 2:30—of 400,000 in the park and 100,000 marchers still on their way from the United Nations.

At 4 P.M. Murphy and McGuire were standing together listening to Linda Ronstadt sing. A cop walked by, holding a lost child by the hand. The worst problem seemed to be lost children. "But they're always found, eventually," Murphy said. Both he and McGuire looked pleased. One of the reasons things had gone so smoothly, they both felt, was that the public had heeded McGuire's warnings not to bring cars into the city and not to come at all unless they planned to attend the demonstration.

A German couple came up to Murphy to tell him how impressed they were with the way the New York police handled crowds. (A day earlier, in West Berlin, demonstrators had battled the police in a violent protest against President Reagan's visit. Demonstrators attacked police barricades, throwing rocks and torches, and the police used water cannons and tear gas.)

An out-of-town photographer snapped Murphy's picture, then said, "You look worried, Inspector."

"It's my duty to look stern," Murphy said. Then he smiled broadly.

The police department of 1982, despite its changes at the top, seemed to be working very much like the police department of 1976. Joe Hoffman was right: it was a well-oiled machine and the chiefs were all more or less interchangeable. (As witness: Joseph Veyvoda held three different three-star commands within three and a half years—first as chief of OCCB, then chief of personnel, and when William Bracey retired soon after the anti-nuke rally, Veyvoda, then sixty-one, was named by McGuire as chief of patrol.) As long as they stayed honest and were committed to a clean and nonviolent department, what was wrong with that?

New York's police were not, however, interchangeable with the police of other cities. New York had a special stature as an international city and a focal point; nowhere else would the police be called upon to deal, for example, with the mixture of confrontational politics and show business that demanded Mickey Schwartz's attention on the morning of March 22, 1982. He had been chief of the Manhattan South area for a little over two years and, like Dan

Courtenay before him, found the job the most rewarding of his career. Courtenay, had he still been Manhattan South commander, would have felt the same sense of trepidation in the face of this potentially volatile event, and would have prepared for it in much the same way—with care and sensitivity, while stoutly upholding the law. The Broadway theater, after all, was a multimillion-dollar tourist attraction, an institution unique to New York. And when its stars chose to challenge the Establishment, everyone watched in fascination. It wouldn't do for New York cops to be seen on television screens using billy clubs on such as Jason Robards, or dragging Geraldine Fitzgerald by the hair into a paddy wagon. Mickey Schwartz was walking a tightrope.

"We will lie in front of the demolition equipment if necessary," announced Joseph Papp, the producer who had hit it big with *A Chorus Line* and whose annual free summer Shakespeare Festival in Central Park had long since established him as one of the city's cultural benefactors. Papp, like Colleen Dewhurst, was a happy warrior in a multitude of political causes; he had participated in civil disobedience protests in Washington during the Vietnam War. He was incensed by the city-approved plan to permit the razing of two of Broadway's most charming and history-haunted playhouses—the Morosco and the Helen Hayes—to clear a site for a fifty-story hotel. The two theaters stood back to back, one fronting on 45th Street, the other on 46th. The Bijou Theatre, once adjoining the Morosco, had already been demolished, leaving a rubble-strewn lot.

Papp organized a group of protestors who gave daily performances from a street platform opposite the Morosco. Christopher Reeve, Tammy Grimes, Celeste Holm, and Treat Williams were among the actors who took their places, day after day, to read scenes from the seven Pulitzer Prize plays performed at the Morosco—including Eugene O'Neill's precedent-shattering *Beyond the Horizon*, produced there in 1920. Placido Domingo came and sang "O Sole Mio," accompanying himself on an upright piano.

"We will have an honor guard of fifty people on duty in the street at all times," Papp vowed, "so they won't be able to start demolition in the middle of the night." The performers exhorted passersby to complain to Mayor Koch, offering dimes and the phone number of City Hall. They appealed to the Supreme Court. It was all to no avail. At 10 A.M. on March 22 all legal avenues were exhausted. Papp, Colleen Dewhurst, Susan Sarandon, Estelle Parsons, and Michael Moriarty were among more than 150 protestors who began occupying the empty lot adjoining the Morosco, where an enormous hydraulic backhoe squatted at the ready. The group was preventing the demolition crew from moving in.

"That's the biggest piece of wrecking equipment I've ever seen," Papp said. The mechanical monster had the name Godzilla stenciled on its flank. As could happen only in New York, the protest was orchestrated. Papp and his lieutenants had held a series of meetings with Schwartz and his lieutenants. Papp's group would be arrested for trespassing in the empty lot, and the television cameras would record their protest. They would not lie down or resist arrest, the police would use no force, and the television cameras would record the police's lack of brutality. Just another New York street happening. To Papp it was a game; for him all the world was a stage, and this particular mock-confrontation was an encounter between Kojak and Peter Pan. It probably did not occur to him that if heads were cracked the blood would be real, not ketchup.

But Schwartz was tensely aware that things could go awry. At 10:30, eyeing the swelling crowds in the street, the proliferating television crews rudely jostling each other and passersby to get their desired angles, Schwartz said: "I'll be happy when this is over. There are too many intangibles. Joe Papp knows what *he's* doing and we know what *we're* doing, but he can't control this, it's getting to be a circus. Some crazy can get in there with them and start something. There are too many television people around."

Across the street a fight broke out, two figures rolling on

the sidewalk. A few feet from me a man inadvertently blocked the view of a television cameraman, who shoved him out of the way so hard that he lost his balance; he was about to lunge in revenge, when an alert cop pulled him away. Schwartz sent for more police, increasing the detail in the street to sixty. Eight of the cops were dressed in riot gear, the sun glancing off their smooth, sky-blue helmets.

Inside the lot Papp and his group were chanting, "Shame on Koch!" On the platform across the street bagpipers set up an accompanying wail.

The agreed-on time arrived—10:45. Schwartz and Papp, flanked by inspectors, huddled just outside the lot. The eight riot police moved to cordon off a path to the police vans parked at the curb. Other police officers formally asked the protesters to leave and were formally refused. Then under Schwartz's personal supervision they were escorted one by one, 170 of them, into the vans and driven away to the nearby Midtown North station house. A woman carrying a child attempted to board one of the vans and Schwartz stopped her. She handed her child to a friend and was permitted aboard.

When the last of the thirteen vanloads was on its way to the station house, I drove there with Schwartz and one of his inspectors. "You always worry about this kind of thing," they told me. "You have to expect the unexpected." Schwartz was still tense. "One mistake and all the accolades are wiped out," he said. It was the price of accepting responsibility. Some of the protesters were leaving the station house as we arrived, wearing their summonses pinned to their coats like badges of honor. They were warned that if they entered the demolition site again they would be locked up. Papp looked pleased with himself. He was smoking a large cigar; he and Schwartz shared that taste. The protesters were ordered to appear in court the following month for sentencing; they expected token fines but were prepared to go to jail. (After lecturing them, the judge ordered the charges dropped.)

Schwartz instructed an aide to have the day's action written up as an Unusual. When things had quieted down, I asked him why he was working out of uniform. He was wearing a trenchcoat over a business suit, and his shield was held to his lapel with a large safety pin. He said he had come to work straight from playing tennis and had not had time to change. "And my game was off because I was nervous about this," he added.

By now I had known both Schwartz and Courtenay for nearly six years, and I understood them, probably, as well as any non-cop could understand a cop. I thought Schwartz had decided to work in civilian clothes in order to shrink the chasm between himself and the theater folk, to downplay his role as "oppressor." His tennis game merely provided an excuse. He was self-conscious about the "gorilla image" that he felt was projected all too often by the police. Courtenay, being less a theater fan than Schwartz and having in general fewer intellectual pretensions, probably would have been less self-conscious and perfectly comfortable working in uniform. For instance, he was not at all embarrassed to admit that he disliked the critically acclaimed *A Chorus Line*. And he had recently seen his first production of *Othello* and found it "Not much of a story, pretty simple, with no mystery or suspense." (When I happened to discuss the *Othello* production with Schwartz and mentioned that Courtenay had seen it, Schwartz said, "Who explained it to him?") Courtenay was a lovable lowbrow. Despite his three stars he was without affectation, still the bone-deep street cop.

Schwartz aspired to greater refinement. By contrast with Courtenay's ankle-holstered, off-duty gun, it was Schwartz's practice not to wear one at all off duty, but to carry it in a trim attaché case. And when Commissioner McGuire, early in 1981, revoked the order mandating that the police go armed at all times, Schwartz seized the option to leave his gun behind on social occasions. Courtenay continued to carry his off-duty gun. "I'm accustomed to it," he said. "I feel naked without it."

I asked McGuire at the end of 1982 if he thought the new

gun rule had proved helpful, and he said that cops liked the option of not having to go armed; but the department had made no study to determine how many cops actually left their guns home when they were out socializing and drinking, or if there were fewer drink-inspired shootings as a result.

News item: On July 29, 1980, a jury continued to hear testimony in one of New York's longest criminal trials—then in its third month—that of Police Officer Kevin Durkin, accused of fatally shooting two unarmed men in a Bronx bar. Amid conflicting testimony from psychiatrists and police officers, the trial also focused on two chronic police problems: psychological pressures on officers who worked in high crime areas and drinking by police officers.

Officer Durkin, 29 years old, testified he believed the men were members of the FALN and wanted to kill him. The bar where the shootings occurred was across the street from the 46th Precinct station house and heavily patronized by police officers. Although Officer Durkin said he was normally a light drinker, two bartenders testified that he had ordered about a dozen beers. On the stand Officer Durkin demonstrated how he pulled out his .38-caliber revolver, which off-duty officers must carry, and fired five shots at the two men. He said he had "no choice" because one of the men moved as if he were reaching for a gun inside his jacket. (Durkin was acquitted on grounds of self-defense.)

Mickey Schwartz was a gentleman cop. He consciously avoided police jargon and was sarcastic when his peers used terms like *racket* for the traditionally stag get-togethers celebrating a promotion or a retirement. He had tried harder than most career cops—as hard, almost, as Joe Hoffman—to launder the street out of his system. And he was thinner-skinned than Courtenay. A *New York Times* reporter, Anna Quindlen, interviewed Schwartz on New Year's Day 1981, after Schwartz had sleekly supervised the 1,200 police at

Times Square during the New Year's Eve celebration attended by 400,000 people. Schwartz arrived at a news conference twenty-five minutes late, she wrote, "looking a little like a used party hat. His two stars glittered, but his eyes were dim." Schwartz was wounded by the frivolous tone and felt his dignity had been impugned. Courtenay would have shrugged it off with a wisecrack.

And yet, in his way—unlike Hoffman—Schwartz was thoroughly wedded to policing. "You know it's going to bother you when you leave," he once said when we were discussing the impending purge of the Top Brass under McGuire and Hoffman.

The women Schwartz began seeing after he was separated from his wife discovered that fact quickly. One or two, impressed by his intelligence, his social poise, his evident enjoyment of cultivated society, attemped to separate him from the police, urging him to do something "better," like going into business. They soon realized their mistake. He knew that policing was what he could do best, was where he could make his most meaningful contribution to society. Eventually he met a woman who understood that and who valued him for it. She was Arlene Wolff, whom he had met as a member of Mayor Beame's administration when she worked in the Department of Civic Affairs and Public Events. They shared a delight in travel, dining on good food with good friends, theatergoing, and keeping fit.

As the date of the primary election approached in the autumn of 1982, the NYPD once again rumbled with rumors. Koch was being challenged for the Democratic nomination for governor by the incumbent lieutenant governor, Mario Cuomo. But even Cuomo's boss, the departing Governor Carey, had endorsed Koch, and all the early opinion polls showed that Koch would win the nomination handily and go on in November to be elected governor. When that happened—few people said *if* that happened—the City Council president, Carol Bellamy, would automatically be appointed to finish out the year as mayor. Then she would presumably run for election to a four-year term and, unless she made a botch of things during her appointive interim term, would be elected as New York's first woman mayor. McGuire let it be known that he would not stay on, even if asked, when Koch left. He said he wanted to go back to his law practice.

The Police Brass trembled at the possibility of Council President Bellamy as mayor. Frequently at odds with Koch, a couple of years earlier she had charged that the police department had far too many mid-level supervisors, and called for the elimination through attrition of 150 sergeants, lieutenants, captains, and deputy inspectors. She had also called for an increased replacement of police by civilian workers. First Deputy Commissioner Devine, while McGuire was out of town, responded tartly that her proposals were based on superficial research, and "conducted by young aides who did not understand the workings of a complicated agency and were only seeking a headline." He said the report was "a real disservice," adding that the department itself felt the need to replace more of its uniformed personnel with civilians and had so informed the council president a month earlier.

Moreover, Devine said, Carol Bellamy did not understand the various functions of mid-level supervisors, many of whom were active in the field as narcotics investigators and homicide detectives and did not sit behind administrative desks.

Carol Bellamy was born into a blue-collar New Jersey family. After graduating from college she worked for the Peace Corps and then entered New York University Law School. Before the mayoralty seemingly became available, she had intended to run for state controller. "Frankly, I have my eye on the governor's office," she told me. Echoing Ed Koch, she said, "That's where the real power is."

As the New York primary drew near, and as Carol Bellamy confidently prepared to take over the city government, the most persistent rumor was that she planned to bring Anthony Bouza back from Minneapolis as her police commissioner. That would certainly finish Courtenay's police career. Schwartz, with his two-star rank, was in the position Courtenay had been in when McGuire came to office: high enough to be advanced to a superchiefdom, or even to chief of operations, but not so high as to be threatened with forced retirement. But, like Courtenay, he detested Bouza.

Joe Hoffman took note of McGuire's intention to resign and speculated idly about his successor. At a restaurant, one day, he chanced to run into Richard Gelb, who, as co-chairman of Koch's search panel, had interviewed him as a possible commissioner nearly five years earlier. Gelb asked him if he had any interest in being commissioner, should McGuire leave. "I told Dick, absolutely not," Hoffman said, adding that he wanted to earn more money than the job paid, that he wouldn't want to "put my family through that again," and that to go back would "just be a tremendous ego trip."

Hoffman had resigned as president of the Health and Hospitals Corporation at the end of May 1980, in protest against the mayor's appointment of a new chairman of the board of directors, who would have superseded Hoffman's powers as principal policy maker. Koch warmly praised Hoffman's work, but he let him go. (Courtenay sarcastically observed that Hoffman finally had reached "his level of incompetence.") By September 1 Hoffman had a new job as executive vice president and chief operating officer of St. Vincent's Hospital and Medical Center.

On September 23, to everyone's surprise except Mario Cuomo's, Koch lost the nomination for governor in the primary election; he was after all destined to finish out the three years and three months of his second term as mayor, at least as far as the voters could determine his destiny. He was chagrined (though not as much so as Carol Bellamy), but he recovered quickly (and so, to all appearances, did she).

The Police Brass collectively sighed with relief. They were luckier than Jim Hannon and the rest of the headquarters High Command at the end of 1977. McGuire found that he was not, after all, that eager to return at once to private practice. He told Koch he would be glad to stay on for an indefinite period of time, and Koch said that was fine with him.

I asked McGuire if he would stay until the end of Koch's second term in 1985, and he replied that he doubted it very much. The commissioner's salary had been raised at the beginning of 1982 to $72,000, which, McGuire said, certainly *should* be enough to raise a family on, even in expensive New York City. Moreover, McGuire said, "This is the most exciting, rewarding, and professionally satisfying job I've ever held." It had originally "been an ego trip," he added, but "that was assuaged in the first two years." Returning to his private law practice was, however, becoming a stronger and stronger temptation; the excitement and professional rewards were considerable there, too, and the earnings (though he tried not to let that issue weigh too heavily in his decision) would be far greater. He had been making a financial sacrifice for the past five years; he and Joan now had two children and he had to consider their future.

McGuire had grown in confidence and stature, secure in the mayor's support, pleased with the men he had promoted to high rank and well-respected by such of his Top Commanders as Courtenay and Schwartz. But he continued to be frustrated by budgetary and manpower problems, and I had heard that he was growing increasingly dismayed by the savagery of street crime, that in fact since taking office his views had changed with regard to the death penalty. When I asked him about that he said, "I've turned around. I think the death penalty should be more broadly applied."

By coincidence he made his comment on November 9, the day after Detective Nat P. Musso was shot in the face through the door of an apartment in Harlem where he and two partners were investigating a robbery. Musso was lucky; the shooting was not fatal.

"There is too much vicious, premeditated murder today,

not just of police," McGuire said. "When I took office it was another era. The kinds of crime were less vicious, the numbers were lower. Now you are seeing criminals with fifteen arrests for violent crimes, a lot of them kids who are hearing a message from society that says there is no serious punishment for killing. They laugh at you if you say you'll put them in jail for life. That just doesn't happen. You can't keep someone in jail forever. He'll be sentenced for life, and in jail he'll get his PhD in ornithology, and some cardinal will say he's rehabilitated, and he'll be paroled.

"Vicious crime is being tolerated by our society and it shouldn't be. No action is being taken, funds are not being allocated, legislation is at a standstill. We are operating under a twenty-year-old criminal justice system and it isn't working. Life has become cheap. Where are our priorities? Society must punish these people."

Apathy may prevail, McGuire pointed out, because the majority of those in power, the influential and vocal members of society, are—at least for the moment—not personally affected by violent crime. "Eighty percent of the victims," McGuire said, "are black and Puerto Rican." So far. He was distressed, that day, about Detective Musso's wounding, and he seemed glad of the chance to air his views. While I had never found him at a loss for words, he was that day seized by a burst of underused courtroom eloquence.

"I believe in the death penalty only for the most vicious types of crime, and I don't believe we will put to death innocent people," McGuire said. "There are today so many controls, so many safeguards, endless appeals. The system has become a laughingstock, it's totally protective of the criminal. Far from an innocent person being killed, we are protecting the guilty from being punished.

"Our government doesn't protect us from violent crime. In the last five years (1977 to 1981) there were 105,331 murders in the United States as compared with the 57,000 Americans killed during the entire sixteen years of the Vietnam War. We *are* in a war. Our enemy is armed with handguns. We take lives in war, in the name of defense. Using the death penalty is a legitimate defense for our society. If, by using the death penalty, by putting to death even ten killers, we could ensure that ten potential victims would survive, it would be worth it.

"I believe in Christian salvation, it's part of my religion and I take it very seriously. But no theology suggests that we must forfeit the right to live. Nothing in the Judeo-Christian ethic says that. We believe in just wars, and in the lesser of two evils. We are allowed, ethically, to kill. I don't think the death penalty will make life cheaper, quite the opposite. We're indulging, *now*, a certain amount of tolerance for killing."

Where were our priorities? "The law," Plutarch once reminded us, can speak "too softly to be heard in such a noise of war."

> News item: In Washington on October 4, 1981, the Bureau of Justice Statistics announced that the number of inmates in prisons in the United States rose more than 20,000 in the first half of the year. This growth rate, if continued for six months, would produce the highest annual rate in 56 years.
>
> Attorney General William French Smith's committee on violent crime recommended in August that the federal government provide two billion dollars in new aid to states to build prisons. The co-chairman of the group, Governor James Thompson of Illinois, called the proposal the linchpin of a series of recommendations designed to lock up more violent criminals for longer periods.
>
> But in a speech on crime in New Orleans on Tuesday, President Reagan made no mention of aid for prison construction. Mr. Smith denied that the proposal was dead but said that the drive to balance the federal budget prevented diverting resources to that purpose.

Chief of Detectives James Sullivan told McGuire he

planned to leave the department early in 1983. He had been offered a job as associate vice president for security of the Alexander's department store chain, which consisted of sixteen branches in the New York area. The security staff numbered 600 and also was responsible for the store's warehouses. The vice president for security was Albert A. Seedman, who had been Commissioner Patrick V. Murphy's chief of detectives and who was planning to retire at the end of 1983, when Sullivan would replace him.

The job paid about the same as Sullivan earned as a superchief, just over $61,000, but he would also have his pension. And presumably there would be perks and increments when he succeeded to the vice presidency. "Al Seedman has built himself a house in Florida near a golf course, and he'll retire there in his early sixties," Sullivan told me, a note of envy in his voice. A retirement home in Florida was the New York police commander's dream.

"I've been in this job for five years," Sullivan said. "There really is nowhere in the department I can go from here. And frankly, even if I could be commissioner, the comparatively low salaries of the New York police department are a factor. Chicago's commissioner makes $83,000. And I hear that the Los Angeles commissioner's salary will be going up to $110,000 next year. The salaries here are just not commensurate with the kind of work we do. One has to make a real personal sacrifice to work for the department, and I feel I've made my contribution. I will leave with no regrets.

"In the five years I've been chief of detectives under Bob McGuire, we did good work, especially with our anti-robbery effort. And we've brought the Detective Bureau's strength up from 1,500, when I took over, to 3,000."

Did he plan to recommend to the commissioner the man he would like to see replace him as chief of detectives? He said he would suggest the area commander of the Bronx, Raymond L. Jones, who had been one of his inspectors when Sullivan was the Brooklyn South area commander.

"His background and training are right for the job," Sullivan said, "and he has a good television presence, which is very necessary for the chief of detectives in this era; the public image is very important." The chief of detectives in New York, where the homicide rate was still close to 2,000 a year, was often interviewed on television. Sullivan, with his good looks, modulated speech, and air of modest self-assurance, had presented a commendable image. But he knew how much-desired his job was by all the other chiefs, and sometimes when I watched him on the screen I had the impression of a man treading water for his life.

Like McGuire (and Courtenay and Schwartz), Sullivan believed firmly in the death penalty. "It has existed since time immemorial," he said. "Only recently was it questioned. But we have seen that the neo-liberal approach just doesn't work. We have to reestablish that prison is for punishment, not rehabilitation. We have been put in the peculiar position of having to defend the death penalty, when it should be the other way around: those who want to do away with the death penalty should have to prove that we can control crime better without it. And in face of the steadily rising homicide rate, that is impossible to do."

His own candidate for his successor was not necessarily the man McGuire would pick. McGuire would make the decision in consultation with his promotions advisory committee, consisting of First Deputy Devine, Chief of Operations Murphy, and the Chief of Personnel, Joseph A. Preiss—the man who, as an assistant chief, ran the security operation for the Democratic National Convention in the summer of 1980. (The Democrats had been so delighted with New York's friendly security in 1976 under Dan Courtenay that they decided to return.)

The new chief of detectives almost certainly would be named from the ranks of the assistant chiefs. There were only ten of them now, two having been dropped as a result of budget slashes, and departmental rumor had it that Mickey Schwartz was the leading contender. He, Jones, and Robert Johnston, one of Dan Courtenay's inspectors during the DNC and now an area commander in Brooklyn, were said to be the three assistant chiefs most highly regarded by the headquarters Top Command.

By the end of 1982 Schwartz was due for promotion. He had been a two-star chief for five years and the Manhattan South area commander for more than three. He had supervised four New Year's Eve celebrations, and, for all he knew, pretty soon he would have to gear up for his fourth St. Patrick's Day parade. He was respected not only by his peers in the department but by the movers and shakers of the business community who dominated the mid-Manhattan area. In addition to being the front-runner for detective chief, it was said that he had also become a contender for commissioner when McGuire resigned. Even Dan Courtenay conceded that Schwartz, with his social grace and popularity, might have acquired the edge.

Mayor Koch felt he now knew his cop supervisors well enough to select a Perfect Police Commissioner (without the aid of a search panel) from within the department, and, indeed, Schwartz's only serious rival for future PC seemed to be William Devine; Devine was esteemed by Koch for his honesty and loyalty in the role of first deputy police commissioner.

Meanwhile, there was little doubt in the minds of those who followed police affairs that Commissioner McGuire was merely awaiting formal notice from James Sullivan of his departure date, before naming Schwartz as chief of detectives. But of course no one knew for sure who would win that most coveted of jobs in the American police community. Schwartz himself modestly declined to speculate out loud on his chances.

ELEVEN

★ The Police Foundation Ball, held every January, was a major social event. It took place in the auditorium of police headquarters and was eagerly attended by the Brass, local politicians, and private citizens who actively supported their police. It was the one day of the year when the moat was bridged, civilians mingling at tables and on the dance floor with cops. It was the one time when cops pretended not to be aliens and the rest of the partygoers pretended they were perfectly at ease among the gun-bearing men they acknowledged as guardians of their society, as good police, as, indeed, the police they deserved.

At the annual ball the Emerald Society pipers piped, the PC danced with his wife, former Mayor Lindsay (a member of the foundation's board) introduced the entertainers, guests received door prizes donated by business organizations, and, ordinarily, a spirit of great bonhomie prevailed. But the celebration on January 27, 1983, was different. It was marred by a recently revealed corruption inquiry involving two precincts in Manhattan South, and Mickey Schwartz was in trouble.

Seated with Arlene Wolff at a table that also held Dan and Mary Courtenay, Schwartz was bravely trying not to look as crushed as he felt. He had spent much of the afternoon at headquarters, summoned before the promotions advisory board.

The corruption charges had been brought by the U.S. attorney's office against fourteen specific targets—thirteen police officers and a sergeant, all but one of whom worked in the 10th Precinct; one worked in the adjoining 9th. Both precincts were under Schwartz's command. He had known nothing about this allegedly corrupt activity or about the inquiry, which was conducted not by the department's Internal Affairs unit but by the Federal Bureau of Investigation.

The suspect cops had been subpoenaed by a federal grand jury, trying to determine whether after-hours club owners were paying off the police. According to the U.S. attorney's office, this investigation was an outgrowth of an earlier one into possible mob connections to certain clubs. During the initial investigation the FBI had placed a couple of undercover agents in the area, and they had stumbled on the crooked cops, who were said to be taking bribes to allow the clubs to operate illegally.

The promotions advisory board asked Schwartz to explain why he should not be held responsible and disciplined for the exposed misconduct under his command.

The events that ultimately were to decide Schwartz's fate had begun a week earlier when the *New York Post*, with ill-concealed glee, had come out with a page-one story claiming that the grand jury was looking into "widespread graft and stealing" and that "the probe, according to sources, could mushroom into one of the largest corruption scandals to shake the Police Department since the highly publicized Knapp Commission corruption hearings of the early 70's."

The next day, again evoking the dread specter of Knapp, the *Post* ran an even more gleeful column recalling the corruption of the past:

"Before folding its tents and fading away," the story said, "the Knapp Commission uttered a premonition—that sometime around 1990, a group very much like it would hold a dramatic series of hearings, declare that the police corruption in the city is 'widespread' and 'standardized,' and recommend basic reforms to eliminate it. . . . But only at the midpoint of that forecast, it would seem the issue of

graft and stealing in the N.Y.P.D. ranks have already surfaced into yet another sensational investigation."

While neither of New York's other major newspapers
made much of the story, Commissioner McGuire was
nonetheless stung into instant Pavlovian defensiveness. The
next day the *Post* let him have his say.

There was no comparison, McGuire protested, with the
Knapp Commission inquiries. The Knapp Commission had
"uncovered institutionalized corruption, pervasive corruption, city-wide corruption which existed throughout all the
ranks of the New York City Police Department," he said,
adding, "The Department has purged itself of that corruption. . . . I think the public should be reassured that to the
extent that corruption exists in any large police department,
as it will exist to a greater or lesser extent, there are agencies
in place to go after it." McGuire also was quoted as saying
that he did view the probe "very seriously," and he promised "a quick shakeup of the manpower" in the 10th Precinct.

The *Daily News*, on the same day, commented, with editorial restraint: "The first thing to be said . . . is that all
reports indicate that whatever graft may exist is strictly
small-bore stuff and limited to a handful of cops acting on
their own, not as an organized ring. So far at least, this
seems a far cry from the wholesale corruption uncovered in
the early 70's by the Knapp Commission."

What the newspapers had not alluded to in their accounts, but what caused McGuire to take the matter more
seriously than an isolated case of misconduct, was the fact
of the corruption incident in the 10th Precinct eighteen
months earlier. That was the incident in which five cops
had been sent to jail for taking bribes, and eleven supervisors had received departmental discipline for not being
aware of the corrupt activity in their precincts. McGuire,
familiar with Chapter Nineteen of the Knapp Commission's report—the one headed "Departmental Disciplinary
Action in Corruption Cases"—believed it imperative that
Schwartz, despite his impeccable record, accept responsibility for the two instances of corruption in his precincts.

As in the case, years earlier, when Assistant Chief Charles McCarthy failed through no fault of his own to effect arrests of the mutinous off-duty cops behaving like hoodlums in the street, McGuire felt that a message had to be sent throughout the department: Manhattan South Area Commander Schwartz would be Held Accountable for the misconduct of men under his command. At the least, he would have to forgo promotion. The New York Police Brass would not be tarnished. It was a warning to all the other area commanders—and to the superchiefs, as well—to increase their vigilance. And it was a signal to the whole criminal justice community that the New York Police Brass treasured the spotless image it had struggled to maintain throughout the past ten years.

On January 26, the day before the Police Foundation Ball, the fourteen targeted cops were placed on modified duty, pending the findings of the grand jury. And on the following day Schwartz made his defense to the promotions advisory committee. By all accounts, it was exemplary. He reminded the committee members that after the first corruption incident in September of 1980, he had brought into the 10th Precinct a tough, trustworthy captain to maintain strict discipline and tight supervision. Also, Schwartz pointed out, he had regularly filed reports specifying possible areas of corruption and enumerating the "measures being taken to reduce those hazards," as was mandated in the Knapp Commission recommendations. Writing such reports, the Knapp recommendations stated, was yet "another step toward holding commanders to account for the conditions in their commands."

The fourteen cops suspended in the current investigation all worked the midnight to 8 A.M. shift, a shift that was dangerously open to bribery from the after-hours clubs flourishing in the area. But no field commander, however vigilant, could monitor the activities of every individual cop under him.

The members of the promotions advisory committee acknowledged that Schwartz was a commander of the highest rectitude, a man who had contributed valuably to the department over many years. He was a logical and obvious candidate for promotion. Nevertheless, he would have to be Held Accountable, he was told by First Deputy Commissioner William Devine. The advisory committee was going to recommend to the commissioner that Schwartz be barred from promotion to three-star rank, and suggest that perhaps he should be relieved of the command of Manhattan South. In fact, Devine implied, Schwartz might even be asked to resign from the department. He was shattered.

Devine was taking the stringent and uncompromising position laid down by the Knapp Commission and by ex-Commissioner Patrick V. Murphy. During the 50s and 60s Devine had been so repelled by the tolerated crookedness surrounding him that he had evolved into one of the department's strictest disciplinarians.

Schwartz, in pain, pretending to enjoy the ball that evening, found himself the center of concern. His friends and supporters both within and outside the department sensed a tragedy in the making. If he were forced to leave, it would be not only a dreadful personal blow, but a deprivation for a police force that badly needed men of his caliber. A number of people spoke to Commissioner McGuire on Schwartz's behalf that evening, among them Gerald Schoenfeld, chairman of the powerful Shubert Organization, which owned many of Broadway's legitimate theaters.

Schoenfeld told McGuire that he hoped it was not true, as he had read in the papers, that there were to be changes "at the top" in the Manhattan South command. He said he spoke as a concerned citizen who had worked with Schwartz on the problems of the theater district. "Mickey has the support and goodwill of the community," Schoenfeld said. "He's doing a wonderful job. He's good for the police department."

McGuire replied to Schoenfeld, as he did to a number of others that evening, that Schwartz was a personal friend, that he knew Schwartz had done nothing wrong, that he was a first-rate commander, that in fact, prior to the discovery of the 10th Precinct bribery incident, he had definitely decided to make Schwartz chief of detectives when Sullivan left. He appreciated Schwartz as not only an intelligent cop, but as "a man able to communicate police lore to influential citizens in the community." Schwartz, McGuire said, was perceived as "the Enlightened Policeman." Gravely, he added, "It was important to the department to have Mickey in that role." He felt terrible, he said, about having to hold Schwartz responsible, but the department's past history of corruption and the Knapp Commission's recommendations made it mandatory.

The next day, Schoenfeld, unpersuaded, telephoned the Reverend George Moore of St. Malachy's Church, in the Broadway theater district, and told him the story of Schwartz's difficulties; he thought that Father Moore might pass on the message to Terence Cardinal Cooke, who, in turn, might say a persuasive word in the ear of the police commissioner. Schoenfeld was convinced that his message had been delivered when, about a week later, he encountered the cardinal at a private viewing of the Vatican collection at the Metropolitan Museum of Art.

"The cardinal greeted me by name," Schoenfeld recalled, "and asked me how things were on 42nd Street."

It was doubtful, though, if even the pope could have turned McGuire aside from what he regarded as his stern duty.

"Before Knapp and Commissioner Murphy," McGuire had expounded to Schoenfeld and others the night of the ball, "the police department was rotten to the core. The fact that everyone turned their backs all the way to the top, that they said entrenched corruption will always be there, that was the real scandal. Murphy reversed that, and if I don't take the same measures, if widespread corruption sets in again, *I'll* be held morally responsible."

McGuire was also thinking of the morale of the honorable street cops who were suffering over their own tarnished image. A few days after the exposure of the corruption inquiry, he visited a cop injured by a bomb on New Year's Eve—the FALN again. The cop, a member of the bomb squad, had lost an eye and injured the other, perhaps irreparably. What he said to McGuire had nothing to do with anxiety over whether he would be permanently blinded.

"Do you think," he asked, "that the public realizes there are honest cops in the department?" The commissioner was moved to tears.

To Mickey Schwartz, McGuire said, "There's just no way I can promote you now." He added consolingly, "You're not derailed, though, just sidetracked." McGuire would not ask him to resign. But Schwartz was severly shaken. He still didn't know if he would be allowed to keep his area command. Would thirty-two years of honorable striving, of battling for acceptance by his peers, end in mortification? He consulted Courtenay. Should he put in his papers? Courtenay advised him to sit tight. The department needed him. All this would blow over.

Somewhat like Jim Hannon when McGuire first took office, Schwartz found himself in limbo. He had heard that Joseph Veyvoda, approaching retirement age, was soon to leave (along with Sullivan), which meant that the chief of patrol's job would also fall vacant. But of course Schwartz would not be promoted to that three-star position either.

"The timing for you is terrible," McGuire told him sorrowfully. McGuire was painfully alive to the tragedy of the situation. Like Hannon, who was ousted at the height of his power through no fault of his own, Schwartz had fallen victim to a system that he himself had vigorously supported throughout his career.

Ex-Commissioner Patrick V. Murphy attended the Police Foundation Ball, as he did every year, flying in from Washington with his wife, Betty. He, too, had heard about Mickey Schwartz's trouble.

"This kind of thing is always painful," he said. "Corruption problems can get out of hand because it's so easy to be overwhelmed by the pressure of everyday planning."

Murphy had promoted Schwartz from captain to deputy inspector. "I know that Mickey is an able administrator," he said. "And I have no doubt he has always understood the police dictum: 'My own career could topple if something breaks in any of my precincts.'"

Murphy acknowledged that in his day, with a considerably larger force, it was easier to allocate more resources to individual field commanders for integrity testing. But, he added, "I assume Mickey had the ability to use whatever staff he *does* have to be constantly testing the waters, taking the temperatures." He described the method he had introduced.

"We had a system where every field commander, once or twice a year, submitted a report which was his estimate of integrity in his command. And of course they then did have resources—a small internal affairs unit of their own. They were expected to use those people out in the precincts even if there wasn't a *hint* of anything wrong, to take the temperature every now and then. And if you don't take the temperature around the 10th Precinct, there's something wrong with *you*, because if you had all *angels* in an area like the 10th . . ." He let the thought trail off. "I mean, you go out and try to *find* something wrong, just go out and pose as an organized crime type or a drug pusher or whatever.

"We should all know from the history of this city that money flows like wine around a lot of activities like after-hours places."

Conceding it would be unfair, without having the facts, to make a judgment about Schwartz's zeal or lack of it, Murphy recalled the opposition expressed toward his administration when he first introduced the Accountability Principle.

"There was an uproar from all the Brass and right down to the sergeant's level," he said. "They said, 'you *can't* hold us accountable.' The argument was, 'We can't follow every police officer eight hours a day when he's working, or the sixteen hours when he's off, when he could be into corruption in his own command or another command. That's impossible for us to do.'"

Murphy's response was, "We won't assume you are automatically guilty, if something happens under your command. But, if something happens, *we will thoroughly investigate the methods you used to prevent it*, and make a judgment as to whether you were *careless*, or not using your resources effectively." And that judgment would be based in part on the regularly submitted report identifying corruption *hazards*.

A few days after the Police Foundation party, while Mickey Schwartz was still awaiting word of his fate, I asked Mayor Koch what *he* thought of the Draconian measures that were likely to be applied against one of the department's acknowledgedly outstanding chiefs.

"I want it known that I will expose and prosecute corruption in *all* of my departments," he said. "And the severest measures must be taken with the police. I thoroughly endorse the Knapp Commission's findings. The police are a military group and rigid accountability, for them, is a must."

He expanded on this theme of military self-discipline and responsibility with an anecdote about the time he was attacked by a heckler, who ground an egg in his eye while clutching him by the throat. Koch, convinced he was being assassinated, desperately found the strength to wrestle his attacker to the ground before the single detective assigned to him at that time could reach him. As the detective sat on the assailant's chest and handcuffed him, Koch, in pain and filled with fury, had an all but overwhelming urge to kick his prone attacker in the head or groin; as he debated which, his rage gave way to statesmanlike prudence, and he refrained.

"I sometimes talk to groups of cops, and I tell them that story," Koch said. "I tell them how I thought about kicking that man. And I say to them, '*You* can't even allow yourself to *think* it!'"

In his retirement home in Florida, Jim Hannon heard sporadic news from friends in the New York Police Department and listened with detachment. Not long after he and Isabel had settled there, he was offered a well-paying security job that would have required his return to New

York. He turned it down. Isabel's health was failing rapidly, and Hannon took her to visit their daughter and grandchildren in a suburb of Philadelphia. She died a few weeks later, shortly before her husband's sixty-second birthday. Hannon spent some time visiting his own and his wife's relatives in New York and New Jersey, then returned to Florida; he had established a comfortable routine there among friends, many of them retired New York cops.

In July 1982 he was remarried, to Isabel's cousin, Dorothy Barrett. By then, one of his brothers had joined him in retirement in Florida and a second brother was building a house there. His life was tranquil and full.

While most news of the New York police left him unruffled, he expressed concern on hearing of Schwartz's difficulties.

"I always liked Milty," Hannon said. "That would be a tough one for me to decide. It would depend a lot on what was going on with corruption in general in the city, if there was an increase in pad situations." A *pad* was that very "cluster of officers assigned to the same command, engaged in a conspiratorial act of misconduct," that John Guido had warned might be proliferating. Being *on the pad* meant being on the take.

"If that was going on, someone would have to be held accountable," Hannon said. "There comes a time when there just has to be a scapegoat, to send the message to other commanders to stay on their toes, or *else.*"

Like Hannon, Schwartz just happened to be in the wrong place at the wrong time. Hannon was sacrificed to send one kind of recurrent police message: that the young, vigorous, forward-looking commanders were now going to run the department (and never mind that the new group turned out to be not very different from the old). Schwartz was to be sacrificed to send another kind of cyclical message: that corruption would not be tolerated (and never mind the possible demoralization of a loyal and able commander).

With the police, the one thing you could always expect

was the unexpected. On February 2, McGuire let Schwartz know he could stay on as commander of Manhattan South. The "corruption scandal" that was going to "shake the police department" had failed to materialize. The day after the Police Foundation Ball the U.S. attorney for the Southern District held a news conference to announce that there was in fact "no evidence of widespread corruption in the police department." When asked by a *Daily News* reporter if he felt the case had been "overblown" in the press, the U.S. attorney answered (according to the *News*), "That's why I'm here." Someone in his office evidently had misjudged the scope of the case.

Not until nearly three months later were any indictments handed down by the grand jury. At headquarters they were saying in April that the investigation was unique among federal probes in that—unlike the Knapp investigation—it seemed, with time, to grow smaller, rather than bigger. Then, on April 28, nine cops—one of them retired—were charged with taking bribes ranging from $300 to $5,000 from illegal after-hours clubs. The payments were made so the cops would overlook double-parking, illegally sold liquor, and patrons' complaints.

The entire operation, according to some irate police officials, had been conducted in needless secrecy by the FBI, had invaded local jurisdiction for no cause, and was a mere sting operation to catch cops, rather than an investigation (as the feds had claimed) into organized crime connections of after-hours clubs.

"We were had by the U.S. attorney's office," one police official said, reflecting the view of the department.

Commissioner McGuire was annoyed at having been kept in the dark about the federal investigation of alleged police corruption, and relieved to find, with the passage of time, that the investigation was considerably smaller in scope than at first appeared. He did not feel, though, that he had initially overreacted.

"The press makes things real," he said. "And in any case, there *is* evidence of some corruption, and I don't ever want to minimize that danger or fail to act against it." He reaffirmed that Mickey Schwartz was "one of the outstanding commanders in the department."

While he was still anguished by his near-dismissal, Schwartz seemed outwardly to recover his spirit. He had other potentially troublesome precincts under his command, and he was grateful *they* had caused him no recent grief.

Meanwhile, he came up with a plan to assign a senior supervisor to every midnight tour in his area. "It's a little like shutting the stable door after the horse has been stolen," he admitted. He and nineteen members of his staff—captains, inspectors, and deputy chiefs—plus the one shoofly permanently assigned to him, would alternate on these tours during twenty-one days of each month. Commissioner McGuire, meanwhile, had initiated a system to beef up the monitoring of corruption citywide, making available several dozen headquarters supervisors, some of whom were to fill the monthly slots left uncovered in Schwartz's area.

"Some of these guys haven't been out in the street in twenty-five years," Schwartz said, chuckling. "They were looking all over for pieces of uniform." He performed his first night patrol on February 23.

A week later, Schwartz was ordered by his doctor into the hospital. He was suffering from a sudden attack of bleeding ulcers. Dan Courtenay telephoned him as soon as he heard the news.

"Listen, Mickey," he said. "We *give* people ulcers, we don't *get* them." But he was concerned.

Schwartz was released six days later, still weak, and advised by his doctor not to go back to work for a while. But he insisted on monitoring plans for the March 17 St. Patrick's Day parade. "He shouldn't be working," said Courtenay, who was planning to march.

Courtenay felt for Schwartz's pain and disappointment. But, though content with his job, Courtenay could not suppress a reflexive hope that once again he himself had a chance to be chief of detectives. Transfers from one three-star bureau chieftaincy to another, while not routine, did occur. And the five Superchiefdoms had their own pecking order: the chief of patrol, because he commanded the most men, was regarded as number one; then came chief of detectives, followed by chief of organized crime control, then chief of inspectional services and chief of personnel.

Detectives would be a decided step up in *prestige*, if not in rank or money. And in fact, now that Schwartz was out of the running, the prevailing rumor in the department once again named Big Dan Courtenay as the leading contender for the job. The thinking was that this would be the tidy hierarchical compromise: if the timing was wrong for Schwartz to be promoted to the job, at least he would not be bypassed in favor of another commander of his own rank. And Courtenay had certainly proved himself beyond any doubt as highly competent to step from one investigative bureau to another. But, as Courtenay said, "This is at least the third time I've been up for chief of detectives, and I'm not counting on it." In spite of his expressed skepticism, though, he decided to ask Sullivan outright when he was planning to leave the department. The raise that Sullivan had been awaiting was imminent, and Courtenay couldn't understand why Sullivan continued to delay naming a firm date for his departure.

Schwartz was out in the street at 11 A.M. on St. Patrick's Day, which was raw and gray. He looked drawn and, throughout the morning, police and parade officials came over to greet him and inquire after his health. They said such things as, "You should have stayed home a few more days." Most of his well-wishers sounded genuinely concerned. One captain said to me, "We don't get really good bosses too often. We have to take care of them." Schwartz, however, was a realist. "Some of these guys are probably hoping I'm sick enough to retire and make room for them," he said.

This particular parade happened to be embroiled in political controversy, and Schwartz, though acknowledging he was still a bit shaky, felt compelled to see it through. (He had time for small jokes. "Arlene packed me a lunch," he told me, "so I can stay on my ulcer diet: a piece of plain, broiled chicken and Maalox.")

The controversy was over the selection of Michael Flannery, a vocal supporter of the Irish Republican Army, as the parade's grand marshal. A number of prominent political figures—Senators Edward Kennedy and Patrick Moynihan, former Governor Hugh Carey—had refused to march, a number of bands had withdrawn from the parade, and it was believed that Terence Cardinal Cooke would stay behind the closed doors of St. Patrick's Cathedral on Fifth Avenue until after the grand marshal had passed by. Since the cardinal, standing on the steps of the cathedral, was one of the enduring symbols of any St. Patrick's Day parade, his pointed absence, it was feared, might lead to some sort of disruptive demonstration.

Schwartz was at pains to keep the front of the cathedral and the steps cleared of *everyone*, including police officials, so that there would be no target for protesters demanding that the cardinal appear. Schwartz had made a bet with his exec, Deputy Chief Michael V. J. Willis, that the cardinal would not appear. Whoever lost would buy the other dinner at an expensive French restaurant (Schwartz expected to be off his restricted diet soon). "I've got the cardinal locked in the basement," Schwartz joked. He won his bet, for Cardinal Cooke did remain within for three-quarters of an hour, until well after the grand marshal had passed by. (When the cardinal emerged, he was booed.)

Schwartz was still in the street when Courtenay, marching in step with Sullivan, went by. "You look pale," Sullivan called to Schwartz. Schwartz smiled. "I *like* parades," he said, sincerely.

Courtenay, as he had promised himself to do, asked Sullivan, as they marched, when he was planning to leave. He got a shock; Sullivan had changed his mind and wasn't leaving after all. He had already informed the commissioner of his change of plans, he told Courtenay.

"As the time to leave got closer," Sullivan later explained to me, "the job at Alexander's seemed less desirable. The larger income seemed less important than doing something that made me happy. My wife and my friends felt I was making a mistake, that I shouldn't be making a purely economic decision. I decided to stay in the job I enjoy, rather than in one that would pay more."

In fact, his raise had come through, as had Courtenay's, and raises for all the department's three-star and two-star chiefs as well. Sullivan and Courtenay now earned $67,000, while Schwartz's new salary was $64,000. (The deputy police commissioners all received raises, too, but the commissioner's salary stayed at $72,000.) Still, Sullivan had, as he put it, "passed up quite a bit of money."

"But I'm not unhappy about it," he said. "I think, in spite of what I said earlier, that I *do* still have a contribution to make to the department." Did Sullivan contradict himself? Well, then he contradicted himself. (At a promotions ceremony soon after, McGuire, who was periodically rumored to be about to resign the commissionership, quipped, "The rumors you've heard about my quitting to become head of security at Alexander's have no foundation.")

And so the name of the commissioner's new choice for chief of detectives was never revealed, and Schwartz's disappointment, as well as Courtenay's briefly held hope, was neutralized by Sullivan's impulsive decision to stay. The next opening for a bureau chief probably would not come until the chief of patrol retired, and that was months away.

When Mickey Schwartz got over the worst of his ulcer condition, he went on his second post-midnight tour, and this time he permitted me to accompany him:

Schwartz picks me up at my apartment building at 12:40 A.M. one day in early May, which has been unseasonably chilly. The cop on his personal staff who always drives him, Joe Morello, is at the wheel of the unmarked, radio-equipped car that goes with the command of Manhattan South. Morello is in uniform and wears his bulletproof vest. Schwartz, in deference to Arlene Wolff's concern, usually wears a vest, too, on this kind of patrol, but he has wrenched his back lifting furniture in his apartment, which is being painted, and has decided a vest would be too uncomfortable tonight. He is in uniform, though, and carries his nightstick, a mean-looking cudgel, close up. And, of course, he wears his holstered service revolver.

"The last time I went on night patrol," Schwartz says, "I asked the driver of a suspicious-looking car for his license and registration, and I kept my hand on my gun. When he handed me his papers, I had trouble with the small print out there in the dim street light. I needed a third hand to put on my reading glasses." He laughs at his own awkwardness. He was a patrolman for nine years, but that was a long time ago.

While he pays attention to street happenings that seem potentially dangerous, his main objective on these night tours is to monitor the behavior of his own cops, he says. Last week an inspector on his staff came across a couple of cooping cops on the midnight tour. They had parked their patrol car—one of the new ones, with individual bucket seats—behind some trucks near the waterfront, and were blissfully asleep, stretched out on the seats' reclining backs. The department had ordered the new cars to accommodate the disparity in leg length of male and female partners; clearly, the seats would have to be modified so as *not* to recline. The cooping cops were disciplined—but not as severely as a couple of other cops who were spotted going into an after-hours bar for drinks; they were docked fifteen days' pay.

"Routine patrol, especially late at night, can get terribly boring," Schwartz says, "and it's hard for the cops not to nap, or, after a while, to look for trouble. I remember I used to devise games when I was on the night shift. I'd pick different blocks each night and test the door handles of all the parked cars. When I found one unlocked, I'd write a note warning the driver to be more careful, and put it on the seat."

We pull up across the street from one of the more notorious discotheques, its neon lights glaring. Bouncers guard its entrance. Waiting limousines and taxicabs stretch out for several blocks, many of them illegally double-parked. We watch as a small police van bearing three uniformed cops, supervised by a sergeant, pulls up, and the men start ticketing the cars—another of Schwartz's innovations. A passing patrol car joins them, and one of the cops puts on his cap as he steps into the street.

"Look, he put his hat on," Schwartz says, pleased that the uniform rule is being obeyed. "Of course, it's probably because he's bald." The sergeant from the van spots Schwartz, crosses the street, and salutes him, as Schwartz, also saluting, leaves his car to exchange a few words.

Returning to his car, Schwartz says, "I'm trying to increase the supervisory presence at night, make the cops feel less isolated, give them a sense of our being there and caring about their work."

Morale, he says, has improved as a result of these night tours by the Brass. During the first weeks there was apprehension, and coded signals of warning were passed when inspectors or chiefs were known to be out on patrol; the most colorful of the warnings was the 9th Precinct's: "The flies are in the shit house!"

Along Eleventh Avenue, at the approaches to the bridges, the prostitutes are out in force, and on one corner a small group of pimps is gathered, keeping a wary eye on them. Many of the "working girls," as Schwartz sometimes calls them, are actually transvestites, and he points them out. I tell him that I recently had a tour of this area from Dan Courtenay. "Dan can't tell the difference between a female pross and a guy dressed as a woman," Schwartz says.

At 2:40 A.M. we cruise through the 9th, which runs from 14th Street to Houston and includes Avenue B and East 5th Street, where Sergeant Reddy and Officer Glover were murdered. "Make sure your door is locked," Schwartz says, locking his own. "This is a *very* bad junkie neighborhood." We glide slowly down the streets of crumbling, abandoned buildings, as the junkies, spotting the uniforms, eyeball Schwartz and his driver, and they eyeball back. It's a little after 3 A.M., and we are on our way now to the 1st Precinct House in Manhattan's toe. Schwartz makes it a point to check in with each of the ten precincts under his command when he does night duty. He intersperses these stops with looks at various after-hours clubs, discos, and all-night game arcades that have been identified as potential corruption hazards for cops. Because this happens to be a Monday, many of the places are closed, recovering from the weekend, and it's a quiet night.

On our way to the Midtown North Precinct on West 54th Street, we pass a suspicious-looking man leaning against a dark building. Schwartz instructs Morello to turn around and cruise by again. The man looks like a car booster, Schwartz says, and Morello agrees. We pull alongside a patrol car, and the cop in the passenger seat says they're tracking the same man. The driver of the patrol car steps through his door, hatless. Suddenly he sees the stars on Schwartz's shoulders, the braid on his cap. He dives back into his car and slaps his own cap on his head, then comes around to Schwartz's car and salutes smartly.

After a brief exchange both cars move slowly down the block, seeking the suspected auto thief. The two cops in the patrol car spot the suspect, toss him, find a bent coat hanger on him, confirming their suspicions. But the man is stoned and apathetic, and they leave him, after confiscating the coat hanger. This is the most exciting thing that has happened all night. "You see what a safe city this is?" Schwartz says.

The next two precinct houses Schwartz visits report arrests for robbery—*good* arrests, with reliable witnesses—three suspects in all, one a prostitute. Schwartz is feeling buoyed and hungry and decides to stop and buy some apples. By now, it's 4:30 A.M. The Manhattan South Area is dotted with fruit-and-vegetable stands that seem never to close. They are brightly lit, often backed up by commodious interiors that sell grocery items, and they all seem to be run by industrious Korean families that spell each other around the clock. No one seems to rob them, and their tidy mounds of gleaming oranges, melons, and tomatoes are never depleted. They are brilliant oases in the grubby streets.

Officer Morello and I watch from the car as Schwartz insists on paying for the apples that are being offered free. The beaming proprietor is delighted by the police presence in his neighborhood and wants to show his appreciation. Schwartz knows he is hurting the proprietor's feelings by not accepting the token gift. But he has to be ruthless. Accepting a free apple would be symbolic corruption. How could he then reprimand a street cop for accepting a free drink? Or a $25 Christmas present from a shopkeeper? Or a $300 bribe from an after-hours club owner? You could no more be a little corrupt than a little pregnant.

One of our last stops, at 5 A.M., is the 5th Precinct in Chinatown, the oldest in Manhattan, built in 1881. It is still heated by a coal furnace that has to be manually stoked.

"We should have torn it down years ago, but the community puts so much pressure on us every time we try to close it, that we just can't do it," Schwartz says.

We stop at the 10th Precinct House. "This precinct, as you know, has been the bane of my life," Schwartz says with a sigh.

On the way to our last stop for the night, we hear a radio call, a signal 10–34: a male is beating a female at Eleventh Avenue and 42nd Street. "Probably a pimp beating up a pross," says Schwartz. We pull up before the Midtown South Precinct House at 35th Street between Eighth and Ninth Avenues, a few blocks from Madison Square Garden. The precinct, commanded by a deputy inspector, is the busiest in the city—"probably in the world," says Schwartz. It gets over 50,000 complaints a year. Tonight, though, it is quiet.

Dawn is breaking and Morello is beginning to yawn. Schwartz, while he believes he has recovered from his recent illness, nevertheless doesn't want to overdo it. He wants to get a couple of hours' sleep. He has secret worries. He decides to call it a night.

TWELVE

★ Having once again swallowed his disappointment at not moving into the chief of detectives' seat—when, at last, it had seemed so closely within his grasp—Dan Courtenay, ostensibly cheerful, settled back into his job and renewed his attack on organized crime. Like Mickey Schwartz, he, too, had acquired some extra manpower as a result of the attention focused on after-hours clubs: a seventeen-member squad, supervised by a lieutenant and two sergeants, that went out five days a week at 3 A.M. to uncover illegal activities in the clubs.

But Courtenay's major area of concentration was getting rid of street-level drugs, particularly around the schools— "For the young people's sake," he said. This area, he tried to make himself believe, was one in which he could have "a real impact."

"We are a city agency and we can't go after the people who transport the drugs here from out of state or out of the country," he said. "Drugs don't originate in New York. But we *can* get the local dealers." In August 1981 he set up a closely supervised street enforcement unit composed of a hundred police officers and dubbed "the three R's program."

"We use very young cops, sometimes right out of the

Academy, males and females, who can pass for students,"
Courtenay explained. "That way we can get in close."

He deployed his troops throughout the five boroughs in
the immediate vicinities of several hundred elementary,
secondary, parochial, and high schools, as well as some
colleges. His teams were in the streets three or four days
each week, and in 144 days they made 5,489 arrests, 71
percent of them for selling narcotics, the rest for possession.
Courtenay noted with interest that only 7 percent of the
dealers arrested were students.

"If we can get these dealers locked up and off the street
for from three to five years at a time," he said, "it can be a
big deterrent." He thought there should be mandatory sentences for drug dealers, but the courts, he said, were not
cooperative.

Courtenay believed in mandatory sentencing for firearms
possession, and, like the commissioner, he believed in the
death penalty, on the ground that a life sentence could
always be mitigated by the courts. (He had little faith in the
backbone of judges.)

"There are people who should be permanently removed
from society to guarantee its survival," he said. "Every human should have the right to protect himself from preda-
tors." (Mickey Schwartz, who had not favored the death
penalty a few years earlier, now felt as strongly about it as
Courtenay. "We've had enough," he said. "We must send a
clear message to the criminals who prey on our society. Life
imprisonment without parole just doesn't happen; it can
always be reversed.")

Courtenay's prestige was now such that he was called to
testify in Washington in May 1983 before the Senate committee investigating organized crime. He felt strongly on
the subject and believed, as did most police officials, that
the public was duped by films and television shows glam-
orizing organized crime figures; he was dismayed by the
evident public adulation of crooks in general. For every
Serpico or *Hill Street Blues* there was a *Godfather* and a

Godfather II. We sometimes talked about the dark fascination that criminals seem to have for artists and intellectuals, and how writers incline to make pets of outlaws, to romanticize them.

Courtenay was scornful, for instance, of Norman Mailer's defense of Richard L. Stratton, who was convicted in March 1983 of conspiracy to smuggle marijuana and hashish. Stratton, when arrested a year earlier, had contended he was a writer researching a book about drug smuggling. Mailer, who had befriended Stratton in the early 70s, testified at Stratton's trial that Stratton was a friend he would "always trust" and that Stratton's writing was "pretty good."

"That guy was carrying a suitcase full of drugs," Courtenay said, with heavy sarcasm, "but he was a 'writer,' and, therefore, innocent. If I caught *you* with a suitcase full of drugs, I don't care what story you told me about doing research, I'd snap you up. You better *believe* I would." (I do, I do, I silently replied.)

As the three-star chief of OCCB, Courtenay put in his habitual long, vigorous hours, just as he had done as an assistant chief, and he seemed, to his colleagues and his family, to be his usual sanguine self: a solid and enduring rock of a man, a man whom Mickey Schwartz, despite his bantering competitiveness, admired deeply as a cop-commander and even, in a way, as a role model. Courtenay was a man who could acknowledge a plague of dragons, and yet return to do battle year after year, his hope undimmed. In my mind, I could still hear him saying, "If I didn't have hope, I wouldn't be in this job. If I thought nothing could be done, I'd be living a lie." I would always see him as a man who had learned to keep his integrity, his faith—and even his rich sense of humor—playing a game that had no rules. But something was gnawing at Courtenay.

Toward the end of May, Chief of Patrol Veyvoda announced he was leaving for health reasons, somewhat ahead of his mandatory retirement date. But to insure his maximum pension, he would continue to hold the rank until the end of June; meanwhile, Commissioner McGuire asked Dan Courtenay to serve as acting chief of patrol, in addition to running the Organized Crime Control Bureau.

"How will you manage both jobs?" I asked Courtenay.

"I'll just work harder," he said. It wouldn't be that difficult, he added graciously, considering the high caliber of the seven area commanders—including Mickey Schwartz—now under his direct supervision. "If they can't resolve a problem, it can't be resolved," he said.

But Courtenay couldn't help thinking back to the time, six years earlier, when Commissioner Codd had made him acting chief of patrol to fill the gap left by Thomas Mitchelson's sudden retirement. And he remembered his chagrin when he learned that Codd did not intend to make the appointment permanent. Courtenay *thought* he had heard McGuire say that the appointment would be permanent once Veyvoda's retirement became official, but he was so nervous about it, he wasn't sure, and he couldn't bring himself to broach the subject again; he would just have to sweat it out once more. McGuire, in fact, *had* told Courtenay the job would be officially his at the end of June; Courtenay had simply not allowed himself to hear it.

Courtenay was gripped by a sense of altogether unfamiliar anxiety. He saw himself going around in circles. He had already achieved his third star. And suddenly he found himself wondering if he even *wanted* to be chief of patrol. With expert area commanders below him, and a vigorous chief of operations younger than he directly above him, would he have any scope for his own style of operation? Somehow Courtenay's optimism seemed to have deserted him. He was getting older, and his elasticity, his buoyancy—along with his optimism—were depleted. After all these years, all his seniority, all his service and vast experience, Courtenay couldn't help feeling demeaned. He was a Good Soldier, yes; but he was also a proud man. There just might come a time when the two would be in irresolvable conflict.

"You can spend your career praying and wishing for your next promotion," he said. "You know you're qualified, and sometimes you get the job you're entitled to, sometimes you don't. After a while you begin to wonder if the anxiety is worth it."

Courtenay recalled the time, not quite four years earlier, when First Deputy Commissioner William Devine had interviewed him for the job of chief of organized crime control.

"He bluntly told me I was one of a number of candidates he was talking to. I *knew* I was the best qualified man for the job, from every point of view, and I felt that should have been recognized. I resented the interview, and I found myself overselling my qualifications. It was humiliating. I really thought I might not get the job. I shouldn't have had to go through that." He grinned ruefully. "You can find yourself wishing your life away."

In May, also, a sudden, serious illness, requiring major surgery, forced Devine to take what threatened to be an extended leave of absence from the department. McGuire, unsure if Devine would recover sufficiently to resume his duties, but not wanting to further demoralize a critically ill man, did not replace him. Instead, he asked Chief of Operations Patrick Murphy to take over some of Devine's duties, in addition to his own. Once again the department trembled on the brink of change.

Would Courtenay become chief of patrol? If so, who would replace him as chief of organized crime control? Would it be Mickey Schwartz? Or was it still too soon for Schwartz to be forgiven? Would Devine return, or would McGuire be obliged to select a new first dep from among his headquarters chiefs (or elsewhere)? The possibilities were open-ended enough to furnish endless speculation at headquarters.

"I'm not going to look into the future," Courtenay said,

with apparent sangfroid. "I've got more than enough to occupy me right now." Perhaps he, himself, did not realize that a wound of the soul had opened. That was in May.

On Friday, June 3, Dan Courtenay arrived at his headquarters office at 7:30 A.M. as usual. He had been conscious of a vague malaise when he kissed Mary good-bye, but he had pushed the feeling aside. By 9:30, however, an increasing sense of what he later described as "discomfort" was making it impossible for him to concentrate on his work. It was a not-clearly-definable sensation of being "boxed in."

"My stomach was in a knot," he said later. He had noticed recently that he couldn't sit at his desk for more than half an hour at a stretch without having to get up and move about. He thought it might be a back strain—not an ache, exactly, but more like a tensing-up that begged for relief. At the same time, he was aware that the tension was not confined to his spine. For the first time in his police career, he felt uncomfortable at headquarters, ill at ease in the police role for which he had cast himself during the past thirty-five years.

Telling his exec that he wasn't feeling well, Courtenay went to see the police surgeon, Dr. Clarence Robinson. He began to describe his symptoms to Dr. Robinson, and suddenly he heard himself saying, "I want to leave the department. I don't want to do what I'm doing anymore. I'm going to quit."

Dr. Robinson pressed for more details and listened sympathetically. He made a preliminary physical examination, found nothing to cause immediate concern, but suggested that Courtenay go on sick leave and undergo a comprehensive medical checkup, including a stress test and an orthopedic examination of his back.

Courtenay agreed. But he insisted he was leaving the department. He would put in his papers, regardless of the medical results, at the end of June. He would not wait to be formally offered chief of patrol—he didn't want it. Dr.

Robinson advised Courtenay not to make such a precipitate decision, but Courtenay said he didn't need to think it over, and he would tell the commissioner immediately that he was leaving.

Courtenay and Dr. Robinson had a long lunch together, during which Courtenay continued to unburden himself. He knew in his bones, he said, that he'd made the right decision. Having made it, he already felt better, felt that a crushing weight had been lifted from his shoulders. Feeling more and more lighthearted, he said that the sense of relief was positively exhilarating.

After lunch he returned to his office, calmly told his exec he was going on sick leave until the end of the month and would not be coming back, collected his personal belongings, and drove home, arriving a little before 4 P.M. Mary was surprised to see her husband back so early. Normally he arrived home at about a quarter to seven. Courtenay told his wife, with a mounting sense of euphoria, that he had quit the department. She was stunned.

On the following Monday Courtenay telephoned Commissioner McGuire to inform him of his decision. McGuire tried to persuade Courtenay to stay, assuring him that the job of chief of patrol would definitely be Courtenay's at the end of June. Moreover, McGuire told Courtenay that if he preferred to stay on as chief of organized crime control, he had that option as well. Courtenay thanked McGuire but said he had made up his mind to leave. McGuire said to think it over; he'd hold both jobs open until June 30.

Despite his offer, McGuire had to consider the probability that Courtenay meant what he said. Illness and defection had invaded the Top Brass, and the commissioner found himself in the unusual situation of having two Superchiefdoms to fill, as well as an incapacitated first dep to worry about.

Had the Brass become so heavily varnished that cracks were beginning to surface? Was the stress of living up to the new Draconian image becoming self-destructive? Was

McGuire, after all, turning out to be too much of an outsider to truly grasp the police psyche, to deal with the subtleties of the Police Experience? Or had he, alternatively, come too strongly under the influence of the unbending William Devine? Undeniably, the Top Brass was showing sudden and alarming signs of disarray. Worse was yet to come.

The furor over the 10th Precinct had died down, and McGuire decided that enough time had now elapsed for Mickey Schwartz to be forgiven. Courtenay had suggested Schwartz to McGuire as his successor, and McGuire was considering that possibility. He was also thinking of Schwartz for the even more prestigious job of chief of patrol, and feeling very pleased about it; he knew what such a promotion would mean to Schwartz, and how it would wipe away the pain he had suffered in January.

Dan Courtenay listed, among the reasons for his decision to retire from the department, his acute concern for his health. (Indeed, to hear him enumerate with relish all the tests he was undergoing was to suspect him of an atypical onslaught of hypochondria; in all the years I'd known him, I had never heard him express any concern about the state of his health.)

"I have to think of myself now," he said, pointing out that too many friends of his, both in and out of the department, suddenly were falling ill. He mentioned Devine, Veyvoda, and Schwartz. Devine's illness, in particular, had shocked him, for Devine was considerably younger than he was.

"I always said, when the job wasn't fun anymore, I'd leave," Courtenay told me. "I suddenly realized it wasn't fun." With pain in his voice he added, "I faced the fact that, with all our best efforts, there are more narcotics in the street today than when I took over OCCB. And being chief of patrol wouldn't be any better, just more of the same. I've had all that. I've gone higher than I ever expected. When I came on the force, I thought that if I ever made sergeant, that would be a dream come true. What's the point of waiting, now, until I'm forced out?"

He was aware that forced retirement, within a few months, was a strong possibility. There was a chance that McGuire might stay on until after the next mayoral election, and even beyond, if Koch were reelected to a third term. But it was widely believed that the commissioner had already made up his mind to leave in December, the end of his fifth year in the job. And with the appointment of a new commissioner, all or most of the Superchiefs might be ousted, as had happened when Michael Codd left.

"I've known chiefs who just couldn't accept the fact that they had to get out," Courtenay said. "I remember one who simply refused to give up his shield. They had to go to his home and take it away from him. I don't plan to get to that point. I want to leave on *my* terms, in my own time." Wryly he added, "A lot of people are lighting candles for me." Such figurative candle-lighting was the departmental version of voodoo, of sticking pins into the waxen effigy of someone you wanted out of the way, so you could take his place.

Approaching his fifty-seventh birthday, Courtenay felt he had only a few more "good years" left, and he wanted to enjoy them. Intimations of mortality strike different men at different ages, and a sense of his own transience had suddenly overtaken him. Like many members of the Top Brass, he felt a nagging sense of guilt at having devoted less time than he would have liked to his family. He and Mary were expecting their first grandchild in October. And they were seriously considering giving up their house in Queens and moving into a condominium or an apartment—possibly in Manhattan.

"Mary and my children were totally surprised by my decision," Courtenay said. "But they are all being very supportive." (To me, Mary Courtenay said, "Thank God, it's about time.")

Courtenay's abrupt departure caused shock waves throughout the department. Mickey Schwartz, in particular, was incredulous. It had been Courtenay, after all, who—less than six months earlier—had advised him *not* to quit the department when his career seemed threatened over the 10th Precinct corruption episode. Courtenay had always been, for Schwartz, as for others, a symbol of unflappable durability.

Dan and Mary Courtenay attended the Police Foundation's boat ride around Manhattan that June 15, an annual springtime event.

"We're not going to give up our friends in the department," Courtenay said. He had no hard feelings toward the department or any of its top officials. He was content to see it run without him. But he was taken aback by the intensity of the reaction to his leaving.

"I guess I've upset a lot of people," he said to Arlene Wolff, who was aboard for the party, accompanied by Schwartz, and who could not bring herself to accept Courtenay's decision, even after he patiently explained to her all his reasons.

By then the rumors had begun to circulate: Courtenay had actually been pushed out; Courtenay was having a nervous breakdown; Courtenay was secretly planning to take a better job. But his manner and appearance gave no credence to any of these rumors. He had pushed *himself* out. Perhaps he was a bit anxious about his health and mortality, but he looked relaxed and happy. He insisted he had no immediate plans to take a new job, but he didn't deny that he might, after a while, look around for one. Meanwhile he was assured of an annual pension of around $48,000. Courtenay was surprised and touched by the "outpouring of feeling and concern."

Mickey Schwartz continued to brood over Courtenay's precipitate resignation. "Dan's leaving really disturbed me," he said. "It left a void. I started reassessing my own life." But Schwartz, in truth, hungered more than ever for that third gold star. And now, with Courtenay's departure, there were *two* Superchiefdoms available. He had to have one of them, had to prove he could rise as high as Courtenay. He would not accept being branded an outsider who never made it quite to the top. He wanted it so much, and he had come so ominously close to losing his chance at it.

The first corruption incident in the 10th Precinct back in June of 1981 had so unnerved Schwartz that he began worrying about the possibility of police misconduct in another precinct under his command. There was a topless bar in midtown that held a compelling allure for some cops. An ugly episode had originated there that ultimately resulted in the dismissal of two men under his command, and Schwartz was deeply concerned about how to keep cops from making surreptitious visits to similar establishments in the area. He could not afford a scandal in yet another precinct under his command. Confronted with a problem that continued to plague him, he took an ill-considered step to safeguard his career and—he truly believed—the integrity of the department as well. But the action, however well intended, was a mistake, and now it was about to boomerang.

By mid-June the P.C. had accepted the fact of Courtenay's retirement and was studying various options. In addition to Schwartz, he was considering Raymond Jones (Chief of Detectives Sullivan's protégé, who was now acting chief of organized crime) and Robert Johnston, Jr. (one of Courtenay's inspectors, along with Schwartz, during the 1976 Democratic National Convention); they were the same two assistant chiefs who had earlier been mentioned as candidates for chief of detectives.

First Deputy Commissioner Devine, partially recovered but undergoing outpatient treatment, returned to the department on a part-time basis June 21. He consulted with

McGuire and Chief of Operations Murphy about the impending promotions. (If two assistant chiefs were appointed as full chiefs to fill the bureau vacancies, they, in turn, would have to be replaced by two deputy chiefs, and so on, down the line. A full-scale promotions ceremony was scheduled for June 30. A lot of people were lighting candles.)

By Wednesday, June 22, Commissioner McGuire had decided to make Mickey Schwartz chief of patrol. Schwartz knew he was the leading candidate for the job and expected to get it. His euphoria did not last long.

The following day the department was given a bizarre piece of secret information about Schwartz. The handful of high police officials privy to the information considered it to be potentially very embarrassing to the department, and they agreed it ended Schwartz's usefulness as a high-level commander. The information was conveyed—in strictest confidence—by another law enforcement agency and involved a case being investigated by that agency. If revealed prematurely, the agency's case would be compromised, and therefore the information had to be handled with extreme delicacy.

It appeared that Schwartz—through his private acquaintance with a local businessman, who he knew had connections to organized crime figures—had passed a word of warning to the owner of a particularly noisome topless bar in the midtown area: Keep off-duty cops out of the place. Schwartz, it seemed, had been so desperately anxious to keep his territory clean that he had been unaware he would compromise the police department by seeking help from mobsters.

Chief of Inspectional Services John Guido, after meeting with Commissioner McGuire, confronted Schwartz on Friday, June 24. Schwartz admitted the truth of the information. He attempted to justify his action on the grounds that the pressure he had brought to bear was good for the department and an effective way of solving what had been a messy problem. He seemed, at first, unable to grasp the commissioner's view that his venture—however well intended—was a patently unacceptable collaboration between the police and organized crime.

Schwartz had suffered an aberration under agonizing pressure. His offense was relative. He did not, for example, abandon a woman trapped in a car at the bottom of a bay. Had he been a U.S. senator, he could have continued to serve his government.

Fifteen years earlier he could have stayed on in the department, where many of his fellow commanders were doubtless committing far worse indiscretions and rising even higher. Even today on most other big city police forces he could have committed a similar indiscretion very likely with no fuss made at all. He had done nothing illegal, nothing corrupt, and his rationale, however askew, was in his view honorable.

But this was the Varnished Brass of New York, the rigidly clean and upright hierarchy that was Frank Serpico's legacy to the police department. Sturdy and dependable cop that Mickey Schwartz had been for thirty-two years, he would now have to go. He had overcome the hostility to his religious background, the stigma of his divorce, the trauma of his childhood, only to be brought down by a single, tragic misjudgment. His high position, the department insisted, was a particular trust; an assistant chief of the NYPD had to be above suspicion.

It was Chief of Operations Patrick Murphy who suggested that Schwartz put in his papers. Angry at being punished so harshly, Schwartz argued the unfairness of it, but he could not be forgiven.

Only a few top police officials knew that Schwartz was being asked to retire and why. McGuire could not publicly reveal how the details of Schwartz's indiscretion had come to his attention, and he was constrained to refuse any comment about his commander's departure. By his silence he let it appear that Schwartz was leaving voluntarily because he had been bypassed for promotion, with the implication that the 10th Precinct episode was still being held against him. Privately, McGuire grieved over the loss. And Schwartz himself, without actually saying so, allowed the same implication to be read into his action. He made himself unavailable to reporters, and they assumed—recalling the widely publicized trouble in the 10th Precinct—that he had, indeed, resigned in a huff over having been bypassed. There was no hint in their stories that he had been asked to leave.

At the time I, too, was unaware that Schwartz had been relieved of his command. But I *did* know, having earlier inquired of the commissioner's office, that Schwartz had been forgiven for the 10th Precinct and had, ever since, been a serious candidate for promotion. Puzzled, I called him to ask what had gone wrong and found him evasive. He had just seen his dream of promotion slip away forever, and he was trying to hide his distress.

"I had a feeling I wouldn't get either of those jobs," he said. "I know Bill Devine is no fan of mine. I'm still young enough to get another job, and I decided now was the right time to leave." Also, he said, his ulcers were again bothering him. "Dr. Robinson said that with my condition, I'd be crazy to stay in the department. I'm pretty sure I'm eligible for a disability pension." Without a disability his pension would be about $45,000; with one it would be $10,000 more.

Still implying that he was leaving the department of his own accord, Schwartz added, "I have absolutely no animosity against the police department. Bob McGuire is a gentleman. Another commissioner might have fired me for the 10th Precinct episode; he did, after all, let me keep my command."

Schwartz even had a kind word for Devine: "The first dep *has* to be a ball-buster; I'm sure if I were in that job, I'd be the same. I lived by the rules and died by them. That is," he caught himself, "I decided *not* to die by them." A few days later, I found out through my own sources why Schwartz had left the department, but he would not discuss the matter with me, being under the same constraint of confidentiality as the other high officials in the know. Although he could not admit it to me, I understood that he had accepted his mistake, had resolved to live with the consequences, and was, understandably, trying to salvage his reputation.

The new appointments were formally announced on the afternoon of Wednesday, June 28: Robert Johnston to be chief of patrol, Raymond Jones to be chief of organized crime control. Neither had been an assistant chief as long as Schwartz, nor held jobs as important as his. That same day Schwartz began the involved process of filing his papers of retirement; he packed his personal office gear, including his Buffet clown, which now, more than ever, seemed to be a soulful symbol of Schwartz's doomed striving.

"This is the single most terrible day in my life," Arlene Wolff told me.

It had been less than a month since Courtenay had startled his colleagues and the press by his abrupt departure, and everyone wondered what was happening to the police department. Schwartz felt hurt by the newspaper stories, which spoke of his having been "snubbed" in favor of other commanders with less tenure as assistant chiefs. And Courtenay (who was unaware of the real reason for Schwartz's departure) was indignant on his colleague's behalf.

"How can they write things like that?" he said angrily. "Mickey gave thirty-two years of his life to the department and there wasn't a better commander than he was. Why didn't they say anything good about his career?"

Schwartz kept his silence. He was ready now to put policing behind him. While Schwartz had ambitions for a new career, and would, perhaps, like Joe Hoffman, soon forget he had ever been a cop, Courtenay would, like Jim Hannon, be forever part cop.

"It's like being a priest," Courtenay said. "Once a priest, always a priest. Once a cop, always a cop." Unlike Hannon, he would continue to carry a gun. Partly it was because he would feel naked without it, could simply not imagine himself *not* carrying a gun. But also, he said, "I feel I might sometime be in a position where I could protect someone." He would never retire to Florida. "I'll always live in this city," he said, "and I'll always be policing it, even as a civilian."

Dan Courtenay luxuriated in the unaccustomed freedom of being out of the daily spotlight, while taking his time to sever his ties with the department. He received a number of job offers and several invitations to explore future opportunities. He took every medical test he could think of and passed them all. He said he was feeling better and better about himself. He decided to take the summer off, to make no decisions until the autumn. Every day his conviction grew stronger that he had been right to stop his police career.

In mid-July Courtenay drove to headquarters to turn in his three-star shield. He submitted his worn identity card to the property clerk, and it was returned to him, stamped "Retired." That gave him a small wrench.

He stopped in for a chat with the P.C. and found him in a low mood about the recent series of illnesses and departures. There were new casualties: Chief of Detectives James Sullivan had briefly suffered a partial loss of vision; he feared he was having a stroke, and the police surgeon was summoned. But the episode passed quickly, and later tests showed no abnormality. Still, Dr. Robinson was being kept unusually busy among the chiefs and superchiefs. And James Meehan, who reported to McGuire in his capacity as chief of transit police, had suffered a heart attack and was in the hospital under intensive care.

Courtenay and McGuire talked about the hideous pressures of police command, the awful responsibility, the virtually unrelieved anxiety. McGuire told Courtenay he might leave the job even earlier than December, that he was staying on largely because Devine was ill and could not take over for him, and he didn't want to leave the mayor stranded.

McGuire was distressed about a congressional hearing scheduled for July 17, during which he was going to have to defend his department against charges that brutality toward blacks was widespread and tolerated. He believed that the charges, brought by black community leaders and elected officials, were politically motivated against Mayor Koch and might stir unrest in black neighborhoods, leading to an eruption of violence. "I'm scared," he said.

McGuire and Courtenay agreed that while it was sad to see so many of the old guard departing, the new Top Brass was just as able, just as honest, just as dedicated. And why not? After all, Courtenay himself had initiated many of them into the intricacies of high command, and inspired them with his own sense of commitment and optimism— just as Jim Hannon, years earlier, had instilled dedication to The Job in Courtenay and his young colleagues.

After a decade spent observing the men of the post-Serpico police hierarchy, I wonder at their fortitude and spirit, at the way they manage, against daunting odds, to do their job, that more of them do not fall victim to one form or another of battle fatigue, of shell shock, seems astonishing. It was for me a long and stirring journey into the arcane.

It was painful to watch Jim Hannon pushed out, startling to see Joe Hoffman's metamorphosis from cop-commander to successful businessman; it was shocking to witness Mickey Schwartz's sudden self-destruction; and it was cinéma vérité to follow the eccentrically self-aborted career of a man as straight and brave as Dan Courtenay.

Today, eight years after I first met Courtenay, I respect the honesty with which he can look into his own soul. And I feel a sense of loss (as indeed I do about Hannon and

Hoffman and Schwartz) knowing he is no longer a member of the police command. No matter what Courtenay says about how the NYPD will endure as an exemplary urban police force, for me the Brass will seem to shine less brightly than it did while he was On The Job.

I will always remember him striding through the streets of his New York, resplendently in uniform, clapping a blue-clad colleague on the back and shoring up morale all the way down the line as he says, with a wink and a grin, "You're doing a helluva job, I've been watching you!"